S

D1355722

COLOR PLATE No. 1

# THE
# COMPLETE
# BOOK OF
# POTTERY
# MAKING

### by JOHN B. KENNY

WITH PHOTOGRAPHS AND DRAWINGS MADE
ESPECIALLY FOR THIS BOOK BY THE AUTHOR

London

PITMAN PUBLISHING

First published in Great Britain 1951
*Reprinted, 1965, 1967, 1968, 1970*

ISBN: 0 273 40803 8

SIR ISAAC PITMAN AND SONS LTD.
Pitman House, Parker Street, Kingsway, London, W.C.2
P.O. Box 6038, Portal Street, Nairobi, Kenya

SIR ISAAC PITMAN (AUST.) PTY. LTD.
Pitman House, Bouverie Street, Carlton, Victoria 3053, Australia

PITMAN PUBLISHING COMPANY S.A. LTD.
P.O. Box 9898, Johannesburg, S. Africa

Printed in U. S. A.
GO (G3118)

# Acknowledgments

To Lyle Perkins, instructor in ceramics at the Rhode Island School of Design, who posed for the photographs of throwing,

to Harold Hunsicker, head of the art department of the Lincoln High School, Cleveland, Ohio, who posed for the photographs of jiggering,

to the students of the School of Industrial Art of New York City, who posed for the photographs of other ceramic processes,

and

to all of my friends and associates who were most generous with their help and encouragement,

my sincerest thanks,

The Author.

# *F*oreword

*W*elcome to the fraternity of potters! Come join the company of those who fashion things out of earth and fire, who work with materials old as time itself. Explore the mysteries of the kiln whose magic changes dull mud into objects as brilliant as jewels. Learn the secrets of the ceramic art—learn about clay.

A wonderful material, clay—probably the first to which man turned his hand when he felt the urge to make things, not for hunting or for war, but just for the pleasure of creating. Out of clay he contrived those first utensils for cooking and storing food which spelled the beginning of civilization. Out of it also he made ornaments, representations of natural forms, objects of religious veneration, even books.

If you learn its simple rules, clay will serve you well, obeying your slightest touch and giving tangible expression to your thoughts. It will remain plastic and responsive, changing as you command; yet when you achieve the form you wish and pass it through the fire, it will hold the impress of your fingers forever.

You may work clay with machinery or you may work it by hand. The experienced potter can use it to produce articles of exquisite design whose making will tax to the utmost his knowledge and his craftsmanship. A little child can use it, also, and make things of real utility and charm. It can be modeled, pressed, or stamped. It can be thrown on a wheel. It can be made into a liquid and cast in molds. It can be carved as a solid. It can be rolled, turned, scraped, incised, pulled, cut. When hardened by fire, it can be glazed with colors, brilliant or subdued, glossy or mat. It may be decorated with designs or given a variety of textures. Its range is almost limitless. It has something to offer to all tastes. It will lend itself to all degrees of skill.

It took a thousand centuries for forces of air and water working on granite rock to form the clay you work with. It took countless centuries more for winds and glaciers and running streams to deposit it in the bed where it was found. It is ready to serve you. Respect it for what it can do. If you are honest and sincere, it will reward you richly, not only in pieces of ware but in that deep satisfaction which comes from making something and knowing that you have made it well.

. . . v . . .

# Contents

Borosilicate, Leadless, Salt, Slip, Lustre. Glaze Calculation. The Molecular Formula. Formula into Recipe. Color in Glazes. Coloring Oxides. Soluble Salts. Prepared Ceramic Colors.

*chapter 11*

Equipment. The Ball Mill. Mortar and Pestle. Hand Mixing. Settling. Gums. Experimenting with Glazes. A Line Blend. A Triaxial Blend. Test Tiles. Applying Glazes. Glazing Raw Ware. Some Glaze Recipes. Egyptian Paste. Special Glaze Effects. Lustre. Defects in Glazes.

*chapter 12*

Engobe. Engobe Recipes. Slip Painting. Slip Trailing. Sgraffito. Spraying. Wax Resist. Terra Sigillata. Ceramic Colors. Majolica. Banding. Underglaze Decoration. Overglaze Painting. Polychrome. Some Points on Ceramic Decoration.

*chapter 13*

Making a Living from Pottery.

# List of Illustrations

. . . xi . . .

# Color Plates

# chapter One

# *I*ntroduction to *Clay*

*T*he true potter loves the feel of clay in his hands. Therefore, the first thing to do is to get some and handle it, in order to learn what it feels like. Buy your clay from a dealer or dig it out of the ground—it doesn't matter which; we'll talk more about that later.

Take a piece of clay slightly bigger than a golf ball and play with it. Squeeze it between your fingers, roll it into a ball, flatten it into a pancake, then roll it into a ball again, making it as round as you can.

Now, holding it in the palm of your left hand, press in the center with your right thumb until the ball begins to look like a little bowl.

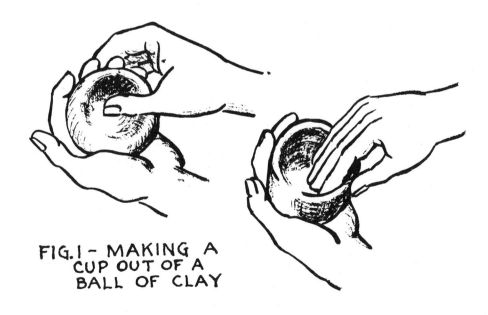

FIG. 1 - MAKING A CUP OUT OF A BALL OF CLAY

Continue the manipulation, using no tools but your fingers, and work the clay until it becomes a cup, wider and taller, with a thinner wall. If the wall starts to crack while you are working on it, moisten your fingers and press the cracks closed. The surface should be damp, but don't let it get wet and soggy.

Keep on working the cup until it is about 3″ high and 2½″ in diameter at the top. Try to keep the sides straight and have the walls even in thickness. Flatten the base by tapping it on a level surface.

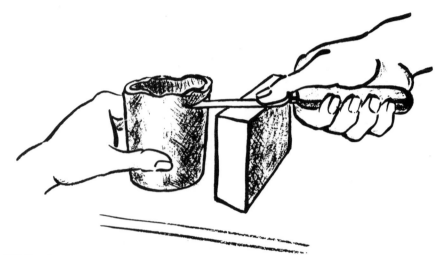

FIG. 2 - TRIMMING THE TOP

The top of your cup will probably be quite ragged. Here you will need the help of a sharp-pointed knife to get it even. Brace the knife on some solid object, such as a block of wood, so that it is at the right height; then, with the cup resting on the table, rotate it against the point of the knife in such a way that a straight cut is made all around the top. Continue rotating until the knife goes through, cutting off the rough edge and leaving a level rim. Smooth this rim with your fingers and continue working on the piece until you achieve a form which pleases you, which feels good in your hand as you hold it, and which stands on the table without wobbling. When you have reached that point, stop—the modeling of the cup is finished. Put it aside to dry. Later you may fire it.

You have just made a piece of pottery. Your little cup is crude (you'll make better ones later on) but it is honest. It looks like what it is—a cup modeled of a plastic material; its form shows how it was made; it is functional.

You have learned something about the way clay responds to your fingers, about what it will do and what it won't do, and something, too, about the relationship which exists between the forms of objects and the materials used in making them. This is a subtle relationship. Years ago when everything people used was made by hand and everyone made something, this relationship was understood and appreciated. In the present day when almost everything is made for us, we have lost a great deal of our sensitivity to form and material. As a potter, you must work to win it back.

*Buying clay*

Any dealer in pottery supplies will have an assortment of clays or clay bodies, either in moist plastic form or as dry powder called clay flour. It is possible to buy small quantities, 10 pounds or so at a time, but of course you pay much more per pound that way. If you plan to do a considerable amount of pottery work, invest in a 100-pound tub of clay at 5 or 6 cents per pound. There is an advantage in buying it this way, for the wooden tub makes a good storage bin.

A clay and a clay body are not the same thing. Clay is a natural product just as it comes from the earth; a clay body is something which has been made according to formula by mixing different kinds of clays and sometimes adding other ingredients to achieve special properties. We shall learn more about clay bodies in Chapter Eight.

In all of your pottery work, bear in mind that shaping clay is only half the job—your pieces must also be fired. This means that you must either own your own kiln or have access to one through some school, club, or community association. Owning your own kiln is not the difficult job it used to be; some of the small electric kilns now offered for sale are quite inexpensive and work very well at moderate temperatures. These kilns are described more fully in Chapter Nine.

Your pottery won't be any good unless it is fired to a temperature high enough to mature the clay, that is, to make it hard and dense. Therefore, when you buy clay, make sure that you get a type which will mature within the temperature range of your kiln. Many clays offered for sale, particularly those which are buff-colored when fired, like Monmouth or Jordan, require high temperatures. Unless you have a high fire kiln, buy a red clay such as Dalton which will mature at cone 04 or lower, or try some of the special low fire clay bodies prepared by the dealers.

Cone 04 is a potter's method of saying 1940 degrees Fahrenheit or 1060 degrees centigrade (the temperature at which earthenware is usually fired). Potters rarely speak of temperatures in any other way. When you fire a kiln you will use cones to measure temperatures, as described in Chapter Nine, and you will soon find yourself thinking of temperature in those terms.

If you live near a brickyard, investigate the possibilities of buying your clay there. A friend of mine who runs a one-man pottery shop does that and pays 2 cents a pound for a clay which is easy to work with, fires to a warm red color, and matures completely in his small electric kiln.

. . . 3 . . .

*Preparing clay flour*

If you buy your clay in plastic form, it won't need any preparation, but you may prefer to buy it dry. It is usually cheaper this way (the price per pound may be the same but you do not pay for water), and it is easier to store until ready for use. Also, if you plan to make any special clay bodies for which the ingredients must be weighed out, you will have to have your clay in dry form. Clay flour may be prepared for use by spreading a layer about ½″ thick on the bottom of a crock or pail, then sprinkling it with water until it is thoroughly moist but not soaking wet. Another layer is then spread on top of the first and sprinkled, the process continuing until the crock is full. After an hour or two, the clay will be ready for wedging.

If the clay you buy dry is not in flour form but comes in lumps, it will be necessary to make a slip out of it. Slip is clay in liquid form. The steps in making slip and converting it to plastic clay are described in Chapter Eight.

*Wedging*

Before clay is used, it must be wedged. This is the oldest method known for getting clay into good working condition, and it is still the best. Wedging makes clay uniform in texture throughout and gets rid of air pockets. If your clay is too dry, you can moisten it during the wedging process; if it is too wet, wedging will dry it.

You will need a wedging board in your studio. This is a heavy slab of plaster with an upright to hold a taut wire and a turnbuckle or some other device to keep the wire tight. The wedging board will receive a lot of rough usage so it should be as solidly constructed as you can make it.

To use the wedging board, hold the lump of clay to be wedged in two hands and pass it over the wire so that it is cut in half. Throw one of the

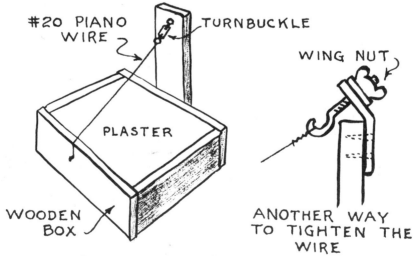

FIG. 3 - WEDGING BOARD

*Below:* Slab built lamp and thrown bowl, majolica decoration.

*Above:* Four thrown pitchers. Front row left, underglaze decoration on white body; right, slip decoration on stoneware. Back row left, slip decoration on stoneware, salt glazed; right, brown lustre glaze on buff clay.

*Below:* Four square plates made in a solid casting mold, majolica decoration.

*Above:* Three porcelain vases, sang-de-boeuf and celadon glazes.

*Right:* A luncheon set of native clay made in drain molds. One surface shows the natural color of the clay under a transparent glaze; the other surface is covered with an opaque glaze containing copper, tin and zinc.

halves onto the plaster surface, then throw the other half on top of it so that one lump is formed. Pick this lump up, cut it in half on the wire, and throw the halves onto the plaster again, one on top of the other. Slam them hard! To get maximum mixing action, keep the layers going the same way. A good device is to throw the halves together with the cut portion always pointing away from you. Cut and wedge at least twenty times before using your clay. You can judge whether or not clay has been wedged enough by looking at the cut portion. If it is even in tone, with no stripes or air holes, the clay is ready for use.

### Storing clay

If you buy your clay in tubs, you may keep it moist and plastic by covering it with a piece of wet burlap, but clay can be kept in good condition in almost any type of container which has a tight-fitting cover. A galvanized iron pail with a lid is good; a large covered crock is excellent. A 4-gallon crock which will hold 50 pounds of clay can be bought for about $2.50. For a small quantity of clay, a bowl covered with a dinner plate makes a perfect storage bin. Damp cloths will help to keep clay plastic; however, look out for two things—coarse fibered cloths will shed particles which cause trouble in the clay, and almost any cloth will rot if it stays wet all the time. So change your cloths occasionally.

### Storing work in progress—the damp box

If you intend to work on a piece for several days, it must be kept moist.

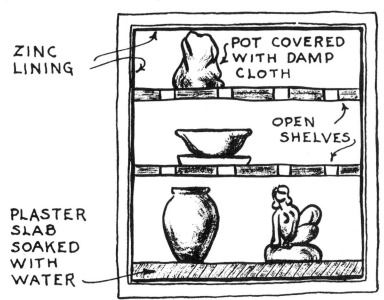

FIG. 4 – CROSS SECTION OF
DAMP BOX

Hence you will need a damp storage closet to prevent drying. A zinc-lined box is best for this purpose—an old ice box is ideal. A large plaster slab in the bottom of the box may be kept water-soaked to maintain the humidity at the right point.

Work stored in a damp box will not remain plastic but will gradually reach a state called "leather-hard," in which it is still damp but too dry to permit changes in form. Clay in this condition can be carved but not modeled. If complete plasticity is desired, the piece must be covered with a damp cloth.

### A place to work

Pottery is not a hobby to carry on in a corner of the living room; you really need a place to work in. If you have a well-lighted, dry cellar, you are in luck, for that makes an ideal pottery studio, especially if it has a concrete floor and running water. You can work in the kitchen if no other place is available, but be careful not to get clay on the floor so that it is tracked into other rooms.

Clay makes a lot of dirt, but it is easy to clean up. The best surface to work on is a plain wooden table top which can be wiped with a sponge or a wet cloth when you are through. A large wooden drawing board provides a good working surface also. You may find it helpful to spread a piece of oilcloth on the table and use the drawing board on top of that.

### Care of tools

Clay will rust steel surfaces, so clean your knives and scrapers promptly. Wooden tools don't rust, but they deserve care also; clean them as soon as you are through using them. Both steel and wooden tools should be rubbed occasionally with a cloth containing a few drops of oil.

### Saving clay

Until it is fired, clay can be used over and over again. Pieces can be made, be allowed to dry, and then be broken up and the clay made plastic once more. Even the clay which you rinse off your hands can be salvaged. Washing under the faucet in the kitchen sink is risky—it will cause trouble if too much clay gets into the drain. A safer method is to have a pail half filled with water into which hands and tools may be dipped to remove surplus clay. After this clay has settled to the bottom of the pail, the water may be poured off and the clay emptied into drying bats. (A drying bat is a large plaster bowl into which liquid clay can be poured and allowed to harden. The method of making such a bat is described in Chapter Five.) When it has hardened sufficiently, it can be wedged and used again.

### Kinds of pottery

Ceramic wares are classified as earthenware, stoneware, china and porcelain. These are not exact terms by any means but are merely generally descriptive.

## Earthenware

Earthenware is usually made from natural clay, fired to some temperature between cone 08 and cone 2 (950° to 1165° centigrade), most of it in the neighborhood of cone 04. The body of earthenware is non-vitreous, that is, comparatively soft and porous; and it will not hold liquids unless it is glazed. Its color is usually buff or red, often quite dark. For this reason it is sometimes covered with a white or colored slip called "engobe" before glazes or decorations are applied. Most of the pottery you make will be earthenware.

## Stoneware

Stoneware is sometimes made from natural clay and sometimes from prepared clay bodies. It is fired to much higher temperatures than earthenware (usually to cone 8 or 1260° centigrade), and as a result is hard and vitreous, able to hold water even when unglazed. Not all natural clays can be used for stoneware, for many of them, especially the red ones, would melt at stoneware temperature.

Pieces of sculpture, tiles, etc., made from natural clay and fired but not glazed are sometimes called *terra cotta.* The word means baked earth.

## China

There is little common agreement on. the dividing line between china and porcelain. In general, the term *china* refers to a type of ware made of a clay body composed of kaolin, ball clay, feldspar, and flint plus a flux (something to lower the melting point). The flux may be a natural ingredient such as talc or a prepared one such as ground glass. China is never made out of a natural clay alone. It is produced in two or more firings at different temperatures. The ware is formed and fired to bisque at a high temperature (cone 10, or 1305° centigrade). The bisque ware is then glazed with a lower temperature glaze and fired again to about cone 2 (1165° centigrade). After the second firing, china is sometimes decorated with overglaze painting or printed designs and fired a third time in a decorating kiln at a very low temperature, about cone 015 (805° centigrade). Some china is fired even more often than this for special decorative effects. The color of the body is usually white, although specially colored bodies are produced.

## Porcelain

Porcelain requires the highest fire among all pottery wares. It is always made from a specially prepared body composed of kaolin, ball clay, feld-. spar, and flint. This is true porcelain, sometimes called "hard paste." Ware made of a body with additional fluxes is sometimes referred to as "soft paste." Porcelain is made in one fire, the body and the glaze maturing together at about cone 13 (1350° centigrade). The product of such a fire, as you might expect, is extremely hard and vitreous.

Porcelain has always held a special place in the thoughts of men. The desire to possess it has sent ships around the world, and the search for its formula has kept potters busy for centuries. The Chinese knew how to make it first, and interesting stories have been told of the efforts made to win the secret from them, stories for example of Père d'Entrecolles, the missionary, who visited the great porcelain city of Ching-te-chen in an effort to convert the porcelain workers and at the same time learn how porcelain was made. His letters are interesting to read. The Chinese are a poetic people. In one of his letters, the good Father tells of a conversation with a Chinese potter in which the latter explained that porcelain must have muscles and bone, the muscles being ka-o-lin and the bones, pi-tun-se. We know now that the potter was talking about kaolin and feldspar but those who read the letter took his words literally and actually mixed some ground-up bones with their clay. The legend has it that this accounts for the discovery of bone china.

Stories could be told, too, of how the dukes of Italy, envious of the wares that Marco Polo brought back, ordered their potters to get busy and produce the same thing, and how the potters, in desperation at being unable to turn out anything but yellowish or brown ware from the clay at their disposal, finally hit upon the expedient of covering their plates with an opaque white glaze containing tin. In this way they imitated the surface, if not the body, of porcelain, and so produced the ware we know as majolica. Stories could be told, too, of the final discovery of kaolin in Germany by Heinrich Boettger (one legend has it that white clay on his horse's hoofs led to the discovery, and another that he found it in the powder he used on his wig); and how when a porcelain factory was finally set up at Meissen, the workers were all locked up to guard the secret.

Yes, porcelain has always been something of romance and glamour. It has even been used as a medium of exchange in place of money. It is worthy of note, however, that the Chinese, the fathers of porcelain, who knew more about it than anyone else, did not regard it with such exaggerated awe. To them a good earthenware pot honestly made and serving its purpose well was just as worthy of respect. Since practically all of the pieces you make will be earthenware, take a lesson from the Chinese. Work your material well, and your pottery can have as much merit as the finest porcelain ever produced.

# $\mathcal{G}$etting Started

$\mathcal{N}$ow let's try out some methods of form-
ing pottery which require direct manipulation of the clay itself, without
the use of molds or the potter's wheel.

*Tools*

You already have a good set of tools for this work—your ten fingers.
In addition, you will need a knife, a wooden modeling tool or two, a wire
loop tool, and a sponge, plus a few plaster slabs and a table on which to
work.

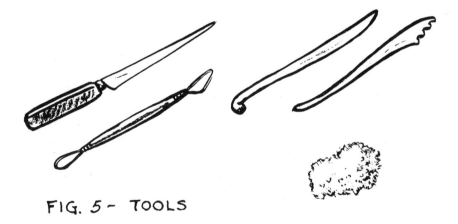

FIG. 5 - TOOLS

*Setting-up exercises*

Roll out a cylinder of clay on a drawing board or on a wooden table top. Make a long thin snake and coil it around itself. If the clay starts to dry and cracks as you bend it, moisten your finger and rub it over the cracking portion.

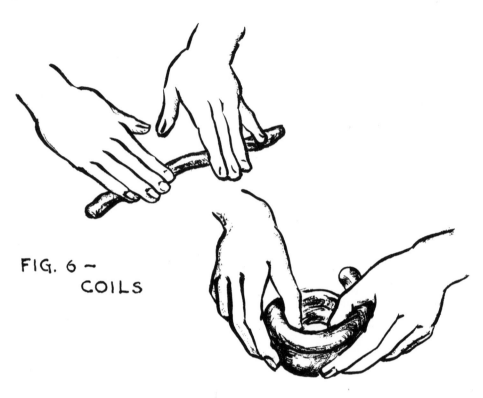

FIG. 6 —
COILS

Squeeze the clay into various shapes. Make a fish, a cat, or a bird.

Make an animal with four legs by rolling two balls of clay, one slightly larger than the other, and then rolling a coil about as thick as your finger. Cut the coil into four pieces to serve as legs. Use the smaller ball as a head and stick them all together. Add ears, nose, eyes, and mouth.

Now using balls and cylinders, try your hand at making some more animals.

Don't copy these sketches, don't even copy real animals, but let your imagination and your hands and the clay itself guide you into creations of pure fantasy. Make things which have never been seen before.

The little animal figures you just modeled serve no purpose. They are merely exercises to acquire freedom and confidence in handling clay; so don't save any of them but mash them all up and throw them back into the clay bin—unless there is an especially amusing one which you are fond of. If so, save him.

FIG.7 - SQUEEZING
CLAY SHAPES

TWO BALLS
OF CLAY ~ A COIL CUT INTO
FOUR PIECES -

FASTENED
TOGETHER

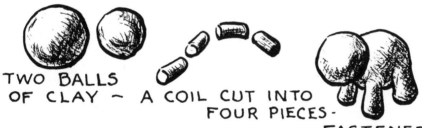

ADD
EARS ~
AND A
NOSE

ADD EYES oo
AND A TAIL

CUT A MOUTH

THERE !

FIG. 8

. . . 11 . . .

FIG. 9 –
FIGURES
MADE FROM
BALLS AND COILS OF CLAY

*Making it stick*

If you plan to keep your little animal for firing, better check to see if the separate parts are well fastened together. If the legs have just been pushed onto the body, they will be sure to drop off in the kiln. To make them stick, roughen the two surfaces to be joined, moisten them, then press them firmly together and weld the joint all around by squeezing the edges tight with a wooden modeling tool.

*Solid masses*

Clay, even when it is bone dry, contains chemically combined water which must escape during the firing. A solid lump of clay an inch or more in thickness, with no openings to let the water out, is almost certain to break apart when it is heated. An accident like this is apt to ruin not only

· · · 12 · · ·

the piece itself but everything else near it in the kiln. So if your animal has a fat tummy, cut him in half, scoop out the inside, and join him together again by welding the joint thoroughly.

A figure with a wide flat base can be hollowed out from underneath without the need of cutting it in half.

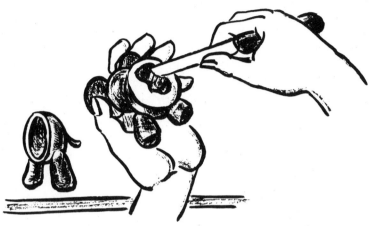

## FIG. 10 - HOLLOWING A FIGURE

### Grog

If you plan to model a small figure and know that there will be solid masses, wedge some grog into the clay before you start. Grog is clay which has been fired, then ground up and screened. It is added to clay to provide openings through which moisture can escape so that thick pieces will not crack during drying or firing. It also prevents thin pieces from warping. For most work, 30-60 mesh grog is used, that is, grog fine enough to go through a screen with 30 meshes to the inch but too coarse to go through one with 60 meshes to the inch. This is a medium grog. For heavy sculpture, coarse grog, 20-40 mesh, is needed. Grog can be bought in 10-pound quantities for about 12 cents per pound. If you use enough of it, your clay will become so porous that hollowing out is not necessary. Use one handful of grog to two of clay, and wet the grog thoroughly so that the two will mix more easily. When you model a figure this way out of heavily grogged clay and fire it, you are actually making terra cotta. Large terra-cotta sculpture, which must be hollow, is usually pressed in plaster molds, but pieces can be built by the coil method, which will be described next.

### Coil building

Before the invention of the potter's wheel, primitive people made vessels by rolling coils of clay and laying them on top of one another in spiral fashion. As the work progressed, the coils were welded together; and when the form was completed, the whole surface was rubbed with smooth stones until the joints between the coils were entirely concealed. Sometimes the surface was decorated by pressing carved sticks into the clay to impart texture. Vessels of good size and considerable beauty were made this way. The method seems to have been used in every part of the world where pottery was made. For some reason, this was always considered woman's work. When the wheel was invented, however, pottery making took on greater importance and became a man's trade. (This is not true today, of course. There are probably as many skilled women potters as men.)

It is a mistake to think that coil-built pottery need look crude or clumsy. Quite the opposite. With time and care, you can produce pieces you will be proud of. Nor is the method limited to simple shapes. Teapots and vases can be made this way, as well as bowls. Let's make a coffee pot with a spout, a handle and a lid.

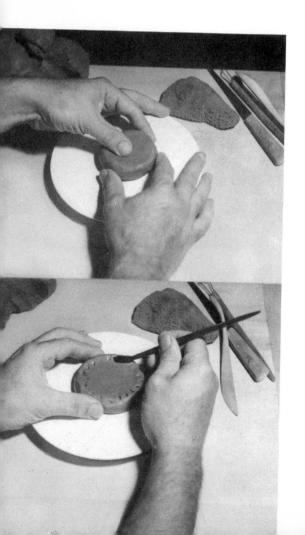

## PLATE I

Before starting, make a full-size sketch of the piece to be built; then trace one side of it on a piece of cardboard and cut out a shape to use as a template or pattern.

Roll a ball of clay and flatten it into a disc ¾″ thick to serve as the base of your piece. For greater ease in working, lay the disc on a plaster bat (a round slab of plaster, cast in a pie tin).

Roughen the top outer edge of the disc and moisten it with a soft brush.

· · · 14 · · ·

Next roll a coil of clay and lay it on the outer edge of the base. Cut the ends of the coil at a slant so that they will join without making a thick spot in the wall.

Weld the coil firmly in place and press it with your fingers until it is about ½″ thick and uniform throughout, then hold the template against it to see how the shape is progressing.

When the first coil is finished, roughen the top and moisten it, then roll a second coil and put it in place on top of the first, welding the joint thoroughly as before. Then roll a third coil and place it in the same manner.

While you are laying the coils, you are also forming the piece, so watch the shape closely. Compare it with the sketch. Keep turning your work, and hold the template against it, not as a scraping tool but as a gauge of your progress. Look at the piece from the top at frequent intervals to see that the coils form concentric circles.

Sometimes you may find it helpful to roll a very thin coil of clay and press it into the joint between the piece and the coil you are adding.

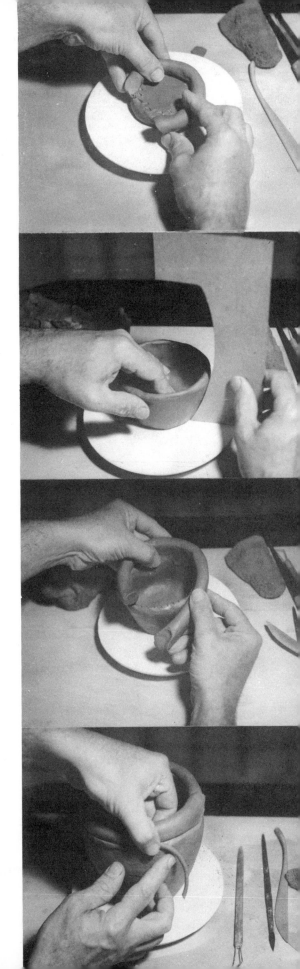

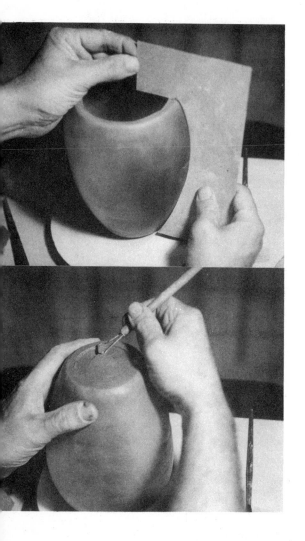

After you have put the fourth coil in place, the walls will be too weak to support any more weight, so set the work aside for a while. You may let it harden for an hour or two and then continue, or you may leave it in the damp box overnight. When you resume building, take care that the top edge of the piece, which meanwhile has dried, is thoroughly roughened and moistened before the next coil is added. Continue adding coils until the shape is completed. If necessary, trim the top edge with a knife as you did with the little cup in Chapter I.

If you want the surface of your piece to be quite smooth, rub it with the flat side of a wooden modeling tool. Don't try to achieve a machined finish, however—let the work bear the mark of your hands.

After the last coil has been put in place and the top edge finished, let the piece dry for an hour or two, then shape the foot. When you made the base you allowed a thickness of ¾". This was so that a portion could be cut out with a wire loop tool, leaving a foot or rim for the piece to stand on. Hold the piece carefully while you do this so that you don't spoil the top edge while it is standing upside down.

It may be possible to support the piece on something tall, such as a milk bottle, allowing it to rest on the inside of the base. Fold a paper napkin over the top of the bottle to form a cushion. The foot should be cut so that in cross section it would look as shown in Fig. 11. So much for the body of the piece, now for the spout and the handle.

. . . 16 . . .

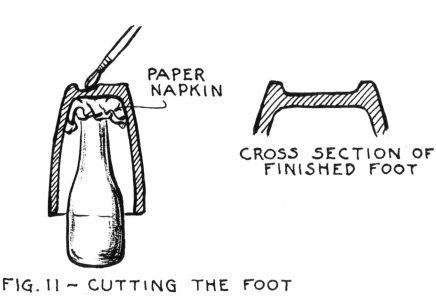

PAPER NAPKIN

CROSS SECTION OF
FINISHED FOOT

FIG. 11 ~ CUTTING THE FOOT

*(Plate I Continued)*

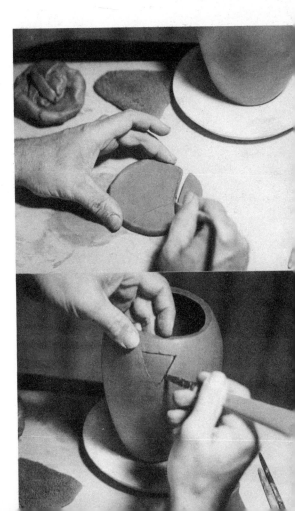

*The spout*

Roll a ball of clay, flatten it, and cut out a fan-shaped piece. This can be folded to make the spout.

Cut an opening in the piece where the spout should be.

. . . 17 . . .

Then take the spout which you have folded, and hold it against the piece to see how it looks. If it is the right size and shape, roughen the edges, moisten them and weld the spout in place.

### The handle

Roll a coil of clay and flatten it into a strip with your thumb.

Bend the strip into handle shape and attach it.

### The lid

Roll another ball of clay and flatten it into a disc about the right size for a lid. Make it slightly dome-shaped.

. . . 18 . . .

Hold the lid against the pot to see if the two go well together.

Make a flange for the under side of the lid by rolling a coil, flatten it into a strip, then cut the ends and join them to form a circle. Be sure that this circle is the right size to fit into the opening of the pot.

Next, fasten the flange in place on the under side of the lid.

Now roll a small ball of clay to serve as a knob and fasten it in place on the top of the lid, using a very thin coil of clay to weld the joint.

. . . 19 . . .

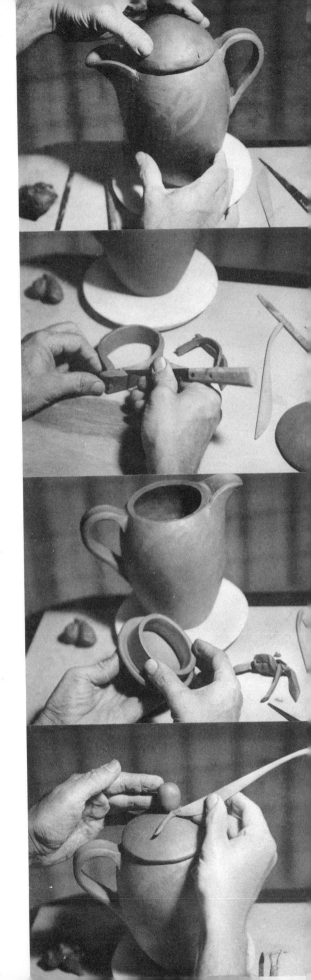

Our job is done. A little sponging on the outside surface and we can put the coffee pot aside to dry.

*Drying*

A piece like the one we have just made should remain in the damp box for a while so that it does not dry too rapidly. Slow drying will help the handle and the spout to stay on and make cracking less likely to occur. After a day or two it can be removed from the damp box and be allowed to dry; stand it on two sticks so that air may reach the bottom as well as the sides. If the top is solid enough to risk it, let the piece dry upside down.

Sometimes, in spite of all your precautions, a piece will crack as it dries. When that happens it is almost impossible to save it, so don't waste your clay by putting it in the kiln, hoping that some miracle during the firing will make the piece whole again. Such things don't happen. Consider the loss as experience gained, break up the piece and prepare the clay for reuse.

*The whirler or banding wheel*

The whirler is useful in coil building because it enables you to turn your work easily while it is in progress and thus see at a glance where

FIG. 12 – THE
WHIRLER

USING THE TEMPLATE
AS A SCRAPER

the piece bulges or is not symmetrical. Mistakes can then be corrected with the fingers.

You may even wish to rotate your work on the whirler and hold a scraper against it as it turns, in order to smooth it, as shown in Fig. 12. It is possible to obtain a highly finished surface in this manner. You could even use the template as a cutting tool to shape the piece as it spins. This is all right to do, provided you remember that you will be making a different kind of pottery that way. Much of the beauty of hand building will be gone, but there may be another kind of beauty in its place. The piece will be more mechanical, but at the same time it can be perfectly honest and pleasing.

Large jars for garden use, too big to be made on the potter's wheel in the usual manner, are sometimes made by a combination of hand building and turning. The shape is first roughed out in coils with extra thickness allowed in the walls; the wheel is then rotated, and turning tools are used to cut the jar to the desired shape. By this method it is possible to form ware which would be difficult to make in any other way.

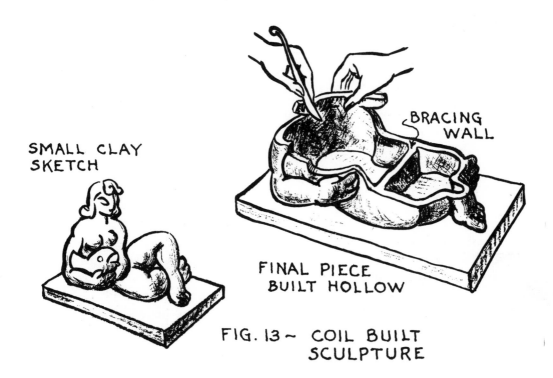

SMALL CLAY
SKETCH

BRACING
WALL

FINAL PIECE
BUILT HOLLOW

FIG. 13 ~ COIL BUILT
SCULPTURE

*Coil-built sculpture*

We know now that any ceramic sculpture bigger than a tiny figurine must be hollow. The best way to achieve this is to make a solid clay model first, then cast a mold in plaster and either pour or press the final piece which is to be fired. If, however, you want to work more directly and fire the original model, you may build it hollow by using the coil method. Make a small sketch in clay and decide upon the ratio of enlargement needed, then proceed to copy the sketch by building clay walls to conform to its outlines, as shown in Fig. 13. Take care to weld the coils firmly together. Use clay with a heavy mixture of grog (one part grog to two of clay) and make the walls about ¾″ thick throughout, slightly thicker if the sculpture is to be over 12″ high. Walls may be built inside the piece to brace it.

As the walls grow, model the form, referring constantly to the sketch to make sure that proportions are right. A pair of sculptor's proportional calipers will be useful here, but if you don't own such an instrument you may make a fairly good substitute out of two strips of wood of equal length, pointed at the ends and fastened together with a bolt and wing nut to serve as a pivot, as shown in Fig. 14. If the pivot is placed so that distance AC is

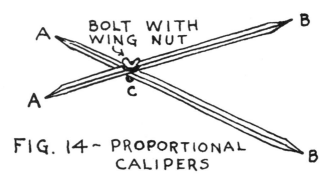

FIG. 14 ~ PROPORTIONAL
CALIPERS

one-half of distance CB, then no matter how the sticks are moved, the distance between the points AA will always be half that between the points BB. To enlarge a small sketch to a figure twice as big, measure the length of a portion of the sketch with the small end of the calipers and lay off the corresponding portion in the enlargement with the other end. By changing the position of the pivot, a different ratio of enlargement may be obtained.

### Slab building

In slab building, clay is rolled flat and cut into patterns which are then folded and joined together to form various ceramic objects. This method is especially suited to rectangular forms, boxes, etc., although cylindrical shapes and irregular ones may be made as well. Let's try making a square cigarette box with a lid.

PLATE II

Add some grog to your clay to make it work better, then roll it out, using a rolling pin and two strips of wood ⅜" thick to serve as guides. Two wooden rulers are good for this purpose. Take a ball of clay the size of a large orange and flatten it into a disc; then place the rulers beside it and roll the clay with the rolling pin. Roll from the center out, lifting the layer of clay from time to time. If the clay sticks to the rolling pin, wipe the surface dry and dust it with a little flint. Continue rolling until the rolling pin rides on the two strips of wood, when you will have an even layer of clay just as thick as the wooden guides.

The next step is to make a pattern of the piece to be built and cut it out of clay. Some ceramists suggest that for a slab-built box, the bottom and each side be cut out separately, with proper allowance for the thickness of the clay, and that the pieces be then connected with butt joints. However, it is hard to make such joints stick. If a piece built that way comes out of the kiln without cracking at the corners, it is almost a miracle. Furthermore, when you cut clay into flat pieces and join them like boards, you are doing cabinet making, not pottery. Clay is a plastic material, it will bend and assume different shapes as you squeeze it. Take advantage of these qualities.

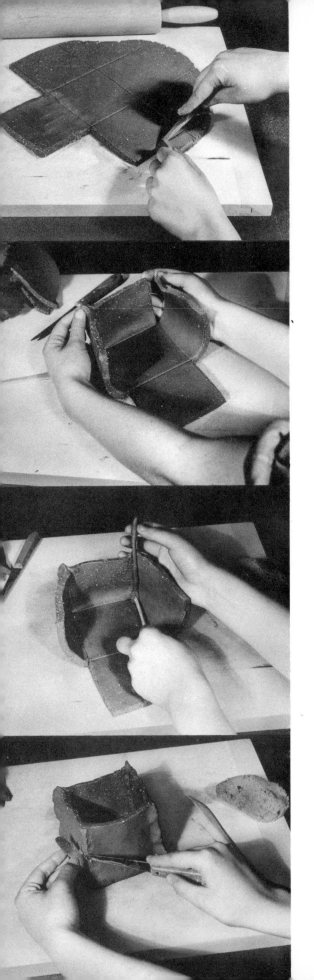

Let's cut a pattern for the box in one piece, shaped like a cross. Since the box is to hold cigarettes, be sure to make it the right size and to allow for shrinkage. A fired piece is about one-sixth smaller than the original clay shape. Here is where a shrinkage rule would be helpful. The method of making such a rule is described in Chapter Eight.

With the pattern cut in one piece, the sides will have to be folded up; as a result, the bottom edges will be rounded, not square. There is no allowance for the thickness of the slab, which means that the sides can be firmly squeezed together, making a ridge of excess clay at the corners. The portions to be joined should be roughened and moistened before they are brought together.

To make extra certain of the joints, roll a thin coil of clay and work it into the inside corner when you squeeze the sides together.

When all of the sides are joined, trim off the excess clay at the corners with a knife.

This method not only gives stronger joints but guards against the finished product being mechanical. The contours of the box will have a soft, claylike quality, the shape will be the result of modeling by your fingers—not cut-and-dried fitting—and that is the way it should be. Finish the surface with a wooden modeling tool.

The lid for the box is easy to make. Cut a piece slightly larger than the box.

Then cut a long strip ½″ wide for the flange, bend it to shape, try it in the box for size (make it a little too small rather than too big), and then fasten it on the underside of the lid.

Make a knob for the lid by rolling a ball of clay and flattening its sides, then attach it and weld it in place with a modeling tool.

FIG. 15 — KNOBS
AND HANDLES

If you prefer, the handle may be made from a strip of clay or from a thin coil bent into a loop like those in Fig. 15. The lid will need support while you are attaching the handle. Cut a little piece off a plaster slab and place it under the lid inside the flange as shown in Fig. 16.

Slab-built pieces must be allowed to dry slowly; leave your work in the damp box for a day or two after it is finished, then let it dry in the room. When the box and the lid are thoroughly dry, see how they fit together and make any necessary adjustment before you fire them. When you put them in the kiln for the bisque fire, have the lid in place. This tends to prevent warping and assures better fit. When ready for glazing, the box and the lid must be put in the kiln separately.

Slab-built pieces lend themselves to gay decoration, majolica, slip painting, or some of the other methods described in Chapter Twelve.

PLASTER
BLOCK

FIG 16 — SUPPORTING UNDERSIDE OF
LID WHILE FASTENING KNOB

(*Plate II Continued*)

The little box whose progress we have watched had a design trailed on in slip, and was then covered with transparent glaze and fired. The body of red clay makes a pleasing contrast to the white slip design.

Note how the grog which was added to the clay to give it better working properties produced an attractive texture in the final piece.

Tall pieces may be made by the slab method if some temporary support is provided to hold the piece until it starts to dry and becomes strong enough to stand by itself. A plaster form can be used, of course, but if you are going to take the trouble to cast plaster, you might as well make a mold and be done with it. Since what you need is merely something to support the piece, and not to help shape it, a crude form made of wood or cardboard will suffice. The lamp shown in Color Plate No. 2 was made by the slab method. It is over 10″ tall. When the clay was rolled out, it was much too soft to stand up at that height, so a temporary support was made by cutting up a corrugated paper carton and pasting together a rectangular block of the right size. This form was then covered with waxed paper, and clay slabs were shaped over it and allowed to stiffen for a few hours. After this, the corrugated paper was withdrawn (the waxed paper made it easy to remove), and the modeling of the lamp base was completed.

Slab building is a lot of fun. The method can be used to make a variety of pottery forms for many different uses. Plate III on page 29 shows a ceramic letter box built by the slab method, and various other containers, and a little farm house whose only purpose is to amuse. Other objects suited to slab construction are shown in Fig. 17.

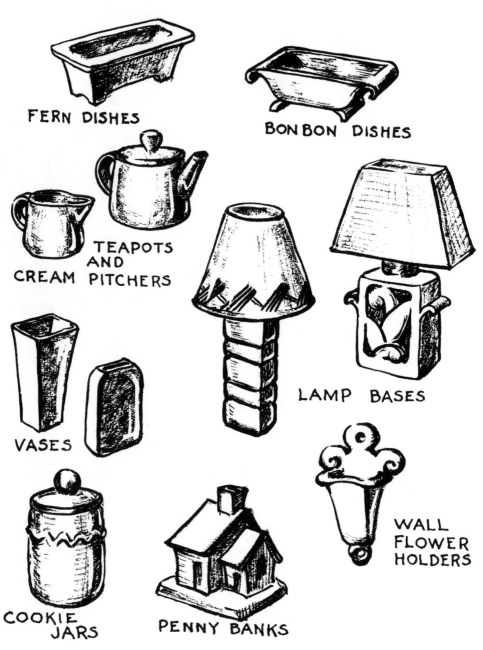

FERN DISHES

BONBON DISHES

TEAPOTS
AND
CREAM PITCHERS

VASES

LAMP BASES

WALL
FLOWER
HOLDERS

COOKIE
JARS

PENNY BANKS

FIG. 17 ~ SLAB BUILT OBJECTS

Boxes.

PLATE III
Examples of slab built ware.

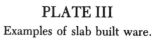

Polychrome knickknack.

Cookie jar, slip trailed decoration.

Majolica letter box.

*Finishing ware*

The surface of a piece of pottery may be smoothed by sponging it before it is fired. This can be done when the piece is leather-hard or even when it is bone-dry, provided care is taken not to let too much water soak in. An elephant s ear-sponge is the best type to use. Too much sponging of a piece will destroy its character, just as too much sandpapering will ruin a wood carving. Sandpaper, incidentally, while a valuable tool for finishing plaster, has no place in clay work—don't use it.

Some of the American Indian potters polish their ware by rubbing it with stones. This gives a slight shine to the surface which remains after the piece is fired, but the effect is seen only in unglazed ware.

The tops and bottoms of green ware (unfired pieces) may be made perfectly level by grinding them on a smooth board or on a sheet of glass, as shown in Fig. 18. To do this, put a few drops of water on the board or glass

FIG. 18 ~ GRINDING
THE TOP OF AN UNFIRED PIECE

and rub the piece over it, upside down, using a circular motion. Have a sponge handy so that after the top has been ground for about five seconds the piece can be lifted up and the rim wiped dry with the sponge. The grinding action is very fast. That is why a few seconds will suffice.

The operation must be done rapidly and the piece of green ware must be kept in constant motion. If you allow it to stand still for a moment, it will glue itself fast to the board and break when you try to loosen it.

*Decorating in clay*

Interesting variations can be made in the appearance of pottery through changes in surface texture. Some of the earliest pots known are beautifully decorated in this manner. Many have a basket-weave pattern, which suggests that the potters may have made reed baskets first and then pressed clay on the inside. It is possible that the discovery of pottery came about when some early craftsmen tried to make a basket hold water by lining it with clay. We can easily imagine how this basket with its clay lining may

FIG. 19 ~
INCISED DECORATION

have fallen into a fire which burned away the reeds and at the same time hardened the clay lining. Later, when pots were made by the coil method, the potters tried to suggest the pattern of a woven basket by scratching the surface with sticks.

The simplest way to ornament clay is to incise a design with a pointed tool. Experiment with this kind of decoration. Try using a three-pronged fork and scratching a crisscross pattern on a pot with it, as shown in Fig. 19.

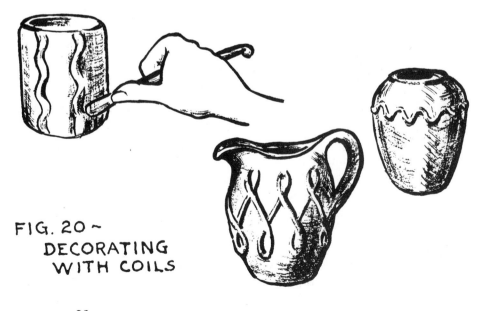

FIG. 20 ~
DECORATING
WITH COILS

Or try almost any kind of notched stick. The possibilities of variation here are infinite.

Try rolling a very thin coil of clay and pressing it on a leather-hard piece of pottery in a decorative way, as shown in Fig. 20. Such coils can be applied as bands around a pot or as vertical lines on the sides. They will need to be moistened before being applied and must be firmly pressed against the pot in order to stick. This very act of pressing may give them decorative quality.

Clay can be decorated with carved figures as shown in Fig. 21. This is a more formal kind of decoration than that just described. When a piece is leather-hard, a design may be drawn on it and the background cut away to leave the design in low relief. When you do this kind of work, remember that you are a potter, not a sculptor, and that the decoration is good only if it enhances the beauty of the form. This means that the design must not be so prominent and demand so much attention that we fail to see the shape of the pottery itself.

FIG. 21 —
CARVED DECORATION

Carving in leather-hard clay can be carried further to produce pierced ware. This is an extremely elaborate kind of decoration—be cautious about trying it. You have seen examples of this work and know how fussy it can become. Obviously, pierced ware is no good for anything which must hold liquids, but it is suitable for certain kinds of purely decorative pieces— lamp bases, etc. You may be interested in trying it. Plan the design and draw it on the surface of the pot, then cut out the background. Do not cut out so much that what remains is thin and weak. Remember, too, that the remaining portions will need to be modeled slightly and given a satisfactory finish.

Some of the first porcelain tableware imported by Europe was shipped from the city of Gombroon and was known as "Gombroon ware." Later the

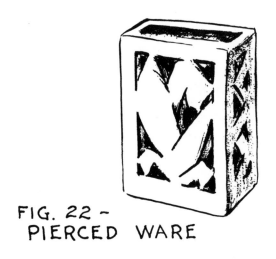

FIG. 22 –
PIERCED WARE

name was replaced by "china." Today, some ceramists use the term *Gombroon* to describe a type of porcelain which is decorated with a pierced design, then covered with a flowing glaze which fills up the openings so that after the firing they appear as translucent windows.

*Ceramic design*

What is good ceramic design? There is no definite answer to this question but here are a few guiding principles:

Pottery should show how it is made and what it is made of.

Clay has plastic qualities; the good potter takes advantage of them.

Make things for use. Don't make bowls and vases—make a bowl for fruit or for cereal, make a vase for daffodils. Let use guide you in planning shape and decoration.

Decoration on pottery must enhance form, not hide it.

Pieces can be made smooth by rubbing or sponging, but don't overdo it. Too much smoothing destroys character.

Clay sculpture intended for firing cannot have a metal frame inside to support it. It doesn't need any. Ceramic sculpture should show its origin in earthy materials. It should be simple in outline and compact. Figures of dancing girls with arms extended, balanced on one foot, are better suited to materials other than clay.

Create—don't copy.

As you grow in experience, your taste will improve. Don't hesitate to use a hammer on any of your pieces which no longer seem good. (The hammer is a valuable tool—use it freely.)

Be yourself. If you like gay, playful pottery, make that kind. If you prefer more formal ware, make yours that way. Make things which are satisfying to you. If you work with sincerity, if you understand the clay and know your tools, the pottery you make will be good.

SOME POINTS TO REMEMBER IN WORKING WITH CLAY:

1. *Clay shrinks. It shrinks as it dries and it shrinks again when it is fired. The total shrinkage may be over 16 per cent. Allow for this in your planning.*

2. *To make two lumps of clay stick, roughen the surfaces, moisten them with water or slip, press them firmly together, and weld the joint tight.*

3. *When joining two pieces of clay, make sure that they are equally moist, otherwise one will shrink more than the other and separate from it.*

4. *A handle and a pot should be left in the damp box for a day or two, so that they will be brought to the same degree of humidity before being fastened together.*

5. *Let finished pieces dry slowly.*

6. *Clay contains water which must have a way of escape during the fire. Heavy pieces should be made with grog, and sculptured figures must be hollow.*

# $\mathcal{T}$he $\mathcal{P}$otter's $\mathcal{W}$heel

$\mathcal{W}$hen a potter works or "throws" at his wheel there is magic in his touch. The clay seems to come to life in his hands as it rises from a shapeless mass to a form of grace and elegance.

The wheel is the potter's true love. With it he can make ware which has a definite character not obtainable in any other way. It is probably the first machine ever invented; we know that it existed four thousand years ago, for there are pictures of Egyptian potters of that period using it. We can guess how it came about; how someone making a pot and turning it constantly hit upon the idea of placing one stone on top of another to make the turning easier; how a pin was introduced to keep the top stone from slipping off; how the pin became an axle; and, finally, how the stones were replaced by wooden discs fastened to a metal shaft supported by a bearing. With this development a new kind of pottery came into being.

There are several different types of wheels. In some, the potter kicks a heavy horizontal disc connected by a shaft to the wheel head. Once he gets

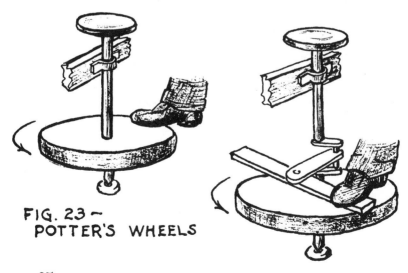

FIG. 23 ~
POTTER'S WHEELS

it going, momentum keeps it turning. In other types, the potter moves a lever back and forth with his foot, operating a crank on the shaft and so turning the wheel head. This is the type usually preferred by studio potters, for it permits full coordination of hands and feet, with the speed of the wheel always under control. Practically all dealers in ceramic supplies offer such wheels for sale. Their catalogs give full details.

Power-driven wheels can be bought, but they are heavy and quite expensive. Don't buy one unless you are planning large-scale production.

### Wheel heads

Most potter's wheels have flat heads, usually of metal though sometimes of wood, on which ware may be thrown directly or on which plaster bats may be fastened to receive the clay. If you throw directly on the wheel head, the piece must be cut free with a wire and lifted off, a difficult trick to do without spoiling the shape. Working on a plaster bat makes it possible to lift the ware by lifting the bat.

Some wheels have a drop type of head, that is, a head with a depression to hold specially shaped bats. This is a big advantage. With this type of head, you can take work off the wheel and put it back on again knowing that it is always perfectly centered. This type of head can also be used for jiggering (described in Chapter Seven), something which cannot be done with the flat head. If you plan to purchase a wheel, get one with a drop head if possible.

A PIECE THROWN ON THE WHEEL HEAD MUST BE CUT OFF WITH A WIRE

A PIECE THROWN ON A BAT CAN BE LIFTED OFF

FIG. 24 ~

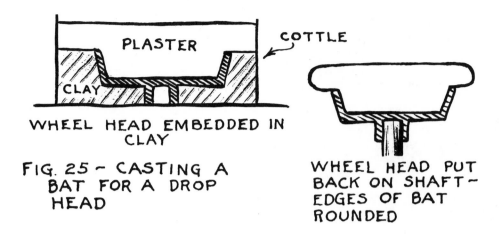

PLASTER

COTTLE

CLAY

WHEEL HEAD EMBEDDED IN CLAY

FIG. 25 ~ CASTING A BAT FOR A DROP HEAD

WHEEL HEAD PUT BACK ON SHAFT ~ EDGES OF BAT ROUNDED

*Casting a bat for a drop head*

To make a plaster bat to fit a drop head, remove the head from the shaft and set it in a ring of clay, making the surface of the clay level with the top of the head, as shown in Fig. 25. The ring of clay should be uniform in width and wide enough to produce a bat of the size you want. Fasten a piece of roofing paper or linoleum around the outside of the clay ring to serve as a retaining wall, coat the exposed portions of the wheel head with oil or vaseline, then mix plaster and pour. When the plaster has set hard, put the head back on the shaft and work on the bat with plaster-turning tools to make the surface level and the edges round. The method of mixing plaster and using turning tools is described in Chapter Five.

When you have finished one bat, it is easy to make duplicates by making a case mold of the first one. The method of doing this is given on page 131.

*Learning how to throw*

You are not going to learn how to throw on the potter's wheel by reading a book about it, any more than you are going to learn to play the piano that way. You will need practice and lots of it, and you should have help from someone who knows how. Whenever you have the chance, watch a potter working at his wheel. Note how he holds his hands, how he controls the clay and shapes it to his will. Let's watch one right now.

PLATE IV

The potter has set the bat in place in the wheel head. In his hand, he has a ball of clay, thoroughly wedged and ready for throwing. He will toss this onto the center of the bat after he has started the wheel.

Centering. The potter's elbows are pressed firmly against his body. His hands have been dipped in water and he holds them against the clay, forcing it into the shape of a truncated cone. His thumbs ride on top.

Opening. The thumbs press downward to make a depression in the top of the clay.

Opening. The potter's left hand is held against the outside of the clay while the fingers of his right hand push down in the center, enlarging the opening made by his thumbs. His right hand is braced against the left.

Raising the cylinder. The knuckle of the right index finger presses against the outside of the clay while the left index finger pushes outward against the inside of the clay wall. Note how the left thumb is braced against the right hand so that the two index fingers will be kept an even distance apart. Starting at the bottom, the potter will bring his two hands straight up, shaping the clay into a cylinder.

The cylinder has been raised. The potter's hands have come up, squeezing the clay into a wall of even thickness.

Starting the final shape. The clay has been raised again, making a taller cylinder with a thinner wall.

Shaping. The left hand presses from the inside while the right hand shapes the outside.

. . . 39 . . .

Finishing the shape. The potter uses his right thumb nail to make a sharp ridge at the neck of the vase.

Cleaning the foot. Using a scraper, he cuts away excess clay from the base of the vase.

The throwing is finished. The bat and the vase are lifted out of the wheel head and put in the damp box overnight.

Next day. After a night in the damp box, the vase is firm enough to be lifted off the bat. It is shown standing upside down at the left. As the wheel turns, the potter holds a pencil against the bat to draw a circle to help him center the piece.

The potter fastens the piece upside down on the bat, centering it in the circle just drawn. Three keys of clay will hold the piece firmly on the bat while he uses the tool shown at the left to finish the base and the foot.

Turning the foot. The potter's hands rest on a turning stick (see Fig. 38 on page 63). Using the loop tool, the potter cuts away excess clay from the foot and makes a depression in the bottom of the piece so that it will stand on a raised ring.

The piece is finished. The potter will now put it aside to dry for five or six days, after which it will be ready to fire.

It looks easy, doesn't it? All right, then, let's try it.

*Tools*

Provide yourself with a bowl of water large enough to dip your whole hand into, a sponge (elephant's ear, if possible), a potter's knife, a wooden modeling tool, a rubber or wooden rib, a stick sponge (a small piece of sponge tied to the end of a stick), a scraping tool, and a pricker. The pricker is a tool you will make for yourself by driving a needle into the end of a small stick of wood so that three-quarters of an inch of the needle remains exposed. This will be useful in measuring the thickness of the wall or the bottom of a piece and it will come in handy for trimming the top edge. Have these tools within easy reach.

FIG. 26 ~ TOOLS FOR
WORK ON THE WHEEL

*Preparing the clay*

Wedge the clay thoroughly; otherwise you will have trouble. A tiny air bubble can ruin your work, and any hard lumps will throw it out of true. Wedge at least twenty times, and do not stop then unless the portion of your clay which is cut by the wire looks smooth, even, and clean. Prepare five or six balls of clay, each as big as a baseball. Don't start with a piece bigger than this at first. Pat each ball of clay until it is round, with no cracks or folds in the surface.

*Starting in*

When the clay is wedged, you are ready to begin. As we have just seen, throwing on the wheel involves four main steps: centering, opening, pulling up, and shaping. Let's practice the first of these.

*Centering*

If your wheel has a drop head, set the bat in place; if it has a flat head, put a plaster bat in the center and fasten it in place with wads of clay (keys). Wet the clay keys and press them firmly against the bat and the wheel head, then start the wheel turning counter-clockwise. Moisten the bat slightly and throw a ball of clay briskly onto the center of the bat as it turns. (For some reason, throwing the clay onto the wheel while it is in motion makes it hold better.) Wet your hands and wet the clay. Brace your left arm firmly against the frame of the wheel or against your body and push the heel of your left hand against the side of the clay. Put your right hand on the other side of the ball opposite your left, and pull the clay toward you while your left hand pushes against it. Keep the wheel turning rapidly during this operation and moisten the clay from time to time by squeezing the sponge over it.

The heel of your left hand does most of the centering, so keep the left arm firmly braced. Grasp the clay in both hands, with the thumbs resting on top, and press it into a cone-shaped mound. This mound must be absolutely true, with no bumps or irregularities. You will know by the feel when the clay is centered. When it is, remove your hands gently. The mound of clay should now look as though it were standing still even when it is turning.

Some potters like to work the clay up and down at this stage by grasping the mound in both hands and pressing toward the center as the wheel turns. This forces the clay to rise into a taller thinner cone. The heel of the left hand is then pressed down on top, pushing the mound back into its original shape. Doing this two or three times improves the texture of the clay. Beware, however, of getting the clay too soft.

Perfect centering is essential for all work on the wheel; so practice it until you have mastered it. Practice kicking, also, so that the motion of your leg will not interfere with your hands. Feet, hands, and body must all work together.

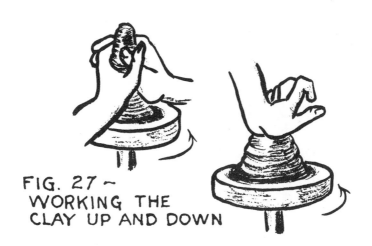

FIG. 27 ~
WORKING THE
CLAY UP AND DOWN

PLATE V

*Opening*

When the ball is centered, press downward with the thumbs to make a depression in the top.

Then brace the left hand against the mound of clay and, resting the right hand on the left, press the fingers of the right hand down on the middle of the mound to enlarge the opening. This opening must be perfectly centered also; and it will be, if you keep your left arm well braced and steady your right hand on your left. The opening should go down far enough to leave a ¾″ thickness at the bottom of the piece. Don't go too far. Until you are able to judge, use the pricker as a gauge to measure the thickness of the bottom. Plunge the needle directly downward, and if the wood goes into the clay, you will know that the base is too thick by that amount. The hole made by the needle will close up as you continue working.

The clay is now shaped like a low, squat bowl with a thick wall. Let this wall turn in your hands for a minute or two, your left hand on the outside and the fingers of your right hand on the inside. Feel it as it turns, smooth and true.

. . . 44 . . .

## Pulling up

Next raise the wall to form a cylinder. The wheel should turn a little more slowly for this operation. Put your right hand on the outside of the piece and your left hand on the inside, with the thumb of the left hand braced against the right wrist.

Then, pressing the clay between the index finger of your left hand and the first knuckle of your right, bring your hands straight up. Your left thumb will help you keep your hands the same distance apart so that the wall of the cylinder will be even in thickness.

Repeat this process two or three times, each time making the wall thinner and higher. Use enough water to keep the work lubricated, but do not use any more than is necessary; if you do, the walls will weaken and slump. From time to time remove the water which collects on the inside of the piece with the stick sponge.

Keep the piece cylindrical. The top will have a tendency to become wider and turn the cylinder into a bowl, but don't let this happen. Using both hands, pull the top together to keep it the same width as the base. Try to make the cylinder 6″ tall (taller, if possible). You should be able to pull it up to the proper height in three or four pullings. If you work on it too long, the piece will collapse.

. . . 45 . . .

### Trimming the top

The top edge of your cylinder will probably be uneven, so it will be necessary to trim off a narrow strip. The pricker is the best tool for this, although you can use a knife. Brace both hands in position and hold the left index finger against the inside of the rim while you press the point of the pricker or the knife blade toward it from the outside.

Keep the wheel turning at a moderate speed and press the point in slowly until it goes all the way through; then raise both hands quickly and lift up the strip of clay which has been cut off. The top of the cylinder will now be perfectly level but slightly rough. Moisten the fingers and hold them against it to smooth it.

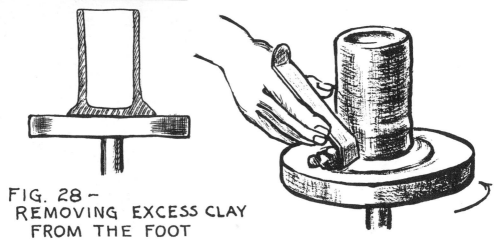

### FIG. 28 – REMOVING EXCESS CLAY FROM THE FOOT

### Cleaning the bat

When you have pulled up the cylinder two or three times, a cross section of the piece will look as shown in Fig. 28. Use a scraping tool and cut away the excess clay from the outside of the foot. This will give your hands a chance to work on the lower portion of the form and will also enable you to see what you are doing. Pull up the cylinder once more after you have trimmed the base.

*The finished cylinder*

Let's see what you have accomplished. Measure the height of the cylinder. Were you able to raise it to six inches? Good! Eight inches? Excellent! More than eight? You're an old hand and ought not to be reading this chapter at all.

*(Plate V Continued)*

Now put your knife on the top edge and cut straight down to the bottom, then do the same thing on the opposite side.

Cut through the base and remove one-half of the cylinder, so that you can look at the cross section. (It will take courage to do this, but remember this cylinder was practice—you did not intend to keep it anyway) Is the wall even in thickness, only slightly heavier at the bottom? Is it free from thin spots? This inspection will tell you what to work for next time.

Don't be discouraged by your first results. Throwing on the wheel sounds a lot simpler than it is. The ease with which a potter does it is highly deceptive, but as you practice, your skill will increase. Don't save any of your first attempts. Keep on throwing cylinders and cutting them in half until you are able to make one 9″ high, with walls no thicker than ⅜″ throughout.

*Shaping*

When you are able to throw a cylinder, you are ready to begin forming special shapes. Most pieces made on the wheel, with the exception of plates and shallow bowls, start out as cylinders, for this form can be easily modified. To make a vase with a narrow neck, throw a cylinder and raise it to full height. Then, pressing on the inside with the left hand and supporting the outside with the right, bring the wall out to the contour you desire. Finish the lower portion before you bring in the neck, because afterward it will be impossible to get your hand inside the piece.

*PLATE VI*

When the lower portion is finished, grasp the top of the cylinder in both hands and using a gentle even pressure, reduce the size of the opening.

Then with the fingers of the left hand supporting the inside, press in with your right hand until the desired shape is obtained.

*Reinforcing the rim*

Thrown pieces are less apt to warp during the firing if they are slightly reinforced at the rim. Fold over a small portion of the top so that it makes a thicker rim at that point.

*Bowls and plates*

To throw a bowl or a plate, you do not need to form a cylinder. Center the clay and open it as usual; then, instead of bringing the wall straight up, start to make a bowl shape by widening the opening, bringing the walls upward and outward at the same time. Let's watch the potter again while he throws a large bowl.

PLATE VII

The potter uses the heel of his right hand to enlarge the opening and force the wall outward. His left hand supports the clay on the outside. Note how the fingers of the two hands are locked together.

Bringing up the wall. The potter makes the bowl wider and taller by pressing the clay between the fingers of both hands.

The wall brought to full height.

Shaping the foot. The index finger of the right hand presses in from the outside. Note how the left thumb rides on the rim.

Removing excess water with a sponge.

Smoothing the inside with a kidney-shaped rubber rib.

Shaping the rim with a sponge.

The throwing is finished. The potter lifts the bat out of the wheel head and puts the bowl aside to dry. Later he will turn it over and finish the foot.

*A pitcher*

To make a pitcher, throw the body exactly as you would a vase, allowing a little extra thickness at the top rim. Shape the spout by supporting the rim with the first two fingers of the left hand, at the same time pulling the top lid outward with the index finger of the right hand until a spout is formed. The clay will need to be coaxed during this step. If you do not handle it gently the rim will crack. Keep the fingers wet.

Making a spout which will pour well is a challenge to the potter. It is annoying to have a cream pitcher which drips onto the tablecloth every time it is used. To keep liquids from running down the side, the spout must be made with a sharp curve downward, as shown in Fig. 29, and the edge of the lip should be quite sharp so that there will be no place for a drop to hang on when you stop pouring.

FIG. 29 — A SPOUT THAT WILL POUR

*Handles*

Handles for thrown pieces may be rolled or pulled. To roll a handle, make a coil just like those used in hand building and flatten it with your thumb. Cut it to the right length and attach it to the pitcher with slurry. (Slurry is thick slip, the stuff which piles up on your hands while you are throwing.)

You will have better luck if you let the handle and the pitcher stand for an hour or two before joining them. In this way there will be less danger of spoiling the shape while putting the handle in place.

Pulled handles are made by grasping a longish lump of clay in the left hand, so that one end protrudes, and pulling the exposed end with the right hand. Pulling is not exactly the word to describe this operation, for the action is similar to milking. The clay is coaxed into shape by squeezing and pulling simultaneously, repeating the processes a dozen or more times. The right hand must be kept wet.

When the clay is drawn out thin enough for a handle, it will be quite pliable; if the left hand is turned, the clay will bend of its own weight into a loop. It can then be set aside to harden for two or three hours, after which a portion of the loop suitable for a handle can be cut off and attached.

This process is not easy; it will take practice. But once you have mastered it, you will be able to make handles in full harmony with your thrown ware. When clay takes shape through its own bending action, the result is more pleasing than anything accomplished by pressing or rolling. A handle which looks as if it had been worked over laboriously spoils the appearance of a thrown piece.

Handles look better when they are not perfectly round in cross section but flattened; they are more pleasing when not uniform in thickness throughout the entire length. Remember, too, that handles must be grasped by hands, so allow room for the fingers and a place for the thumb. Practice making lots of handles before you actually fire one.

Now let us watch the potter as he goes through the steps.

*PLATE VIII*

The centering and the opening have been completed. The potter is bringing up the wall.

Forming the cylinder.

. . . 52 . . .

Narrowing the top.

Reinforcing the edge.

Making ridges in the neck with the fingernail.

Starting to pull the handle.

Pulling the handle.

Turning the left hand so that the clay bends of its own weight.

Forming the spout. The first two fingers of the left hand press against the outside while the right index finger pulls the clay out between them. Meanwhile the handle is drying.

The spout is finished. The potter cuts off a piece of the loop to use for the handle.

. . . 54 . . .

Attaching the handle.

The finished pitcher. The potter lifts the bat out of the wheel head and puts the pitcher in the damp box.

This completes the throwing, but just for fun let's see what happens later on.

The potter has put the pitcher back on the wheel upside down and has turned the foot. With a brush he applies a layer of colored engobe to the lower portion.

Slip trailing a decorative band. (This process is described in Chapter Twelve.)

The pitcher in the kiln ready for salt glazing. Note the cones.

Bricking up the kiln.

Putting salt into the kiln through one of the openings for the burners. (Salt glazing is described in Chapter Ten.)

The firing completed. Note the cones.

The finished pitcher with typical salt glaze finish.

*A teapot*

Here is where the potter meets a real challenge to his skill. Throwing a teapot presents technical problems which call for expert craftsmanship, but at the same time the potter has much freedom in his choice of design. If he is an artist as well as a craftsman, he can create something truly original, graceful, light, easy to hold and to pour. It's a big order.

The body of a teapot is thrown in the same manner as a vase—first a cylinder, then shaped, then brought in at the top to form a seat for the lid. Care must be taken to make the wall thin enough and even throughout, and to finish the outer surface in its final form; for after spout and handle are attached, no changes are possible.

There are two ways in which the lid may fit. These are shown in Fig. 30. Whichever is chosen, the seat must be made accurately. Use a straight piece of wood with a square end in shaping it.

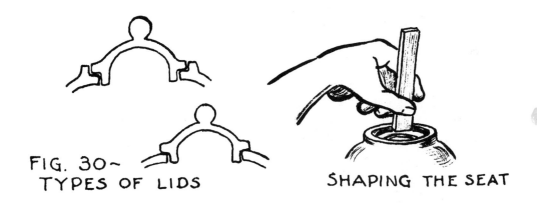

FIG. 30—
TYPES OF LIDS

SHAPING THE SEAT

To make a spout, take a ball of clay, center it, and open it as if you were going to make a cylinder, but instead of bringing the walls straight up, draw them upward and inward until you have formed a cone-shaped tube. Be careful not to make the opening too small. Use a wooden tool as shown in Fig. 31 to smooth the inner surface of the tube and make the

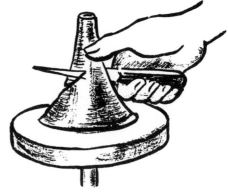

FIG. 31 ~
MAKING A SPOUT

opening the right size. Allow this tube to harden for an hour or two, then cut off a piece of the proper length for the spout.

It is good to roll some coils of clay first and roughly shape a number of spouts from them. By holding these against the body of the pot you will get a good idea of proper size and placing.

When you have decided on the position, mark it and cut a hole equal to the opening of the spout, leaving a rim to which the spout may be fastened with slurry.

Take care not to mar the surface of the pot when you attach the spout. Knuckle marks, however, may be preserved. Better let the pot and the

FIG. 32 ~
ATTACHING
THE SPOUT

FIG. 33 ~
THE SPOUT MUST
BE HIGHER THAN THE
TOP OF THE TEAPOT

spout harden for an hour or two before putting them together. Weld the joint carefully, using a long modeling tool with a ball-shaped end to close the seam on the inside as shown in Fig. 32.

Be sure that the top of the spout is higher than the top of the pot, otherwise tea will spill out when the pot is filled.

The handle for the teapot may be made in the same manner as the handle for the pitcher, either rolled or pulled. Some people prefer the bail type of handle which is made out of a piece of split bamboo and fastened to two loops on the pot. If you want to make the handle this way, roll two small coils of clay and fasten them to the shoulder as shown in Fig. 34.

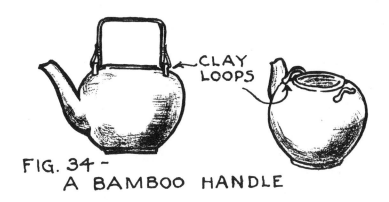

FIG. 34 -
A BAMBOO HANDLE

*A lid for the teapot*

The lid for our teapot presents a special problem because both top and bottom must be shaped. It may be thrown right side up or upside down, but in either case, it will need turning after it is leather-hard, to form the other side (turning is described on page 61). If it is thrown right side up, its shape and that of the knob may be formed in the plastic clay and the turning limited to forming the under side and the flange where appearance is not so important. Usually better design results this way.

Throw the lid as a solid, as shown in Fig. 35.

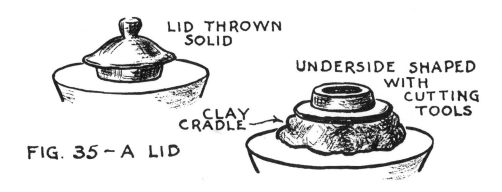

LID THROWN SOLID

UNDERSIDE SHAPED WITH CUTTING TOOLS

CLAY CRADLE

FIG. 35 – A LID

Use calipers to get the size of the flange equal to the size of the opening in the teapot. Allow the solid lid to become leather-hard, then set it in a clay chuck as shown in Fig. 35; center it carefully. The inside of the flange and the inner portion of the lid can then be cut with turning tools.

If the lid is thrown upside down, the flange may be formed and finished with a rib In this case the lid will have to be finished without a knob. After it is leather-hard, some kind of coiled or rolled knob may be attached.

Before the teapot is fired, make sure that the lid fits properly. When both pot and lid are bone-dry, put the lid in place and twist it carefully, thus grinding it to a perfect fit. Remember that the glaze will add thickness; hence, the lid should be rather loose in the raw state. When the teapot is put into the kiln for its first firing, the lid should be in place.

And that's all there is to making a teapot.

### Surface treatment

Much of the charm of thrown ware comes from the fact that the marks of the potter's fingers show in the finished piece, either as rings around the sides or as spirals on inside surfaces. Note the pitchers and the teapot illustrated on Plate IX. As we have seen, the potter may deliberately use his knuckles or his fingernails to make such ridges.

At times you will leave your finger marks on the piece; at others, you will want smooth surfaces, and it will be necessary to remove the ridges with a rib. The rib is a piece of wood, either straight or curved, which is

FIG. 36 ~ USING A RIB

## FIG. 37 - FORMING RIDGES

held against the side of the piece as the wheel turns. A kidney-shaped piece of rubber or a small piece of leather is suitable, also.

A tool with a round head held against a piece will make a groove, while a stick with a depression in the end will produce a raised bead. It is easy to make such a tool by notching the end of a thin flat piece of wood with a round file. A tongue depressor is excellent for this purpose.

### Turning

Before a thrown piece is fired, it usually needs to be trimmed slightly. The shape of the foot must be finished and any extra-thick portions of the wall must be shaved down. The piece is allowed to become leather-hard before this is done. It is then carefully centered on the wheel and fastened in place with keys of plastic clay. The wheel is then rotated and the piece is shaved with a cutting tool.

Such a tool can be made out of a strip of steel bent at the ends and shaped with a file. It is good to have one square end and one round end, both sharpened. Almost any other cutting tool can be used in this process—a potter's knife with a hooked end, or a wire loop modeling tool, or a flexible steel scraper.

To steady your hand, you will need a turning stick like the one shown in Fig. 38. You can make this out of a broomstick about three feet long. Put a spike on one end and a flat piece of wood about 3″ x 5″ on the other. In use, the spike is driven into the wall or into a wooden board erected for that purpose in back of the wheel, and the other end is braced against the chest. The hand can then rest on the stick.

A piece is ready for turning when shavings can be cut off in long curls.

. . . 61 . . .

PLATE IX
Examples of thrown ware.

*Above:* Pitcher and mug glazed with a low firing natural clay made by Alabama potter described in Chapter Thirteen.

*Upper right:* Stoneware teapot, engobe decoration.

*Lower right:* Vase, engobe decoration sprayed against stencils.

*Below:* Brown lustre pitcher and stoneware bowl. Note finger ridges on the pitcher. Bowl made by Pat Lopez.

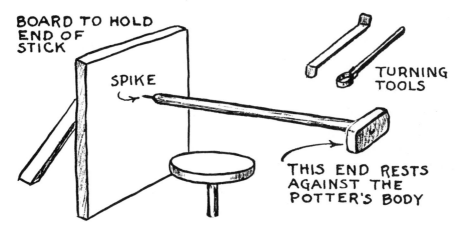

## FIG. 38 ~ TURNING STICK

If the piece is still sticky, it is too wet. If the clay cut off by the cutting tool is a powder, it is too dry. If you leave a piece in the damp box for a day after it has been thrown, it will be just right for turning.

When you fasten a piece to the wheel upside down to turn the foot, look out that you don't spoil the top edge. A vase with a narrow neck, or a pitcher with spout and handle, will need a cradle of soft clay to support it. A piece of oiled paper between the piece and the cradle will prevent the soft clay from sticking to the piece.

There is no set pattern for the shape of a foot. It may be high or low, depending upon the design of the piece. As a rule, a shape like the one shown in Fig. 11 on page 17 is best.

Practically every piece you throw will need some turning, but don't do too much. It is easy to destroy the character of thrown pottery this way. Limit yourself to turning the foot, relying upon your fingers to form the rest of the piece while the clay is plastic.

SOME POINTS ON WHEEL WORK:

*1. Practice, practice, practice. Work to develop skill, not to produce pieces. Nothing you make will be worth saving until you have thrown for an hour or two every day for a period of several months.*

*2. Wedge your clay thoroughly.*

*3. Pulling the clay up and down on the wheel before opening the ball is helpful but do not get your clay too soft.*

*4. Keep the work wet but don't use any more water than is necessary to lubricate it.*

*5. In centering, brace your arm.*

*6. Every one of your fingers is an important tool.*

*7. Your whole body plays a part in throwing.*

*8. Keep the clay turning true at all times. Whenever it starts to wobble, stop forming and center it again.*

9. *Avoid sudden movements. Do not remove your hand from the work abruptly.*

10. *Use the thickness gauge to help you judge the thickness of the bottom but stop using it when you no longer need it.*

11. *Throw pieces and cut them in half to see the thickness of the wall. Work for a uniform wall ⅜" thick.*

12. *Use the rib and the potter's sponge with restraint.*

13. *Avoid strains. A piece which has been pulled up too rapidly will show spiral twists on the side after it is fired.*

14. *Be careful in lifting pieces off the wheel. A sudden jar will cause a delicate bowl to collapse.*

15. *Avoid thin edges. Reinforcement at the rim will help to prevent warping.*

16. *Do not depend upon turning for form. Get form by throwing.*

17. *Be sure your wheel is steady. If it is shaky, fasten it to a wall.*

18. *While you are throwing, bear in mind the use to which the piece will be put. What purpose will it serve and how can its form be suited to that purpose?*

19. *Consider structural elements. Make shapes which will be able to support their own weight during firing.*

20. *Watch a potter at his wheel whenever you have a chance to do so.*

21. *Practice, practice, practice.*

# chapter Four

# *Plaster of Paris*

laster of Paris is useful to the potter because it will absorb moisture from clay either in the liquid or the plastic state. If a lump of clay is left on a slab of dry plaster for only a few minutes, the portion touching the plaster will become dryer and harder than the rest, while a drop of slip falling on the same slab will turn into a dry, hard button almost immediately. Any scratches in the slab will be faithfully reproduced as ridges on the underside of the button.

Let us try an experiment. Suppose we gouge a depression in a plaster slab, making it roughly the shape of a small cup, and then pour clay slip into it. The plaster will begin immediately to draw water out of the slip, and the surface of the liquid will be lowered. If we turn over the plaster slab at the end of five minutes and empty out all of the slip which will still pour, we will note that a thin layer of clay remains lining the inside of the depression and taking its shape. In a few minutes, as the plaster continues to absorb moisture, this clay layer will begin to harden; in an hour it will have shrunk and pulled away from the plaster, so that we can lift it out. In a few hours more it will be hard enough to pick up, and, behold, we have a clay cup. In a day or two it will be dry enough to put into a kiln and fire.

This is the property which makes plaster of Paris essential to the pottery industry—makes it, in fact, the basis of practically all commercial ceramics. Don't think, however, that its use is restricted to the factory. Not at all; it is a valuable aid to the individual craft potter as well; and when used with appreciation and understanding of what it can do, it will help him to produce ware highly individual, which has no suggestion whatsoever of commercialism.

### What is plaster of Paris?

Briefly, plaster of Paris is gypsum rock which has been heated. When mined, the rock is hard. The heating process drives off chemically combined water and reduces the rock to a soft material that is easily crushed into a fine white powder. Unlike clay, which once it has lost its chemically combined water will never take it back, this powder has an affinity for water; when mixed with water, it sets or crystallizes once more into a hard, white solid just about like the original rock. And there's the whole secret of plaster of Paris.

### What plaster to buy

Many different kinds and brands of plaster are sold. The best type for the potter is the U.S. Gypsum Company's pottery plaster. This comes in 100-pound bags or 250-pound barrels. If it is not easy to get pottery plaster, buy Red Top or Sunflower. Don't buy more plaster than you can use within a few weeks. Unless you are able to store it in an absolutely air-tight container, it won't keep.

### Mixing

Best results in plaster work are obtained when both plaster and water are accurately measured. The correct proportion for mold work is 2¾ pounds of plaster to 1 quart of water. A greater proportion of plaster produces a mix which is hard and dense, not absorbent enough for molds. A smaller proportion of plaster makes a weak substance which crumbles easily and is not strong enough for use.

In mixing, measure the water first and put it in a pail or a bowl, then weigh the plaster and sprinkle it into the water. *Sprinkle* it in—don't dump it; otherwise you'll have a lumpy mess on your hands that will be hard to stir. When all of the plaster has been sprinkled in, allow it to slake for two minutes. This slaking period is important, for if you stir too soon the plaster will form lumps. After the slaking, stir.

The stirring should be done by hand in such a way that the whole mass is agitated and air bubbles are driven out. Don't whip the mixture, for that will get more air bubbles in. If a pail is used, a good method of stirring is to put the hand palm upward on the bottom of the pail and wiggle the fingers vigorously so that the plaster is constantly forced up to the top. For a smaller batch, stir so that the fingers rub the bottom of the bowl, or, if you prefer, use a large spoon.

Stirring should continue for another two or three minutes. By that time the plaster will begin to thicken. When the mixture is thick enough so that a finger drawn over the surface leaves a slight trace, it is ready to pour.

You will soon be able to recognize the feel of plaster and be able to judge the proper pouring time. You will also be able to tell when you start the stirring if the proportions are right. Any lumps in the mix should be broken with the fingers. Incidentally, such lumps indicate that the plaster was put into the water too rapidly or that not enough time was allowed for slaking; perhaps, too, the plaster itself was lumpy. Examine your plaster

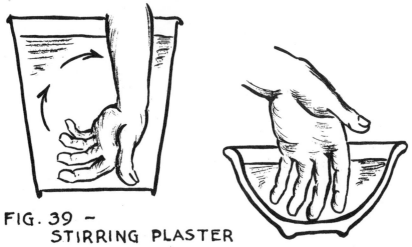

## FIG. 39 ~ STIRRING PLASTER

supply, and if you find lumps in it, screen it through a sieve before you use it.

### Pouring

Plaster must be poured smoothly without any splashing. The trick is to pour it so that no air bubbles are trapped and so that no vacant spaces are left next to the model. It is good to work on a table which can be jarred right after the plaster has been poured so that air bubbles can be forced to the surface. The plaster can be stirred with a small stick immediately after it has been poured, provided you are careful not to touch the model.

### Making a plaster slab

In your pottery work you will always have use for a number of flat rectangular plaster slabs and for round plaster bats. Let's learn how to mix and pour plaster by making some of these. Prepare four strips of wood ¾" thick, 1" wide, and 12" long. Fasten them together so that they make a frame enclosing a 9" x 12" area, and lay it on a sheet of glass. This will act as a retaining wall for the plaster. The wood should be coated with oil or vase-

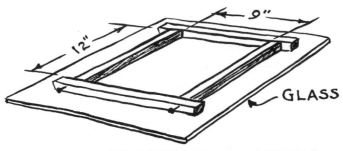

## FIG. 40 ~ FRAME FOR CASTING PLASTER SLAB

line. If the glass is clean it need not be oiled. When the plaster is poured it will lift up the frame and flow out underneath unless the wooden strips are fastened down with clay or held in place by some heavy objects, such as a pair of bricks, placed on top.

Now put one quart of water in a large bowl, weigh out 2¾ pounds of plaster, and mix as directed above. When it is ready, pour the plaster into the frame. The sheet of glass should be on a table whose top is absolutely level, so that when the plaster flows it will make a layer of even thickness. Jar the table vigorously immediately after pouring to cause the plaster to flow into all corners. If air bubbles come to the surface, blow on them to break them.

In a few minutes the plaster will begin to set and the surface will lose its shine. If you were to stick your finger into it now, you would find it to be of the consistency of cream cheese. It is passing through its period of plasticity, which potters call the cheese state. Later we shall learn how to use this period of plasticity to model in plaster or to run forms with a template; but for the present, leave the plaster undisturbed. In a few more minutes it will harden, then it will begin to get warm. This is the period of crystallization. Let it stand until it begins to cool. When it is once more cold to the touch, crystallization is completed and it is safe to remove the wooden frame and lift up the slab.

### Computing amount of plaster needed

You will note when you have completed the slab that the quantity of water and plaster you mixed was just enough to fill the frame. The slab is 9″ x 12″ x ¾″ thick, or 81 cubic inches. Remember this figure—one quart of water plus 2¾ pounds of plaster equals 81 cubic inches. This will help you compute the amount of plaster to mix for other mold jobs.

### Plaster bats

Round plaster bats are useful for wheel work and coil building. To make them, use a pie tin about 6″ or 8″ in diameter. Use oil or vaseline on the pan but wipe off all of the excess before pouring the plaster. Bats of even thickness can be made if the table is absolutely level and the plaster is poured soon enough so that it can flow. Another way of making sure the bats are even in thickness is to pour just a little too much plaster into the pan; then when it begins to set, draw a straight edge or a ruler across the top as shown in Fig. 41.

### Drying plaster

Freshly made plaster will need to dry for five or six days before it is ready for use. The drying process can be hastened if the plaster is placed near a warm radiator. Don't let it get hot—that weakens it and causes it to crumble. A good way to dry plaster molds (clay, too, for that matter) is by

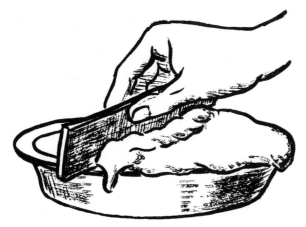

FIG. 41 ~ LEVELING THE TOP
OF A PLASTER BAT

using infra-red lamps. The rays from such lamps penetrate solid objects, causing them to dry on the inside as well as on the surface. You will find a pair of these lamps useful in your studio. Set them up so that they shine on the object to be dried from a height of three feet, and arrange shades so that the rays do not reach any other part of the room.

*Sizing*

Plaster can be poured over moist clay or onto a clean sheet of glass, and when it hardens, it will come away without sticking. If it is poured onto another piece of plaster, however, it will stick fast unless we use size as a parting. Size is soap. A good grade of soft soap suitable for this purpose can be bought for about 25 cents per pound. When you buy it, it has the consistency of axle grease. Don't use it in that form. Size should be thin, almost as thin as water for the first application, slightly thicker for those that follow. To prepare it, boil up about a pound of soft soap in two quarts of water and then thin the resultant syrup by adding two more quarts of water when it is cool. An easier way of preparing size is to put a lump of soap as big as your fist in the bottom of a gallon jar, then fill the jar with hot water, cover it, and shake violently. Let it stand overnight. The next day there will be some thick size at the bottom of the jar while at the top will be a clear honey-colored liquid just right for use. When most of this has been used up, add more hot water and repeat the process.

If you can't get soft soap, a fairly good substitute can be made from brown laundry soap.

Any size which gets on the working surface of a mold will spoil it because the absorption of the plaster will be killed at that spot. If this happens, remove the size by wiping the mold several times with a cloth soaked in vinegar.

### Stearine

Mold makers sometimes prefer to shellac plaster and then use stearine as a parting compound. This works a little better than soap size, but it must not be used on surfaces from which drain molds are to be cast, for any stearine which gets on the mold kills the absorption at that point and hence spoils it for use.

Stearine is made from stearic acid. Put about two tablespoons in a can and heat it until the stearic acid melts, then remove the can from the fire and add eight tablespoons of kerosene. Be sure to extinguish the fire before you add the kerosene. Stir for fifteen minutes, then put the mixture aside to cool. When you are ready to use it, whip it up with a brush until it forms a creamy mass just right for applying. Add a little more kerosene if necessary.

Shellac the plaster before you use stearine, applying three or four coats in succession and allowing each to dry before the next is put on. Use the shellac thin. When the last coat of shellac is dry, brush a coat of stearine on the surface, then wipe off all of the excess.

Plaster can be cast against a dry clay shape if the clay is given several coats of shellac then coated with size or stearine.

### Applying size

Much of the craftsmanship of the mold maker depends upon proper sizing. Size must be put on in several successive applications, each of which is thoroughly wiped off. It may be put on with a soft brush and wiped off with a sponge, although some potters prefer to use the sponge for both operations. In the first application, the size should be very thin. Apply it quickly and wipe it off at once. This reduces the absorption of the plaster surface. The second application may be made with size which is slightly thicker. Rub it in well with the sponge, then squeeze the sponge dry and wipe it all off. Repeat this process at least five times. At the end of the last application, squeeze the sponge as dry as you can and wipe off every bit of size. *Don't* rinse the sponge in water. Don't even rinse your hands. Keep a clean cloth handy, and when you are ready to take off the last coat, roll the sponge in the cloth to get all of the size out.

Is it really necessary to be so fussy? Yes—the smallest trace of size left on a plaster model will spoil the surface of the mold which is cast from it. When you have finished sizing, the model should look like a piece of old ivory. Flick a drop of water against it. If the size job is good, the water will skip as it would on a hot stove.

Don't size a model and then leave it for an hour before pouring plaster— by that time the size will no longer be effective. Sizing must be done just before plaster is poured.

*Plaster tools*

You will need a few special tools for working in plaster—a steel scraper with a saw-toothed edge, two flexible steel kidney-shaped scrapers (one with a saw-toothed edge and one plain), a spatula, a chisel, and half a dozen steel plaster carving tools. If you plan to do any plaster work on the wheel, you will need two turning tools, one with straight sides and one curved. The toothed edge of the scraper is valuable for smoothing surfaces. The best way to get a perfectly level surface is with such a tool. After the saw-toothed edge has been used to take down any bumps and make the surface level, the straight edge can be used to take off the scratches.

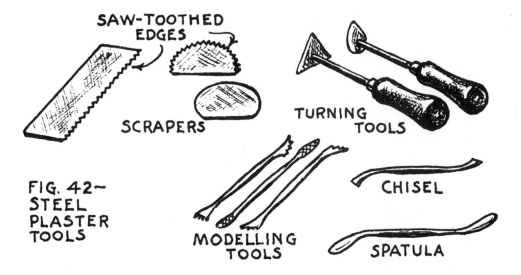

SAW-TOOTHED EDGES

SCRAPERS

TURNING TOOLS

FIG. 42— STEEL PLASTER TOOLS

MODELLING TOOLS

CHISEL

SPATULA

When plaster is wet it is comparatively soft and easy to cut. When it is dry it can be worked on with sandpaper. For final finishing of plaster surfaces, use the finest grade of sandpaper you can buy. Number 6-0 garnet paper is best.

*Adding new plaster to old*

When making plaster models, you will sometimes want to add new plaster to old. Whenever you add plaster this way, be sure to soak the old plaster thoroughly and scratch the surface where the new plaster is to be attached. Unless the old plaster is saturated it will draw water out of the new batch causing it to "short," that is, set extremely hard like a mix with too much plaster and not enough water. When this happens, the new plaster won't hold on.

*Disposing of plaster waste*

Let's not ruin the plumbing. If you clean a bowl in which plaster has been mixed by rinsing it in the sink, you will almost certainly have an expensive repair job on your hands. Don't let a bit of plaster get into the drain!

For small amounts of plaster work, the disposal problem can be solved by wiping the mixing bowl with old newspapers as soon as the plaster is poured and before it begins to harden. Another method is to allow what remains in the mixing bowl to set completely hard, then fill the bowl with cold water. If the surface of the bowl is perfectly smooth, the water will cause the plaster to crack off in chunks which can be disposed of as ordinary refuse.

If much plaster work is to be done, the studio should have a special sink trap like the one shown in Fig. 43. When plaster accumulates in the large container, it can be removed and emptied. A simpler arrangement is to rinse all plaster bowls in a large pail of water, disposing of the accumulated plaster the same way as above.

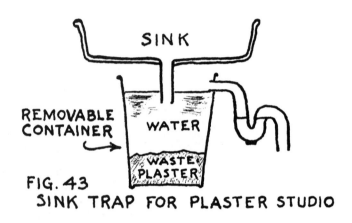

FIG. 43
SINK TRAP FOR PLASTER STUDIO

Plaster which gets on the clothes should be allowed to dry, and then be rubbed off. If necessary, the material may be soaked in cold water, but don't use soap—that makes plaster stick to the fabric.

SOME POINTS ON PLASTER:

*1. When mixing, sprinkle the plaster into the water slowly. Never pour water into plaster.*

*2. Have proportions right. If you have no scale, add plaster to the water until a mound of plaster projects above the surface. After the plaster has slaked, pour off any free water which remains on top. This will give a mix approximately right.*

*3. Store plaster in an air-tight container, otherwise it will absorb moisture from the atmosphere.*

*4. If your plaster contains lumps, sift it before using it.*

5. *Old plaster won't work. A dirty scum on the surface of the water when you are mixing indicates that the plaster is no good.*

6. *Plaster can be cast against moist clay or glass without the use of a parting compound. Wood and metal surfaces should be oiled or greased before plaster is cast against them, and plaster surfaces should be sized.*

7. *Be thorough when you apply size.*

8. *Plaster tools deserve good treatment. Clean them each time they are used and oil them occasionally.*

9. *Take pride in your work. Even though the things you make of plaster are for temporary use, make them with care and accuracy.*

# chapter Five

# *M*olds

*P*laster molds can be made in many different ways. They may be cast from clay shapes or plaster models, or even natural objects. In fact, a plaster mold can be made of practically anything at all.

Potters as a rule prefer to make their molds from plaster models because better surfaces are possible that way. In making a mold of a small figure or of a rectangular plate, the potter would first model the shape in clay, then make a waste mold and cast the shape again in plaster. This plaster shape would then be carefully finished with plaster tools and sandpaper, and the final mold cast from it.

Plaster models can be turned directly on the wheel, or on a lathe, or they may be carved by hand. Models are sometimes made by running templates over plaster while it is setting.

Some molds use liquid clay, while others require clay in plastic form. The simplest molds are "drain molds." In these, clay slip is poured into the mold and allowed to stand until a clay wall of the proper thickness is built up on the inner surface of the mold, after which all of the slip which is still liquid is poured out. The clay wall remaining in the mold is then allowed to dry, after which it is removed from the mold, finished, and fired.

*A one-piece drain mold for a bowl*

A bowl or a cup can be cast in a one-piece drain mold, provided the shape is widest at the top and diminishes steadily from top to bottom like those shown in Fig. 44. Such a shape is said to have "draft." It can be easily lifted out of a mold.

The model for such a mold may be shaped on a potter's wheel out of a solid lump of clay. Wedge the clay well to remove all air bubbles and use a plaster bat about 3″ greater in diameter than the shape you are making. After fastening the bat to the wheel head, throw the ball of clay and center it just as if you were going to make a vase. However, instead of opening the ball of clay, mold it to the shape of the outside of your bowl, upside down. Remember to allow for shrinkage. The shape must be at least one-sixth larger than the finished bowl.

SHAPES LIKE THESE CAN BE MADE
IN ONE-PIECE MOLDS

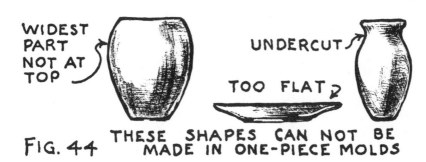

WIDEST PART NOT AT TOP

UNDERCUT

TOO FLAT?

FIG. 44  THESE SHAPES CAN NOT BE
MADE IN ONE-PIECE MOLDS

## A *waste rim*

A mold works best when it contains a waste rim, that is, a small collar on the form which can be trimmed off and discarded. In making the shape, allow an additional piece about ½″ high and ½″ wide for this purpose as shown in Fig. 45. This can be easily formed with a wooden modeling

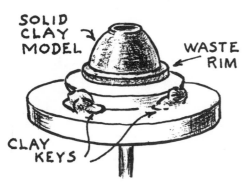

SOLID CLAY MODEL

WASTE RIM

CLAY KEYS

FIG. 45- MAKING A
MOLD OF A BOWL

COTTLE

READY TO POUR
PLASTER

tool. Use the wooden tool, also, to finish the foot, and smooth the sides with a rubber rib.

When the shape is finished, the mold may be poured. This can be done without removing the work from the wheel head. Size the plaster bat thoroughly but don't get any size on the clay. It will now be necessary to erect some type of retaining wall to hold the plaster. For this purpose, a piece of heavy roofing paper answers well. The paper should be cut slightly wider than the height of the mold and long enough to wrap around the plaster bat three or four times. Roofing paper used this way is called a cottle. The cottle may be tied with a length of twine or fastened with a snap-on clothes pin. A roll of clay pressed firmly around the base of the cottle as shown in Fig. 45 will prevent plaster from leaking out.

When the cottle is in place, mix the plaster and pour. Immediately after pouring the plaster, jar the wheel head by striking it sharply with your fist several times. This will get rid of any air bubbles adhering to the clay form. When the plaster has reached the consistency of cream cheese, remove the cottle and smooth the outside surface of the mold by holding a scraper against it as the wheel is turned. This must be done before the plaster gets hard, otherwise the work will come loose from the wheel head. After the outside of the mold is reasonably smooth, allow the plaster to set, then remove the mold from the clay model. It is finished. Set the mold aside to dry for five or six days. We shall learn in Chapter Six how it is used.

### A plaster drying bat

In Chapter One mention was made of plaster drying bats into which liquid clay could be poured and allowed to harden. The method of making such a bat is the same as that described for the bowl above, except that you may work directly on the wheel head and the clay model should be wider and shallower, as shown in Fig. 46.

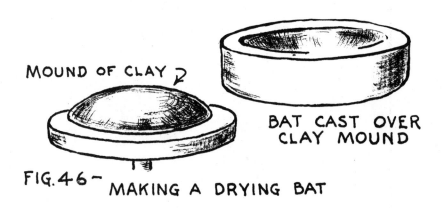

MOUND OF CLAY

BAT CAST OVER CLAY MOUND

FIG. 46 – MAKING A DRYING BAT

*A mold for a box*

Rectangular shapes can be made in one-piece drain molds just as easily as round ones, provided we allow draft. In designing a rectangular box, we should remember that we are potters, not carpenters. We work with clay, and so our box must not look like wood—corners should be rounded rather than square and surfaces should not be too flat. There is a sound structural reason for this. Sharp corners do not cast easily nor take glaze well, and surfaces absolutely flat tend to sag and become concave during the firing.

For a mold of a box we shall need a flat plaster slab which is perfectly smooth, preferably one cast against glass. Cut the slab into a rectangular shape 3″ longer and 3″ wider than the box. Take care in cutting the slab to have the corners square and the sides true. Accuracy here will help in making the mold later on.

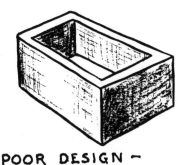

POOR DESIGN —
LOOKS LIKE WOOD

FIG. 47-
A CERAMIC BOX

BETTER DESIGN —
BOX HAS A "CLAY"
QUALITY

Draw a line with indelible pencil through the center of the slab, dividing it in half the long way, then draw another line through the center of the first one at right angles to it. It is important that these two lines be perpendicular to each other, for our box will be lopsided if they are not.

The next step is to draw an outline of the top of the box on the plaster slab. Remember to allow for shrinkage when you plan the size. You will find it helpful to fold a piece of paper in quarters and cut out a pattern for the top. In this way you can be certain that the shape is symmetrical. Keep on trimming the paper pattern until the shape pleases you. When the pattern is right, lay it on the plaster slab so that the folds in the paper are on the lines previously drawn, then trace the outline with indelible pencil.

Now comes the job of building a solid clay form shaped like the box

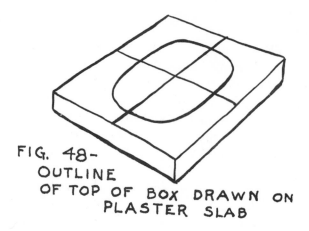

FIG. 48-
OUTLINE
OF TOP OF BOX DRAWN ON
PLASTER SLAB

upside down. This clay form must fit the outline you have drawn and must slope up evenly on all sides to a height equal to the depth of the box. There is no short cut here—patience and a lot of careful modeling are needed.

Use a piece of wood about 2″ x 2″ x 4″ to block out the form, then finish it with modeling tools. Draw a flexible steel scraper up the sides to make them smooth and uniform. Use a cardboard template as a guide. The top of the form must be flat or else slightly concave, otherwise the box will not stand level. Lay a ruler on the clay to make sure that the top is not convex. You can, if you wish, model a raised rim for the box to stand on, or else make four feet, one in each corner. Feet of this type must be small and must taper sharply to avoid trouble in the casting.

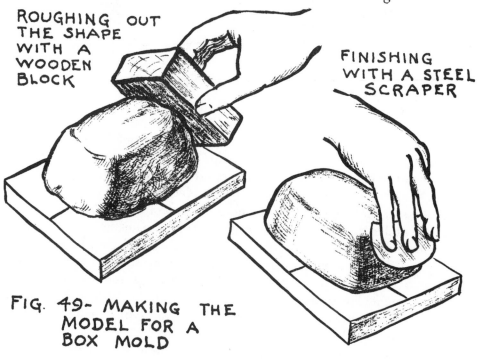

ROUGHING OUT
THE SHAPE
WITH A
WOODEN
BLOCK

FINISHING
WITH A STEEL
SCRAPER

FIG. 49- MAKING THE
MODEL FOR A
BOX MOLD

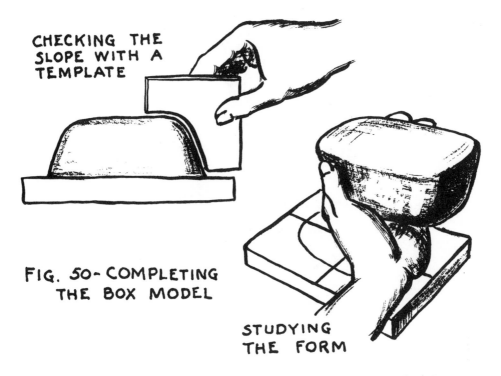

CHECKING THE
SLOPE WITH A
TEMPLATE

FIG. 50- COMPLETING
THE BOX MODEL

STUDYING
THE FORM

Study the shape as you work by looking at it from all angles. Compare opposite sides for symmetry. Look straight down on it. Study it by feeling as well, for your fingers will often tell you more about form than your eyes.

For a final check, lift the clay model off the plaster slab and look at it right side up. Is the shape pleasing? Does it feel right in the hand? Does it stand well on the table? If so, you are ready to pour the mold. Size the slab, and put the clay form back in place, then set the retaining wall at the edge of the slab and pour the plaster for the mold.

The retaining wall may be made out of four pieces of wood. When you pour plaster to a depth of several inches, the pressure on the retaining wall is greater than you may think, so fasten the pieces of wood securely, either by tying or nailing them together. Put clay at the joints to keep the plaster from seeping out.

*A casting box*

This is a good place to describe a simple device for casting rectangular shapes which mold makers call a casting box. This consists of four pieces of wood about 6″ x 15″ x ¾″ thick, each with a piece of strap iron fastened to the end as shown in Fig. 51. These four pieces fit together to make a box of any size up to 15″ square; and four wedges, used as shown, hold them tightly together while the plaster is poured.

When the retaining wall is in place, mix plaster and pour. Allow the plaster to set, then remove the casting box and take out the clay model. Try to remove the clay form without destroying it. This may not be easy.

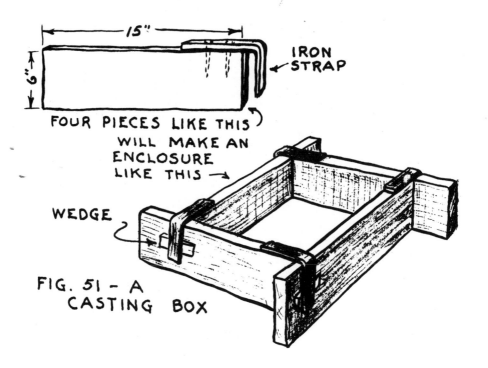

FIG. 51 — A
CASTING BOX

If you have to break it to get it out, patch the pieces together again, for you will need the model to help you in the next job, which is designing a lid.

### A mold for the lid

A lid for the box we have just designed must have a flange or collar to fit into the box. Hence, we cannot make it in a one-piece mold. We can, however, make a simple two-piece mold which will work.

Start as before with a flat plaster slab. In fact, the same slab that was used for the box may be used again. This time draw an outline about ⅛″ larger all around than the outline of the box. This is to allow the lid to overhang slightly. Now build up a clay form for the lid, forgetting the flange for the time being. The lid should not be entirely flat but slightly domed in the center. The thickness may be about ¼″ at the midpoint, tapering to ⅛″ at the edge. Model this just as you did the box, using a steel scraper for the final smoothing. When you have it as you think it should be, take it off the slab and try it on the clay model of the box to see if the two go well together and if the lid is pleasing when in place. If it is, size the slab, put the lid back in position, set the casting box or the retaining wall, mix plaster, and pour.

This is only one-half of the job. When the plaster has set, remove the original slab, allowing the clay shape of the lid to remain embedded in the mold. Turn the mold upside down so that the clay lid is on top, and make a shape for the flange. The flange can be cut out of a layer of clay

. . . 80 . . .

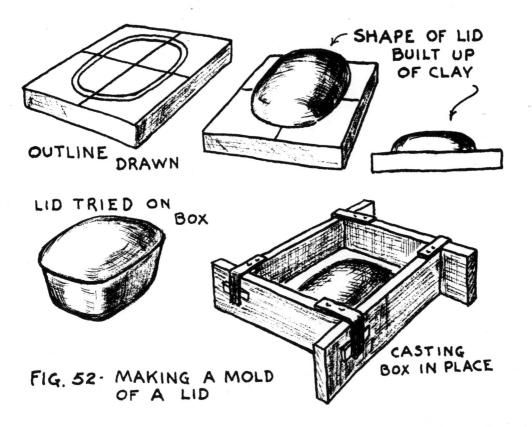

OUTLINE DRAWN

SHAPE OF LID BUILT UP OF CLAY

LID TRIED ON BOX

CASTING BOX IN PLACE

FIG. 52· MAKING A MOLD OF A LID

rolled flat, ½″ thick. It should be the same shape as the box itself, but ½″ smaller all around. This may make the flange a trifle too small, but it will be possible to enlarge the opening in the mold later if the finished lid fits too loosely. The sides of this piece should be almost vertical, tapering slightly toward the top. Lay this piece in place on the underside of the clay lid which is still embedded in the plaster mold.

Before pouring the second half of the mold, cut some notches in the first half so that the two will fit together. A knife with the end of the blade bent into hook shape is a good tool for this purpose. Such knives can be bought from ceramic supply houses. (*Note:* Don't cut the same number of notches on each side. If you do, you will always be annoyed when putting the two halves together, for somehow or other, you will be sure to try them the wrong way first. Put two notches on one end and one on the other. That way it will be quite evident which way the halves fit.)

When the notches are cut, size the exposed portion of the first half of the mold, set the casting box and pour the second half. This half will be quite thin since it should not extend higher than the piece of clay which forms the collar.

When the molds of both the box and the lid are dry, pour trial pieces. As we mentioned above, the lid may fit too loosely. If it does, the portion of the mold making the flange may be enlarged by scraping or rubbing

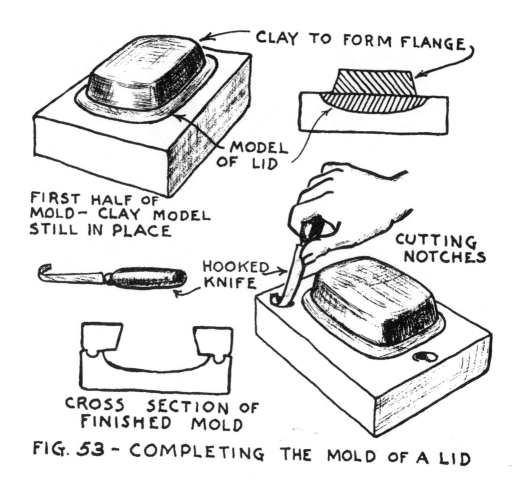

CLAY TO FORM FLANGE,

MODEL OF LID

FIRST HALF OF MOLD - CLAY MODEL STILL IN PLACE

CUTTING NOTCHES

HOOKED KNIFE

CROSS SECTION OF FINISHED MOLD

FIG. 53 - COMPLETING THE MOLD OF A LID

with sandpaper until a good fit is obtained. Remember that the finished box will have a coating of glaze; so the lid must not fit too tightly in the raw state.

*Drain molds from plaster forms*

The drain molds described so far, the bowl, the box, and the lid, were made directly from clay models. Each of these would have been a better mold had the model been made in plaster first, for plastic clay does not permit the finish which is possible with plaster.

To make a plaster model of the box, start as described above, first making the shape as carefully as possible out of clay; then instead of casting a mold from the clay, make a waste mold. As the name suggests, this is a mold which will be thrown away after one use; so it is not necessary to take too much care in making it. A ¾″ shell will suffice. When this has hardened, remove the clay, smooth the inside of the waste mold with sandpaper, size it, and pour in plaster. When this plaster has set, remove the waste mold (break it away if necessary), and the model of the box is ready for finishing with plaster tools and sandpaper.

In describing the method of making a mold for the box directly from a clay form, no mention was made of a waste rim. This was not overlooked; it was left out to make the job less complicated. The mold can be used without a waste rim, but it is better to have one. Before pouring plaster over the model, make a layer of clay ½" thick, place the box upside down on it, and cut the layer so that it forms a band ½" wide all the way around. Put this on the plaster slab with the model on top of it, then size the slab and the model, set the casting box, and pour the mold.

To make a model of the lid, proceed as before, shaping the lid in clay without a flange; then make a waste mold and cast the lid, still without flange, in plaster. The models of the box and the lid may then be studied together, and any changes needed to improve appearance can be made. In making the mold for the lid, the first half is cast over the plaster model, then the second half is made as before, with a layer of clay cut to form the flange and notches cut so that the two halves will fit together. The mold for the lid will not need a waste rim.

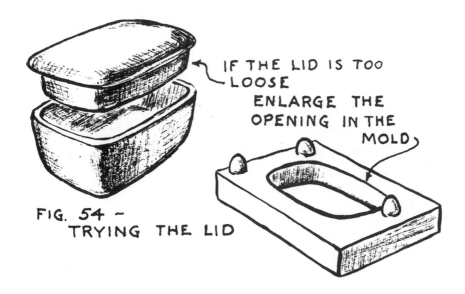

IF THE LID IS TOO LOOSE ENLARGE THE OPENING IN THE MOLD

FIG. 54 –
TRYING THE LID

*Plaster work on the wheel*

Molds for round objects can be made from plaster models cast and turned on a wheel, but it is quite difficult to operate a foot-power wheel and cut plaster at the same time. A motor driven wheel is almost a necessity for this kind of work, because a speed of 200 revolutions per minute is required. A kick wheel can be used, however, if someone is willing to turn it for you while you do the shaping.

Plaster work on the wheel requires a working surface of plaster; it is, therefore, essential to have some means of fastening a large plaster bat firmly on the wheel head. For a wheel with the drop type of head, cast a bat to fit according to the method described in Chapter Three, but make the bat larger and thicker. If your wheel has a flat head, it will be necessary to fasten some lugs of metal or wood to the surface so that a large plaster bat cast on the wheel head will be held in place.

*Tools*

You will need a turning stick like the one shown in Fig. 38 on page 63 for this work and a board to hold it. You will need some turning tools (one with straight and one with curved edges), a flexible steel scraper, a knife, and a chisel, as illustrated in Fig. 42 on page 71.

*A chuck*

The first step in making a mold on the plaster wheel is to make a chuck. This is merely a projection on the wheel head over which a cylinder of plaster can be cast and held while it is worked on. The chuck must be shaped so that the form cast over it can be easily lifted off and replaced. A truncated cone with a slot cut in it as shown in Fig. 55 serves well. The base of the chuck can be used to fasten the cottle when the mold is poured.

FIG. 55 — A CHUCK

To make a chuck, place the plaster bat on the wheel head and start the wheel. Then brace the turning stick in the board and hold a pencil against it so that it draws a circle on the plaster bat about 7″ in diameter. Next, size the plaster bat and set a cottle on the circle just drawn, fastening it firmly with clay. Mix enough plaster to fill the cottle to a depth of three inches (a quart and a half of water plus 4 pounds and 2 ounces of plaster will do the trick) and pour it in. As soon as the plaster is firm enough to stand by itself, remove the cottle and start cutting the chuck.

Don't let the plaster get hard. Remember, you have sized the bat; therefore, as soon as the plaster hardens, it will come loose. As long as it is soft you can work on it safely.

Hold the triangular cutting tool as shown in Fig. 56, the left hand grasping the handle of the tool against the turning stick and the right hand squeezing the shaft of the tool and the turning stick together. A firm grip like this will give you perfect control of the tool. Keep the point of the stick tight in the board and brace the other end firmly against your body. By moving your body slightly you will be able to move the stick and the tool without loosening your hand grip.

While the plaster is still soft, cut the cylinder into shape as shown in

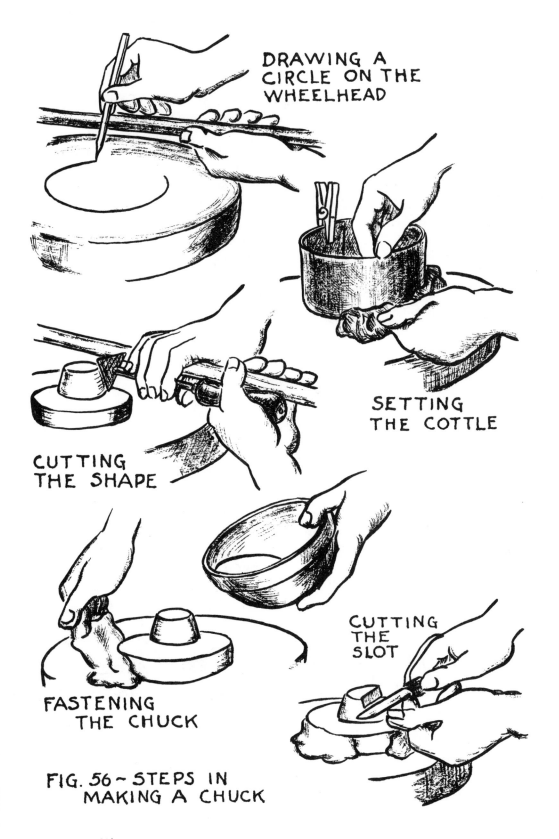

DRAWING A CIRCLE ON THE WHEELHEAD

SETTING THE COTTLE

CUTTING THE SHAPE

FASTENING THE CHUCK

CUTTING THE SLOT

FIG. 56 ~ STEPS IN MAKING A CHUCK

Fig. 56—cut straight up for half its height, then cut in to make a small truncated cone about 3″ in diameter at the base and 2″ at the top. (The size of the cone will vary according to the size and shape of the piece you plan to make.) As soon as you have this shape roughed out, stop cutting and fasten the chuck to the bat by mixing a small quantity of plaster extra-thick and using it to make wads or keys to hold the edge of the chuck to the bat in three places. These plaster keys will stick firmly against the chuck; but in order to have them hold on the bat, it will be necessary to scrape through the coating of size and wet the plaster bat at each point where a key is to be placed.

It may seem odd that we took the trouble to size the plaster bat before pouring the plaster for the chuck, and that we then mixed fresh plaster to hold the chuck in place, but there is a reason for doing so. We want the chuck held firm while we work; but when we are finished, we want to be able to chip away the keys and lift it off the wheel.

When the keys have set, work on the chuck some more. It will be hard by now, and you will be able to cut a perfectly smooth surface. Be careful to remove any little ridges. When this is done, stop the wheel and cut a slot in the top of the cone as shown. Now the chuck is finished and you are ready to make some shapes.

*A one-piece drain mold for a simple vase*

To make a vase like the one shown in Fig. 58, size the chuck thoroughly, then set a cottle around its base and pour enough plaster to make a cylinder slightly wider and taller than the vase will be (Fig. 57). Take away the

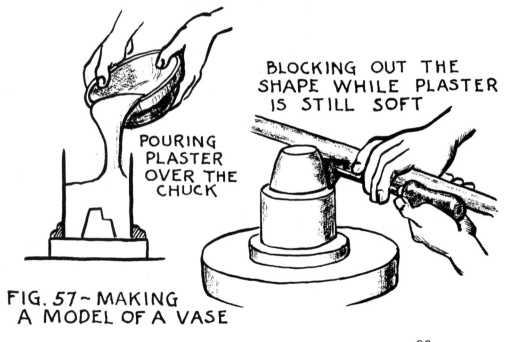

POURING PLASTER OVER THE CHUCK

BLOCKING OUT THE SHAPE WHILE PLASTER IS STILL SOFT

FIG. 57 ~ MAKING A MODEL OF A VASE

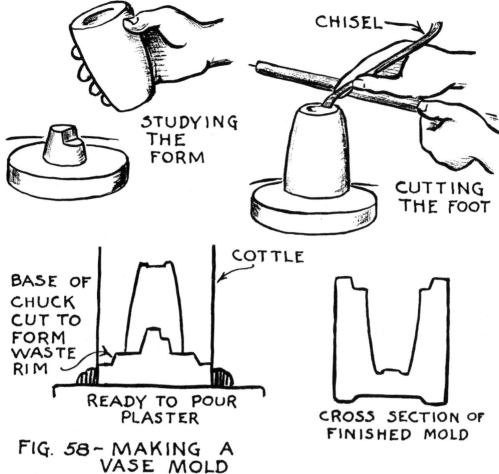

STUDYING THE FORM

CHISEL

CUTTING THE FOOT

BASE OF CHUCK CUT TO FORM WASTE RIM

COTTLE

READY TO POUR PLASTER

CROSS SECTION OF FINISHED MOLD

## FIG. 58 – MAKING A VASE MOLD

cottle as soon as the plaster is firm enough to stand and start roughing out the shape before it gets hard. Finish the shaping after the plaster hardens.

Here is where the chuck comes in handy. When you have the shape just as you think it should be, lift it off the chuck and study it right side up. You will be surprised to see how different it looks and how defects which you did not notice before are now glaringly evident. Put the model back on the chuck and correct the mistakes, then take it off for further study. The flexible steel scraper is a good tool for final shaping because it can be bent in the fingers and adapted to almost any curve. It gives a good surface, too. The chisel will be useful in shaping the foot.

Before the mold is poured, cut a step on the chuck, as shown in Fig. 58, to serve as a waste rim in the mold. Size the model, place the cottle around the base of the chuck, and pour plaster for the mold. As soon as this starts to stiffen, remove the cottle and use the turning tools to trim up the outside surface. Make the bottom of the mold slightly concave so that it will stand level on a table without rocking. When that is done, the mold is finished— put it aside to dry.

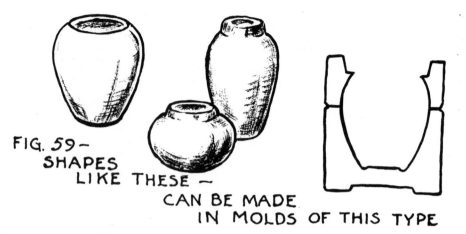

FIG. 59 – SHAPES LIKE THESE – CAN BE MADE IN MOLDS OF THIS TYPE

*A two-piece mold on the wheel*

Shapes like those shown in Fig. 59 which have their widest diameters somewhere between the top and the bottom, and whose profiles do not have undercuts, can be made in two-piece molds divided horizontally. The model for such a mold is made in the same manner as the model for the one-piece vase mold. Prepare a chuck, size it, cast a cylinder of plaster over it, then cut the shape upside down. Take it off the chuck to study the form. When it is just right, finish the foot, and polish the surface.

Here is where a new step comes in. Before you cast the mold, it will be necessary to determine accurately the position of the widest part of the model. To do that, use a try square as shown in Fig. 60 and mark the spot where it touches the side. (If you haven't a try square, cut a right angle out of cardboard and use that.) Rotate the wheel and hold an indelible pencil at the point just marked so that a line is drawn completely around the

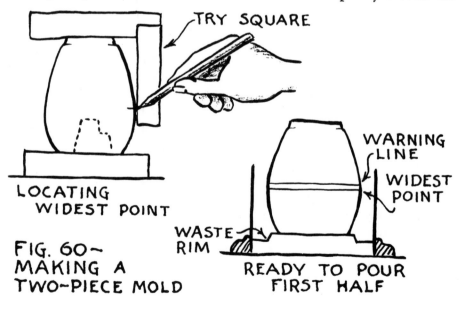

TRY SQUARE

LOCATING WIDEST POINT

FIG. 60 – MAKING A TWO-PIECE MOLD

WASTE RIM

WARNING LINE

WIDEST POINT

READY TO POUR FIRST HALF

model. Then make another line ¼″ above the first to serve as a warning line.

Now you are ready to cast one-half of the mold. Cut a step in the base of the chuck to form the waste rim, size the model and the base of the chuck, and then set the cottle in place. Mix plaster and pour enough into the cottle so that it just covers the two lines you have drawn on the model. Pour the plaster a minute or two sooner than you would ordinarily, while it is still fairly liquid, and jar the wheel head vigorously after you pour, for bubbles tend to collect on the underside of curved surfaces like this one.

The next step is to cut the top surface of this half of the mold until it is exactly level with the line drawn at the widest point. As soon as the plaster is firm enough, remove the cottle and start cutting the mold. It is

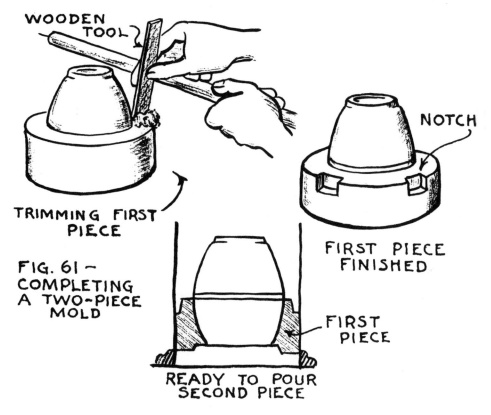

WOODEN TOOL

TRIMMING FIRST PIECE

NOTCH

FIRST PIECE FINISHED

FIRST PIECE

FIG. 61 – COMPLETING A TWO-PIECE MOLD

READY TO POUR SECOND PIECE

important not to cut into the model, so for the first part of the cutting, use a wooden tool. This will cut the fresh plaster which is still soft but won't mar the model. Lower the surface of the mold until your warning line is visible. This tells you that you must go exactly ¼″ farther. Use the steel tool now and continue cutting until the second line is just visible. Stop! You can trim up the side of the mold, but don't take any more off the top edge.

Before the second half is poured, cut some notches in the first part so that the two halves will fit together. Now you are ready to pour the second half. Size the model again (the first size coat is no longer any good), set the cottle in place, mix the plaster and pour. When the plaster has set, remove the cottle and trim up the outside surface of the mold. The job is done.

*Another type of two-piece mold*

A shape with undercuts or returns, like the vase shown in Fig. 62, cannot be made in the type of mold just described. Such a shape requires a mold which separates laterally. If the form has an indentation in the base it needs a mold of three pieces, but if you are willing to accept a vase with a flat bottom, you can use a simple two-piece mold, easy to make. Fig. 62 illustrates the steps.

Make the model by casting a cylinder of plaster over a chuck and cutting the shape, upside down, in the same manner as that described for the simple vase on page 86. When the form is finished, remove it from the chuck and cut a template to fit its profile. In order to get the correct profile, you will need to draw center lines on opposite sides of the model, dividing it exactly in half. This can be done with a try square as shown in Fig. 62. (A more accurate method of drawing the center line will be described later.)

The template may be cut out of a thin sheet of plaster or out of heavy cardboard. Cardboard is easier to handle because it is less apt to break. If it is given three coats of shellac and then sized, a cardboard template will work very well.

Lay the template on a bed of soft clay and put the model in place so that it is embedded exactly to the centerline. Any space between the model and the template should be filled with clay so that a perfect fit is secured. Make a plug of clay to form the opening in the mold and put it at the top of the model. This plug will form the waste rim, also; so make it carefully and see that it projects a half-inch beyond the top rim of the model.

When the plug is in place, size the model and the template, set the casting box and pour the first half of the mold. When this has set, turn it over, remove the clay backing and the template, but leave the model embedded in the mold.

Put another plug of clay at the top of the model, cut notches in the first half of the mold, size the mold and the model, set the casting box again, and pour the second half. The mold is finished.

*A three-piece mold*

If you want an indentation at the foot of the vase, you can make a three-piece mold by adding one additional step, as shown in Fig. 63. In this case, the foot of the model must be carefully finished. When the model is set in the template, put a second plug of clay at the foot and proceed to cast two parts of the mold as described before.

When these two parts are finished, each will have an opening at the base made by the second plug of clay. If we pour plaster into this opening,

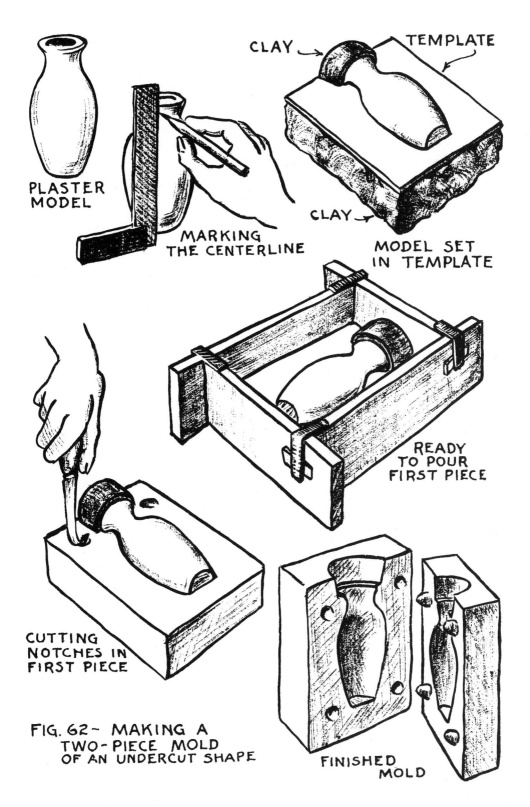

PLASTER MODEL

MARKING THE CENTERLINE

CLAY

TEMPLATE

CLAY

MODEL SET IN TEMPLATE

READY TO POUR FIRST PIECE

CUTTING NOTCHES IN FIRST PIECE

FINISHED MOLD

FIG. 62- MAKING A TWO-PIECE MOLD OF AN UNDERCUT SHAPE

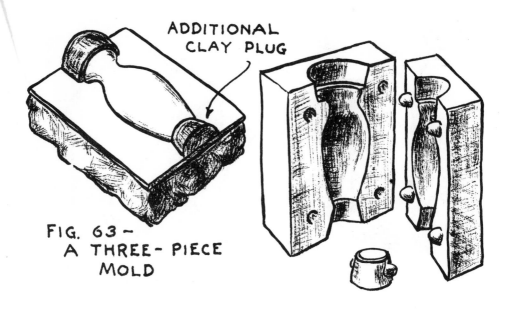

ADDITIONAL CLAY PLUG

FIG. 63 –
A THREE - PIECE
MOLD

it will make the third piece of the mold. Cut notches so that the third piece will be held in place, then put the two halves of the mold together with the model between them, size the foot of the model and the opening, and pour plaster for the third piece.

*A three-piece mold made on the wheel*

A mold for a vase can be made directly on the wheel. Such a mold may

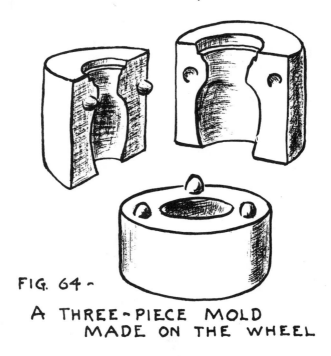

FIG. 64 –

A THREE - PIECE MOLD
MADE ON THE WHEEL

be divided all the way down the side with a plug at the base, like the mold shown in Fig. 63, or it may be made in two parts, from the top down past the widest point, with a third piece forming the entire lower half, as shown in Fig. 64. The second type is easier to handle and easier to make.

Here are the steps. Make a chuck, size it, pour a cylinder of plaster over it, and cut the shape of the vase. Next cut a template to fit the profile.

It was mentioned before that a more accurate method of drawing centerlines on a vase shape would be described later. Fig. 65 illustrates this method.

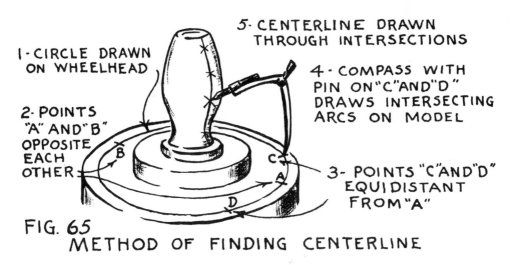

**5· CENTERLINE DRAWN THROUGH INTERSECTIONS**

**I· CIRCLE DRAWN ON WHEELHEAD**

**4· COMPASS WITH PIN ON "C"AND"D" DRAWS INTERSECTING ARCS ON MODEL**

**2· POINTS "A" AND "B" OPPOSITE EACH OTHER**

**3· POINTS "C"AND"D" EQUIDISTANT FROM "A"**

## FIG. 65
## METHOD OF FINDING CENTERLINE

Make a circle on the plaster wheel head near the outside edge, by holding a pencil against it as it turns. Locate two points on this circle exactly opposite each other (let's call them A and B). You can do this by marking one point A, then stepping off distances with a compass in each direction until the point opposite A is reached. Now put the pin of the compass on A and mark off two more points (C and D), one on each side of A and equidistant from A. Next put the pin of the compass on C and draw an arc on the model. With the compass set at the same radius, put the pin on D and draw another arc crossing the first one. Change the compass setting and draw two more arcs on the model crossing each other in a different spot, then change the compass setting again and repeat the process. Each pair of arcs you draw will cross exactly on the centerline of the model. Make as many of such intersecting arcs as you wish, setting the compass to a larger or smaller radius as needed to reach all parts of the model, then connect the points of intersection. You have drawn one center-line. To draw the other one, repeat the process on the other side using two points equidistant from the point B.

When the centerlines are drawn, cut the template to fit the model at that point. Before you set the template in place, mark the widest part of

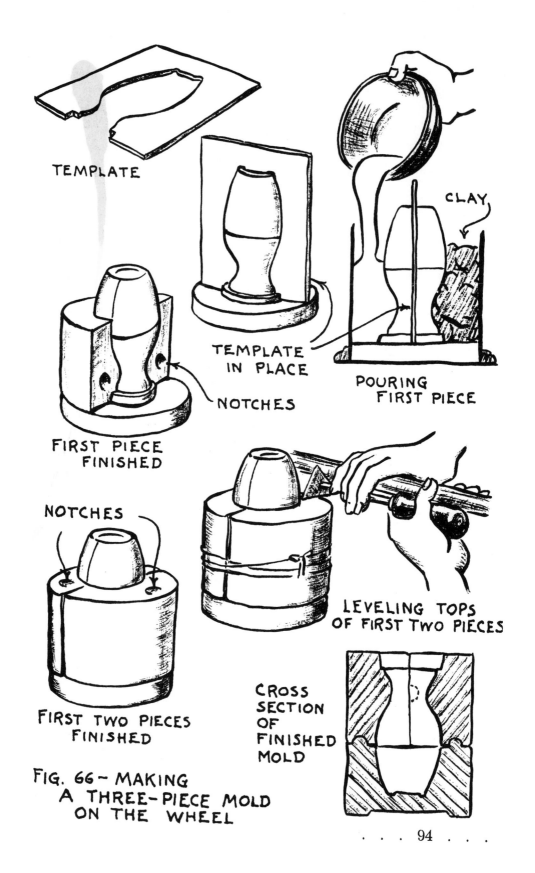

TEMPLATE

TEMPLATE
IN PLACE

CLAY

POURING
FIRST PIECE

NOTCHES

FIRST PIECE
FINISHED

NOTCHES

LEVELING TOPS
OF FIRST TWO PIECES

FIRST TWO PIECES
FINISHED

CROSS
SECTION
OF
FINISHED
MOLD

FIG. 66 - MAKING
A THREE-PIECE MOLD
ON THE WHEEL

the model. It will not be necessary to do this with great precision, since the two halves of the mold which you are going to pour will extend slightly beyond this point.

Now set the template in place as shown in Fig. 66, backing it firmly with clay; size the entire model, the base of the chuck, and the template; wrap the cottle around the base of the chuck, and pour enough plaster to cover the widest point mark to a depth of about an inch.

When the plaster has set, remove the cottle and the template. Cut notches in the first half of the mold just poured, so that the second half will lock in place. When this is done, size the model, the base of the chuck, and the first half of the mold; then set the cottle in place again and pour the second portion of the mold level with the first.

When the second portion has set, remove the cottle and true up the top surface of both halves of the mold. You can do this by turning the wheel and using a cutting tool in the usual way. Look out that you do not mar the surface of the model; also take care that the two halves of the mold do not separate and fly off the wheel. To guard against this, tie them firmly together with a piece of heavy twine as shown.

Before pouring the last piece of the mold, cut notches in the first two pieces so that the three parts of the mold will lock.

Size the model and the tops of the two parts of the mold already completed, set the cottle in place again, and pour plaster for the last piece of the mold. As soon as this has set, remove the cottle and true up the outside surfaces of all three parts of the mold. Make the base of the bottom piece slightly concave so that the mold will stand level on the table. When this is done your mold is finished.

A vase like the one shown in Fig. 67 would need a mold of the type shown in Fig. 63, with two pieces separated all the way down the side and a plug at the bottom. To make such a mold, cut the model with a projection shaped like the plug left at the base, then make the two side pieces of the mold exactly as described above, but cut the template to include the profile of the plug. The two halves of the mold will extend from the waste rim to the bottom of the plug. When these are finished, cut the projection off the model and finish the shape of the foot. Cut notches in the two halves of the mold so that the plug will be locked in place, then put the two halves of the mold together with the model between them and tie them. Size the opening for the plug and pour in plaster. This completes the third piece. These steps are illustrated in Fig. 67.

### Narrow-necked shapes

Forms with narrow necks like those shown in Fig. 68 cannot be made upside down on a chuck but they can be made right side up. To make a mold for such a form, proceed in the manner described before. Make a chuck, size it, cast a cylinder of plaster over it, and then cut the shape.

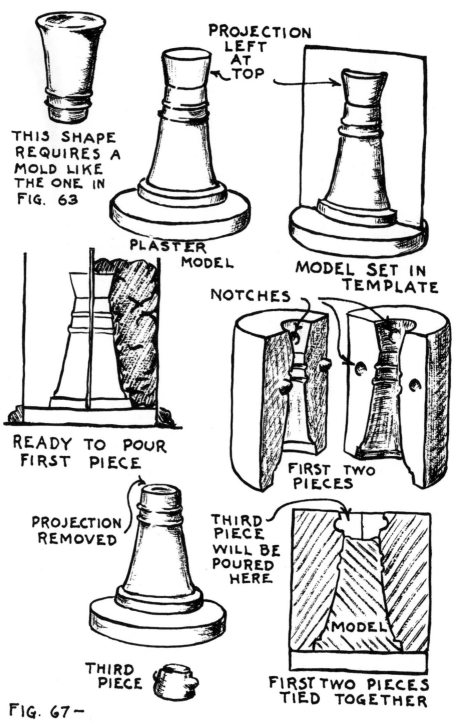

THIS SHAPE
REQUIRES A
MOLD LIKE
THE ONE IN
FIG. 63

PLASTER
MODEL

PROJECTION
LEFT
AT
TOP

MODEL SET IN
TEMPLATE

READY TO POUR
FIRST PIECE

NOTCHES

FIRST TWO
PIECES

PROJECTION
REMOVED

THIRD
PIECE
WILL BE
POURED
HERE

MODEL

THIRD
PIECE

FIRST TWO PIECES
TIED TOGETHER

FIG. 67 —
ANOTHER TYPE OF
THREE-PIECE MOLD

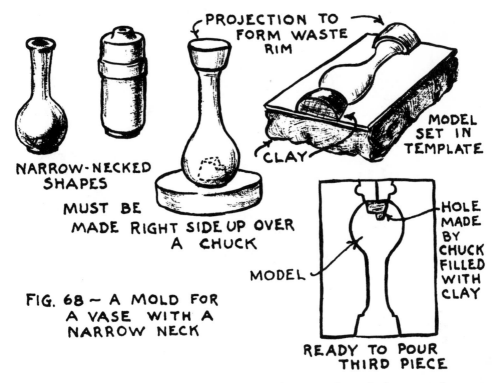

NARROW-NECKED SHAPES

MUST BE MADE RIGHT SIDE UP OVER A CHUCK

PROJECTION TO FORM WASTE RIM

CLAY

MODEL SET IN TEMPLATE

MODEL

HOLE MADE BY CHUCK FILLED WITH CLAY

FIG. 68 – A MOLD FOR A VASE WITH A NARROW NECK

READY TO POUR THIRD PIECE

This time cut the shape right side up and leave a plug of plaster at the top to form the opening in the mold and the waste rim.

When the form is completed, fill with clay the opening in the bottom made by the chuck, and finish the shape of the foot by hand. After this is done, a three-piece mold can be made by the steps illustrated in Figs. 62 and 63.

*A mold for a pitcher*

To make a model in plaster of a pitcher with a spout, turn the body of the pitcher on the wheel as if you were making a vase; then model a spout and a handle out of clay and stick them in place as shown in Fig. 69. Look at the pitcher from all angles and make any necessary adjustments in design. When the form suits you, remove the handle and make a mold of the spout, so that it can be cast in plaster attached to the body of the pitcher. Size the surface of the plaster model next to the spout, build a retaining wall of clay, and pour a layer of plaster to form a little mold around the spout. When this has set, take out the clay and pour plaster in its place; but before doing so, make sure that the little mold is held securely. Fasten it with string if necessary. Size the inside surface of the little mold, but don't get size on the part of the model where the spout is to be attached, for you want it to hold fast there. Roughen that portion of the model, and wet it, then pour plaster into the mold. When this has set, take the mold away. You now have the spout, in plaster, attached to

. . . 97 . . .

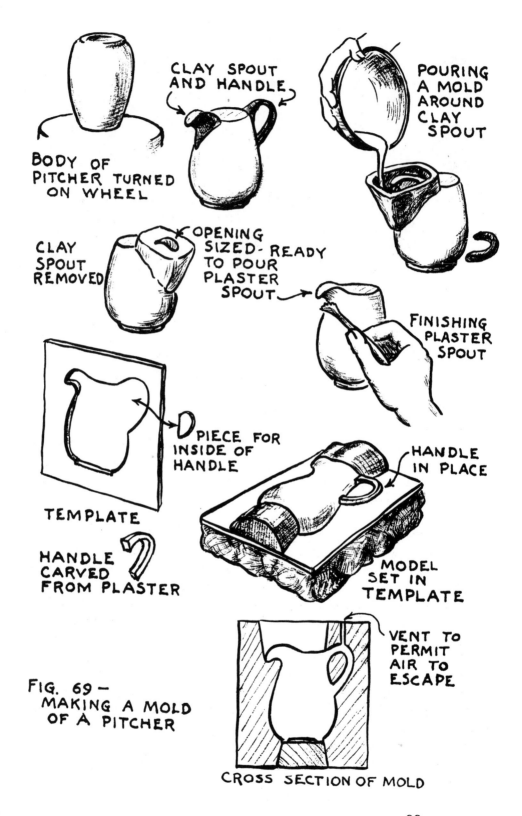

BODY OF PITCHER TURNED ON WHEEL

CLAY SPOUT AND HANDLE

POURING A MOLD AROUND CLAY SPOUT

CLAY SPOUT REMOVED

OPENING SIZED-READY TO POUR PLASTER SPOUT

FINISHING PLASTER SPOUT

TEMPLATE

PIECE FOR INSIDE OF HANDLE

HANDLE IN PLACE

HANDLE CARVED FROM PLASTER

MODEL SET IN TEMPLATE

FIG. 69 — MAKING A MOLD OF A PITCHER

VENT TO PERMIT AIR TO ESCAPE

CROSS SECTION OF MOLD

the body of the pitcher. Perfect the form with plaster tools and sandpaper.

Handles for small pitchers are usually pressed and attached in the manner described for cup handles in Chapter Seven. In larger pitchers, however, the handle is often formed in the mold. Carve a handle out of a piece of plaster and attach it to the pitcher when you make the mold.

Make a three-piece mold for the pitcher by cutting a template out of a thin slab of plaster or heavy cardboard. This template should have the shape of the centerline of the pitcher passing through the spout and the handle. Lay the template on a bed of soft clay and put the model of the pitcher in place so that it is embedded exactly to the centerline. Now, if you are careful, you can put the handle in place in the template without the need of fastening it to the pitcher itself. Cut a small template for the portion inside the handle. Next make a plug of clay to form the opening in the mold and the waste rim and put it at the top of the pitcher. Make another plug for the base and proceed to cast three pieces for the mold by the method illustrated in Fig. 63 on page 92.

In pouring this mold, you may have trouble if air gets trapped in a pocket at the top of the handle, preventing slip from filling all of the space. If this happens, cut a tiny vent as shown in Fig. 69 to allow the air to escape. The cast pitcher will have a projection on the handle where the vent was placed, but this can easily be trimmed off.

### Re-surfacing the wheel head

The plaster working surface of your wheel will be cut and chipped as you work on it. When it gets too ragged, re-surface it by tying a cottle around the edge and pouring a layer of fresh plaster on top, first taking care to soak the old plaster surface thoroughly.

### Molds for irregular pottery shapes

Not all pottery shapes can be turned on a wheel. Some are oval rather than circular, some are square or hexagonal, others follow no definite pattern. To make molds of shapes like these, model the form in clay, then make a waste mold, and cast the shape in plaster. This plaster model can then be carved, if necessary, and finished with plaster tools and sandpaper; after that, the mold can be made in the usual manner.

### Drain molds for small sculpture

In Chapter Two, we saw how to hollow out a little figure of an elephant so that it could be safely fired. A better method would be to make a plaster mold of the figure and then cast it in slip. In this way we would be sure that all parts were hollow and all walls even in thickness. Let us see how a mold for this elephant would be made.

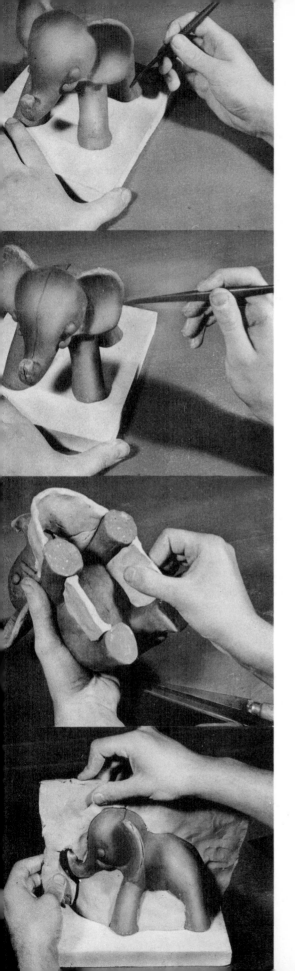

## PLATE X

The figure has been modeled and allowed to become leather-hard. The potter studies it to decide how many pieces will be needed for the mold. This takes imagination, for the pieces must be planned so that they will "draw," that is, come apart without marring the delicate figure inside.

A line has been drawn through the center of the back and over the head and down through the trunk; the mold must separate along this line. Another line of separation is drawn through the edge of the ear.

One piece of the mold will have to be contained within the four legs and the portion under the trunk. The potter builds a wall of clay to block off this area.

The elephant stands on a plaster slab while the potter sets another wall of clay along the centerline.

A clay wall has been set along the line of separation which follows the edge of the ear and passes down the center of the front leg. The separating walls are now all in place. Layers of clay were rolled with a rolling pin and cut to shape to make these walls.

The casting box is set in place so that it comes tight against the edge of the plaster slab on which the elephant stands. The clay separating walls will be pressed tightly against the sides of the casting box. To save time, two pieces of the mold will be poured at once in the next operation, the right front and the left rear.

Pouring the plaster. The sides of the casting box and the plaster slab were sized beforehand.

The plaster has set, the casting box and the clay separating walls have been removed. The clay blocking off the portion under the trunk and between the legs remains. The potter cuts notches in the two portions of the mold just poured, so that the next pieces to be poured will fit securely.

. . . 101 . . .

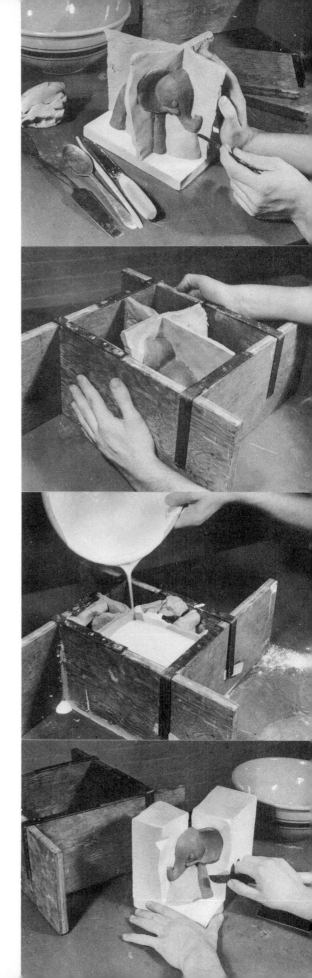

The notches are complete. The potter sizes the sides of the two finished pieces of the mold and the plaster slab preparatory to pouring two more parts.

Setting the casting box again.

Pouring the right rear and the left front portions of the mold.

Four pieces of the mold have been poured. The plaster has set, the casting box has been removed, and the mold has been turned upside down. The potter has taken out the clay which blocked off the portion under the trunk and between the legs. He now cuts notches so that the last piece of the mold will be held in place. When this operation is finished, he will size the exposed portions of the mold and pour plaster into the opening, making the surface level with the other four parts of the mold. This will form the last piece.

. . . 102 . . .

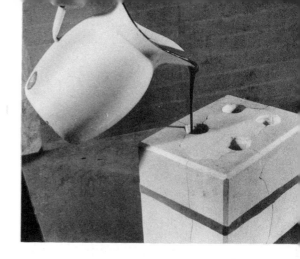

Several days later. The mold has been completed, the pieces have been taken apart, the figure of the elephant removed, and the separate parts of the mold allowed to dry. Now the five pieces of the mold are together again, fastened with a heavy rubber band cut from an inner tube, and the potter pours slip into one of the openings left by the legs.

This is a drain mold. The slip will be allowed to stand until a wall of a proper thickness is built up, then poured out again. This means that the bottoms of the feet will be open. The potter can close these openings by rolling little balls of clay and using them as plugs, pressing them in place after the slip has set but before it becomes hard. Thus no opening at all will be left in the figure.

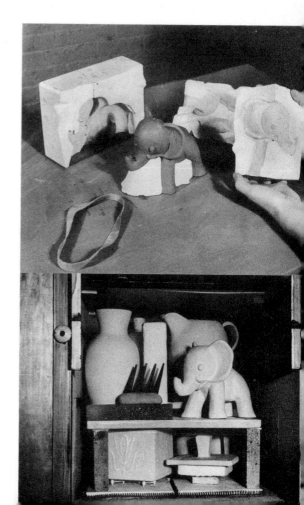

The slip has dried sufficiently to allow the potter to take off the rubber band and separate the pieces of the mold. The little elephant is now ready for trimming and firing.

There he is in the kiln.

. . . 103 . . .

The finished product.

NOTE: In high fired work, porcelain or stoneware, a hollow figure like this would need an opening; otherwise, as the clay matured during the firing and became vitreous the air inside the figure would be trapped. Continuing to expand as the temperature of the kiln rose, this trapped air would cause the figure to bloat or even blow up. For low temperature work, however, the body is porous enough to allow air to get through; so it is not essential to leave an opening in the surface of the piece.

A difficulty sometimes encountered in molds of this type is that during the pouring, air is trapped in some portion such as the bottom of the trunk or the lobe of the ear and slip is not able to fill all parts of the mold. If you have this trouble, make a vent to allow the air to escape like the one for the handle of the pitcher shown in Fig. 69.

*Thread separation*

Silk threads can be used to separate the pieces of a mold which must be made in several parts. This method is not as good as that just described but it is much quicker. The threads are placed on the clay model along the lines of separation of the mold as shown in Fig. 70, and the retaining walls are placed so that the ends of the threads remain outside. Plaster is then poured over the entire model. When the plaster has started to set, but before it becomes hard, the threads are pulled upward and out so that they divide the plaster into the separate parts of the mold. Such molds will not fit together as well as those made in the regular way, but they can be tied and made to work.

CRAFTSMANSHIP

Plaster work demands good craftsmanship. Carelessness is sure to cause trouble. Here are some things to watch out for:

1. *Measure the water and weigh the plaster. If you rely upon guesswork, some of your guesses will be wrong.*

2. *Be sure to mix enough plaster for each operation. When in doubt, compute the volume in cubic inches and divide by 81. That will tell you how many quarts of water you will need.*

3. *Do a good job when sizing. Apply at least five coats and wipe each one off thoroughly. Don't allow any size left on the model to spoil the mold.*

4. *Stir the plaster well.*

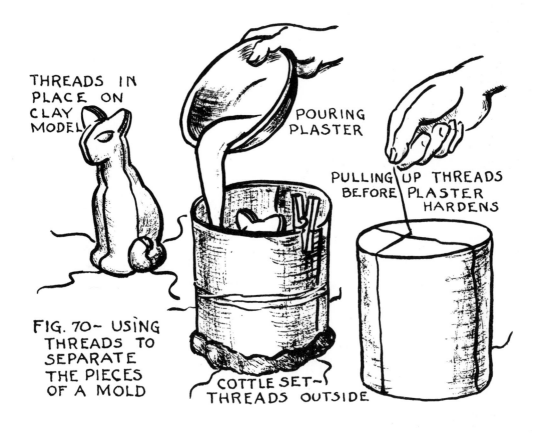

THREADS IN PLACE ON CLAY MODEL

POURING PLASTER

PULLING UP THREADS BEFORE PLASTER HARDENS

FIG. 70~ USING THREADS TO SEPARATE THE PIECES OF A MOLD

COTTLE SET~ THREADS OUTSIDE

5. *If the cottle gives way—what a mess! Be sure it is secure before you pour.*

6. *Immediately after pouring, jar the work by rapping the wheel or the table with your fist to loosen air bubbles.*

7. *Look out for undercuts. The merest scratch, almost invisible to the eye, will be enough to lock the model firmly in the mold.*

8. *If there is trouble getting the model and the mold apart, try putting the model back on the chuck and twisting the mold. When this doesn't work, hold a piece of wood against the outside edge of the mold and strike it sharply with a hammer, or, if you have a spray gun, disconnect the hose and shoot a stream of air at the crack between the model and the mold. This should get them apart. Next time do a better job of sizing and don't have any undercuts.*

9. *Let the mold dry thoroughly before pouring slip in it. Several days will be needed for this. Warm it slightly if you are in a hurry but don't let it get hot.*

# $S$lip $C$asting

$\mathcal{N}$ow that we have made a number of drain molds, let's see how they are used. The series of pictures on Plate XI will help to clarify the process. These show the pouring of two different molds, a one-piece mold for a cup and a two-piece mold for a bowl with bulging sides.

By now you know that a mold must not be used until it is thoroughly dry. If in doubt, hold it against your cheek—the least suggestion of coolness means that the mold is still damp. If it is the same temperature as other objects in the room, you are ready to pour.

### PLATE XI

*How a drain mold is used*

Pour a steady stream of slip into the center of the mold until it is level with the top. Get it just level—don't slop over. As the mold starts to absorb moisture from the slip, the surface will fall in the mold, so more slip must be added from time to time to keep the mold full.

The longer the slip stands in the mold, the thicker the wall of the cast piece will be. It is not possible to tell you how long the slip must remain in the mold in order to build a wall of the proper thickness; it may be five minutes, it may be thirty, depending upon the consistency of the slip, the density of the mold, and the thickness of wall desired. You can judge the progress of the casting by scraping away the slip with a knife and cutting into the waste rim. That's one reason why a waste rim is provided.

When the proper thickness has been built up, pour out the excess slip. The smoothness of the inside surface of the piece depends to a large extent upon the skill with which this is done. Take the mold in two hands. Now, holding it over a bowl or a pitcher, rotate it with a slow steady motion until it is almost, but not quite, upside down. Hold it in that position until all of the excess slip has run out —don't shake it—then rest it on two sticks laid across a bowl until the slip starts to harden. One of the sticks should be higher than the other so that the mold tips slightly. This prevents drops of slip from collecting on the inside of the bottom and forming lumps.

When the slip starts to dry, the shine will disappear from the surface; now the mold may be turned right side up and the edges cleaned with a knife.

As the casting continues to dry, it will shrink away from the mold. It is important that the shrinkage be even all the way around; otherwise the piece will warp. Watch the casting as it shrinks and carefully loosen it at any point where it tends to stick. Allow the piece to dry for an hour or so, then trim off the waste rim, using a bent knife. (This is a handy tool. To make one, bend the end of a potter's knife at right angles.) Run the knife around the edge of the waste rim and lift out the ribbon of clay trimmed off. Now the casting is complete. In another hour the piece should be hard enough to remove from the mold.

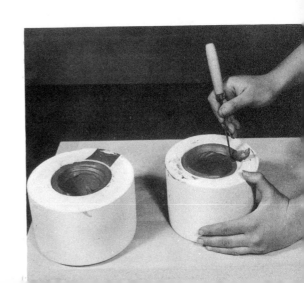

To remove a casting from a one-piece mold, place a flat slab of plaster on top of the mold and reverse the two together; then lift the mold. The piece will remain upside down on the plaster slab, where it may be left to dry. In the two-piece mold, the top half of the mold has been lifted off and the piece left to dry in the bottom half.

A simple two-piece mold of the type illustrated does not have to be tied together before it is poured. More complicated molds, however, must be held together with heavy twine made tight by wedges, or fastened with strong rubber bands.

### Finishing the top edge

After the waste rim is trimmed off, the top edge of a cast piece will need smoothing. Do this by grinding it on a piece of glass in the manner described in Chapter Two.

### Deflocculation

Clay mixed with water makes slip, but this is not the best material for casting. The water content of the mixture is high (usually 100 per cent of the dry weight of the clay, since equal parts of clay and water are required to make a slip which will pour); consequently, there is a large amount of shrinkage. This is not so bad in simple drain molds; but in more complicated molds, casting with ordinary slip is extremely difficult. Some way must be sought to make a casting slip with less water. The answer is deflocculation.

We are not certain what makes clay plastic. It is believed that the very minute particles of clay substance have a static electrical charge which makes them flock together just as bits of paper stick to a rod when it is rubbed. Ordinary water is a non-conductor of electricity, but if a small amount of alkaline substance is introduced, it becomes a conductor. When this is done to a clay slip, the static electricity of the clay particles is discharged, they lose their attraction for each other, and they no longer flock together. The slip is then said to be deflocculated. Alkaline substances used in deflocculation are called electrolytes.

This phenomenon can be illustrated dramatically with certain types of clay. When 1000 grams of dry clay are mixed with 400 grams of water, the result is a thick, sticky mass. If a few drops of sodium silicate (the alkaline substance or electrolyte) are added, the mixture will suddenly change into a smooth creamy liquid easy to pour. It has become a deflocculated slip, suitable for casting.

Unfortunately, this does not work the same way for all clays. Some are temperamental and require a mixture of two or more electrolytes, while others cannot be deflocculated at all. If you have a natural clay or a clay body which you want to use for casting, the only thing to do is run a series of experiments.

A well-deflocculated casting slip should have about the same percentage of water as plastic clay, namely 35 to 45 per cent. There are several substances which may be used as electrolytes. The best are sodium silicate and soda ash, which work well in combination. The percentage of electrolyte needed is extremely small, ranging from 1/10 of 1 per cent to 3/10 of 1 per cent (percentages are based on the weight of dry clay). It is important not to add too much, for a slight excess of electrolyte reverses the process, and instead of making the slip more liquid causes it to jell into a semi-solid mass.

Here is one way to conduct your experiment. Take 1000 grams of dry clay and 400 grams of water and mix them together. Put 25 cc. of water in a glass graduate and add 3 grams of soda ash and 3 grams of sodium silicate. Soda ash is a powder, but sodium silicate is a liquid. To weigh it, put the graduate containing the water on the scale and note its weight, then drop sodium silicate into the water until three grams have been added. After both electrolytes are dissolved in the graduate, add enough water to bring the quantity up to 30 cc. Now you know that 1 cc. of this solution contains 0.1 gram each of sodium silicate and soda ash. Add the solution, drop by drop, to the mixture of clay and water, stirring it constantly as you do so. If the clay suddenly turns liquid, your experiment has been a success. By consulting the graduate, you can tell how much of the electrolytes you have used. In preparing future batches of casting slip you can put that amount into the water before you add the clay.

If the mixture starts to become liquid, then thickens and starts to jell, you have added too much electrolyte. Prepare another batch of clay and begin again. If the electrolytes make the mixture partly liquid but not thin enough to pour, try adding another 50 grams of water and, if necessary, 50 grams more. This will bring your total water content to 500 grams or 50 per cent—don't go higher than that. If you still don't have any luck, try adding a few drops of sodium tannate. Sodium tannate can be made by boiling 100 cc. of distilled water and adding 10 grams of soda ash and 10 grams of tannic acid. Next try Calgon (a commercial water softener). If none of these work, you may have a clay which cannot be deflocculated at all; however, as we said before, some clays are temperamental in this respect, so keep on trying. You may hit the right combination.

Another way of conducting a deflocculation experiment is to put 40 grams of water into each of several containers (glass tumblers will do) and then add various quantities of different electrolytes. To one container, add 0.2 gram of sodium silicate, to another 0.3 gram of sodium silicate, to a third 0.1 gram of sodium silicate and 0.1 gram of soda ash, and so on, keeping a record of what goes into each container. Then add 100 grams of dry clay to each solution and stir it thoroughly. The resultant mixture which is thinnest and pours most easily is nearest to correct deflocculation.

## Aging

Casting slip works better when it is allowed to age slightly; so wait three or four days after preparing a batch before you use it. Keep it in a covered container meanwhile, and stir it often. Screen it through a 40- or 60-mesh sieve every time you cast with it. If you have trouble with air bubbles, use two pitchers and pour the slip back and forth from one to the other several times until the bubbles are all driven to the surface and broken.

Sometimes natural clays contain sulphur which causes trouble by making blisters in the glaze. If you have this difficulty, add a small percentage of barium carbonate to the slip (1 per cent will be enough). This will not affect the working properties of the slip but will prevent the sulphur from bubbling out under the glaze during the firing.

## Grog in slip

If you plan to cast large pieces with thick walls, you can add grog to casting slip just as you would to clay. When slip is properly deflocculated, grog will not settle to the bottom but will remain suspended almost indefinitely. A piece cast this way will have a smooth surface, as though the slip contained no grog at all. If you want the grog to show in the texture of the finished piece, sponge the surface after it has dried.

## Prepared casting slips

In Chapter Eight, recipes are given for clay bodies for various temperatures. Some of these make excellent casting slips. Instructions for deflocculating them are given along with the recipes.

Many ceramic dealers offer prepared casting slip for sale. It comes in dry powder form with deflocculating agents already added.

## Fettling

Pieces cast in molds of two or more parts will have ridges at the seams where the parts join. These ridges are called "fettles" and the process of removing them is called "fettling." Trim the ridges off with a knife and remove any remaining traces with a sponge.

These ridges are a good measure of your craftsmanship. If they are hardly noticeable, you are a good mold maker. If, however, they are quite prominent, better take more care with the next mold you make.

SOME POINTS ON SLIP CASTING:

1. *Pouring a mold must be done with care. Otherwise pieces will be warped, lumpy, or marred by air pockets.*

2. *Stay with your casting. Don't pour a mold and then go away and forget it.*

3. *Casting slip must be screened just before it is used to eliminate lumps.*

4. *Air bubbles in slip cause trouble. Get rid of them by pouring the slip back and forth in two pitchers.*

5. *Pour excess slip out of the mold with a steady even motion. Shaking the mold will spoil the inner surface of the piece.*

6. *Time yourself when you pour a new mold so that you can know about how long it takes to cast a piece.*

7. *As a mold is used, it absorbs moisture; therefore, each successive casting requires more time. After six castings, a mold will be too damp for further use. Set it aside to dry overnight.*

8. *A one-piece mold must be turned right side up as soon as the slip starts to harden to keep the piece from falling out when it shrinks.*

9. *Clean the top edge of the mold immediately after the slip has started to harden.*

10. *Release the edge of the casting so that it can shrink away from the mold evenly. If it sticks in one spot, the piece will be warped.*

11. *An infra-red lamp can be used to hasten the drying of cast pieces.*

12. *Keep casting scraps separate from other clay. These scraps can be mixed in with the dry ingredients when a fresh batch of casting slip is prepared.*

13. *Deflocculation is a tricky business. Don't be discouraged by lack of success at first—keep on trying.*

# chapter Seven

# *More About Plaster*

*A*ll of the molds described so far have been for drain casting. Now it is time to learn about some other ways of using molds—solid casting with slip, pressing with plastic clay, and a special method of forming plates called "jiggering." Also, let us study some different ways of working with plaster—the mold maker's method of "running" it under templates while it is setting, and the sculptor's method of building up molds over clay models by applying plaster directly without the use of retaining walls.

## Solid casting

Solid casting is different from drain casting in that the mold shapes both the inside and the outside of the cast piece. This method has many advantages, among them the fact that both surfaces of the piece can be controlled, as can the thickness of the wall. In drain casting, the inside of a cup always shows a ring at the foot, while in solid casting the inside is perfectly smooth. In drain casting, two pieces poured in the same mold may have walls of different thickness, depending upon how long the slip

CROSS SECTION OF A
SOLID CASTING MOLD

FIG. 71· SOLID CASTING

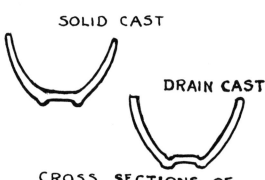

SOLID CAST

DRAIN CAST

CROSS SECTIONS OF
CUPS

was left in the mold; but in solid casting, every piece is identical. In solid casting, also. the thickness of the walls may be made greater at the base. Plates and shallow bowls which cannot be made in drain molds can be solid cast. Obviously, a solid casting mold must be in two parts.

## A *solid casting mold for a rectangular dish*

Here are the steps in making a solid casting mold for a rectangular dish.

### PLATE XII

Start by drawing the shape of the inside edge of the plate with indelible pencil on a slab of plaster; use perpendicular axes and paper templates to help you, as you did in making the mold of the box. Use a plaster slab about 3″ longer and wider than your dish will be.

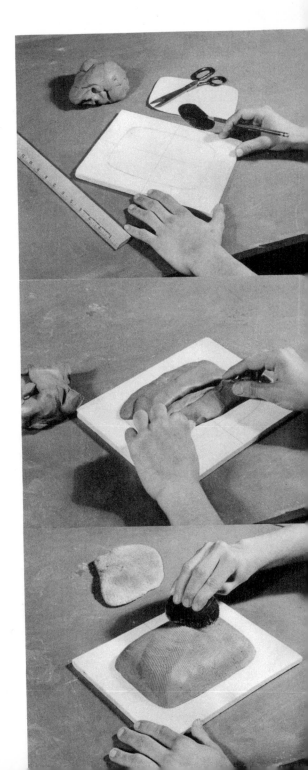

Next build up a clay mound on the slab shaped like the inside of the dish in reverse. Make this as smooth and as symmetrical as you can.

A small steel scraper with a toothed edge will be helpful in forming the mound. Drawing the toothed portion over the clay in different directions will take down any irregularities and help pull the form together. The scraper can be bent in the hand to conform to the curve of the corners and can be drawn upward over them.

. . . 113 . . .

It is an easy matter to smooth the scratches when the proper shape is obtained. Cut a cardboard template with which to judge the slope of the sides.

In making a mold of this type, there is a temptation to make it too flat. Since the final dish will become flatter during the drying and the firing, make the mound higher than you think it should be—and don't forget shrinkage when you plan the size.

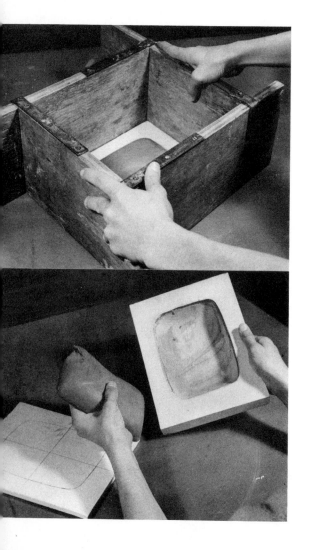

When the mound is finished, size the plaster slab, put the casting box in place at the edge of the slab and pour a layer of plaster about ¾" thick to make a waste mold.

When this has set, remove it and take out the clay.

Finish the inside surface as well as you can with a scraper.

For an extra-fine surface, use sandpaper. Ordinary sandpaper won't work on wet plaster; so if you have plenty of time, let the waste mold dry thoroughly before finishing it. If you can't afford to wait, use 6-0 garnet paper (sometimes called wet-and-dry sandpaper) which will work pretty well on the wet plaster. The inside of the waste mold is the shape of the inside of your final plate. Study it carefully and make any alterations needed to improve the design.

When the waste mold is as good as you can make it, size it, place the casting box again, and pour plaster to a depth of about 1½″. This will be one-half of the final mold. When this has set, remove the waste mold. (If you have trouble getting the waste mold off, try prying the two apart with the straight edge of your steel scraper. If this does not work, break the waste mold.) This half of the mold is similar to the mound on a slab which you started with, except that now the mound is of plaster. Here you have still another opportunity to smooth the form.

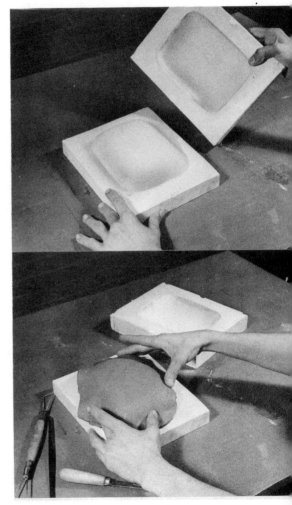

The next step is to roll a layer of clay and put it over the mound to form a plate. Use a rolling pin and two strips of wood 3/16″ thick as guides in making the layer. Draw an outline with indelible pencil around the edge of the mound, ¼″ away from it, then work the layer carefully against the plaster and trim it to conform to the outline you have just drawn.

. . . 115 . . .

The shape which you make out of this layer of clay will be the shape of your final plate. Taper it toward the edge so that it is slightly thinner at that point. It will be good to let the clay harden a bit on the plaster so that you may take it off and study its thickness, its weight and its general contour.

You may even cut the clay plate in half to study the cross section. The two halves can be put together again easily on the plaster mound.

The second half of the mold must have an opening or "gate" through which to pour the clay slip. This opening usually coincides with the foot of the piece. When the clay slab is shaped, put it on the mound and build a column of clay to make the gate. Since this will form the foot, it should start at the point where the curve of the plate changes from horizontal to vertical—in other words, where the bottom joins the sides. The column should taper toward the top and should be high enough to project beyond the plaster which will be poured for the second half of the mold.

Now for the final step. Cut notches in the plaster slab. Remember not to put one notch in each corner; cut two at one end and one at the other so that it will be easy to see which way the halves fit together. Size the plaster, set the casting box, and pour the second half of the mold.

. . . 116 . . .

When this has set, remove the clay. The two pieces of the mold are finished.

*Pouring a solid casting mold*

The mold you have just made requires a deflocculated slip—clay and water won't work. Tie the two halves of the mold together and pour in slip until the mold is half full. Tip the mold from side to side so that no air pockets are trapped, then stand it on a level surface and fill it to the top. As the slip settles, keep adding more so that the mold is always full.

You will have to pour the mold a few times before you know just how long the slip must stand in it. Watch the thickness of the wall which builds up at the edge of the gate. When this is as thick as the wall of your plate or a little thicker, pour out the slip and let the mold dry upside down on two blocks of wood.

When the slip has hardened, remove the top half of the mold, leaving the cast plate in position on the bottom half. The plate will have a foot over 1″ high which must be cut down to a height of about ¼″. Use a ruler as a guide and trim off the excess with a knife. The height of this foot is a matter of taste. You may want it a little higher, or you may prefer no foot at all, in which case trim the bottom level.

. . . 117 . . .

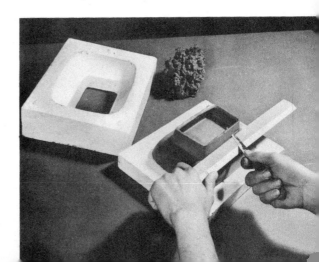

When the foot is trimmed, the cast plate is finished. Put it aside to dry.

### Loosening the cast piece

Sometimes a solid cast plate sticks to the bottom half of the mold. This is bad, because unless the cast piece is able to loosen and rise off the mold it will split as it shrinks. If you have this trouble, study the mold to see if there are any undercuts which grip the piece—if there are, remove them with fine sandpaper.

Dusting the surface of the mold with flint before you pour in the slip will help to prevent sticking. Sometimes you can loosen the plate by holding the mold in one hand and rapping it sharply with the other fist. Strike downward and avoid hitting the clay piece. You may use the hose of your spray gun in the manner described at the end of Chapter Five to shoot a stream of air under the piece and lift it free. Be careful, however, that the piece is not blown off entirely and destroyed.

### Free form

Contemporary designers have produced some pieces of pottery which are a complete departure from all conventional shapes. This pottery is neither round nor square, it is not symmetrical, the walls are not uniform in thickness, yet some of these pieces (not all) are beautiful indeed. Have you had the opportunity to hold a well-designed, free-form dish in your hands? If so, you know how good it feels, how well it balances. The lack of conventional symmetry gives the piece an individual charm. To be sure, such ware is not suited to all uses—there are times when we want conventional shapes to eat from (round cups to hold our coffee); but for occasional dishes—ash trays; bowls to hold fruit—free form serves well.

While this type of work apparently frees the designer from many restrictions, it actually imposes greater demands upon him. His pieces must show originality and imagination—roundness and smoothness will not be enough.

Before you start to create a free form, go out into the fields and study stones. Pick up a number of them and turn them in your hands. See why some are easier to hold than others and note the differences in texture. Bring home one or two which are especially interesting—they will suggest shapes which you can adapt to ceramic ware.

When you have thought out your design, take a lump of clay and shape

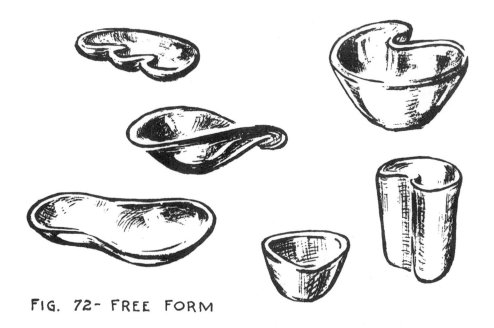

FIG. 72- FREE FORM

it as you did the little cup in Chapter One. The model will be rough at first, of course; but make it the right size, and plan how it will stand on a table, how it can be picked up, where the walls need to be thick and where thin. As you continue to work with the plastic clay, it will begin to respond to your thoughts, and the form will grow in your hands. Carry the modeling as far as you can with the soft clay. Then set the piece aside to dry for a day or two.

For the best results, a waste mold should be made of the clay shape and a new model cast in plaster. However, this time we shall try a short cut and make the final mold directly from the clay. When the clay has hardened, work on it with a toothed scraper and sandpaper. (We said before that sandpaper has no place in clay work, but here you are merely using the dry clay as a substitute for a plaster model.) Keep studying the form until you feel that it is just right. Try it not only in your hand but resting on the table. Pick it up, put things in it, judge it for utility and for beauty.

Since the clay has been allowed to dry, it must be shellacked and sized before plaster is cast against it. Give the model three or four coats of shellac and allow at least twenty minutes for each coat to dry.

The free-form dish must be solid cast. This means that the mold will have to be in two parts. Bed the model in clay up to its widest point, size it, set the casting box, and pour one-half of the mold. When this has set, remove the clay, leaving the model in the plaster, turn it over, and set a column of clay where the foot will be, just as you did in making the mold of the rectangular plate. Next cut notches in the plaster, size the bottom of the model and the plaster, then pour the second half of the mold. When this has set, the mold is finished.

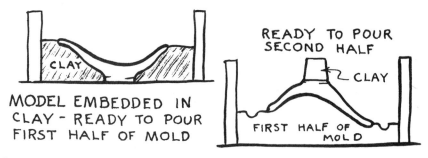

MODEL EMBEDDED IN
CLAY - READY TO POUR
FIRST HALF OF MOLD

READY TO POUR
SECOND HALF

FIG. 73 ~
A MOLD FOR A FREE FORM

This is our first experiment with a new kind of artistic expression. Explore the possibilities of this type of design, based not upon symmetry and mechanical perfection but upon the subtle relationships of free-flowing lines and balanced masses. Such work is a challenge to you—it may open new fields.

*A press mold*

A small figurine of fairly simple design can be made in a two-piece press mold, provided its widest part is along the centerline. For example, the little squirrel shown at the top of Fig. 74 could not be made in a press mold because his ears stick up above the top of his head and his legs project beyond his body; but if we can get him to pull in his ears and his legs a bit, a press mold will work.

To make a press mold, model the figure in clay and let it get leather-hard. Then mark the centerline and cut a template which will have the profile of the figure at that point. The template must be cut large enough to allow a 2″ space all around the figure.

When the template is cut, place the figure in it so that the top of the template is even with the centerline, and lay them both on a bed of clay, as shown. You are now ready to size the template, set the casting box, and pour one half of the mold. When this has hardened, turn it over, leaving the figure embedded in the plaster; remove the clay backing and the template, cut the notches, set the casting box, and pour the second half.

The job is not yet finished. When the mold is used for pressing, it must have a trough in each half, completely around the figure, into which the surplus clay will be squeezed when the two halves are pressed together. This trough will have to be cut by hand. Bring it right up to the figure, but be careful not to break the edge. If the edge is left sharp, the surplus clay will be cut off when the mold is pressed, and the figure will come out clean.

To use a press mold, take a lump of soft clay the right size (experience will help you to judge), and lay it in the depression of one-half of the mold; then put the other half in place and press. In about a minute, you should

. . . 120 . . .

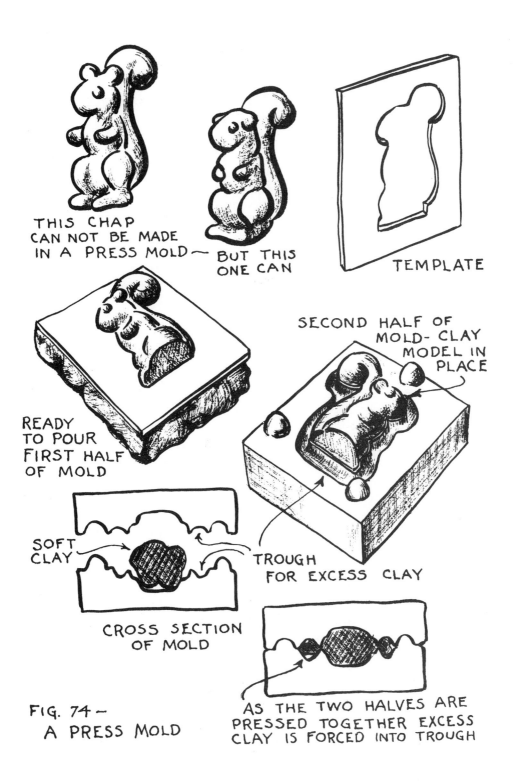

THIS CHAP
CAN NOT BE MADE
IN A PRESS MOLD ~ BUT THIS
ONE CAN

TEMPLATE

READY
TO POUR
FIRST HALF
OF MOLD

SECOND HALF OF
MOLD- CLAY
MODEL IN
PLACE

SOFT
CLAY

TROUGH
FOR EXCESS CLAY

CROSS SECTION
OF MOLD

FIG. 74 ~
A PRESS MOLD

AS THE TWO HALVES ARE
PRESSED TOGETHER EXCESS
CLAY IS FORCED INTO TROUGH

be able to open the mold and take out the little figure. If there is any trouble with sticking, dust the mold with flint before pressing.

A press mold gets a lot of rough treatment, so make it extra-thick and make the notch holes large enough so that the projecting lugs don't break off.

*A press mold for a cup handle*

Cups may be made in drain molds or by jiggering, but cup handles are almost always pressed. A press mold for a handle is made in the same manner as the figurine mold just described, except that the original model is carved out of plaster and not modeled in clay.

The steps in carving the model are these. Starting with a slab of plaster ⅜″ thick, cut a profile which fits exactly against the edge of the cup, then draw the outline of the cup handle on the slab as shown in Fig. 75; cut the slab along the outline which you have drawn.

Your handle will now have the right profile but will be square in cross-section. The next step is to make it round. Mark the centerline along the outside and inside edges with indelible pencil. Then use a sharp knife to trim the corners until the handle is completely rounded. Use the centerline to guide you in this operation, cutting toward it from each edge until the handle is finished.

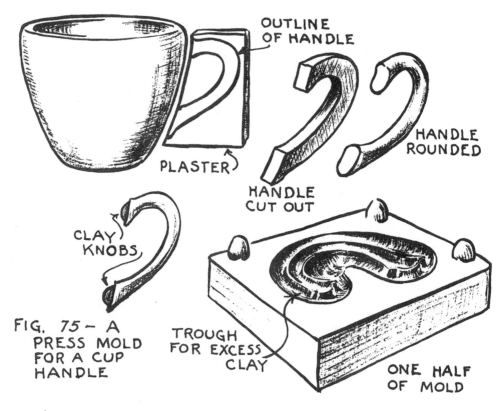

OUTLINE OF HANDLE

PLASTER

HANDLE CUT OUT

HANDLE ROUNDED

CLAY KNOBS

TROUGH FOR EXCESS CLAY

ONE HALF OF MOLD

FIG. 75 – A PRESS MOLD FOR A CUP HANDLE

Carving a cup handle is a delicate operation which requires a lot of patience. You will probably break one or two before you are finished, but don't be discouraged. It takes a little practice. Cut the handle from a thoroughly dry slab of plaster, so that fine sandpaper may be used for the finishing operation.

The ends of the handle which touch the cup will cause difficulty in the press mold because they are flat and do not allow draft; therefore it is helpful to put little knobs of clay at the ends of the handle before the mold is made.

The press mold for the handle is made in the manner already described. Cut a template out of a thin plaster slab or out of cardboard; embed the handle up to its centerline in the template, and back them both with clay; then size and pour half of the mold. When the first half has set, turn it over, remove the template and the clay backing, cut the notches, size, and pour the second half. After this has set, cut the trough for the excess clay as described above.

To use the handle mold, roll a small cylinder of clay and lay it in the depression in one-half of the mold, then press the other half firmly on top of it. In a few minutes, the mold can be opened and the pressed handle removed. Before it is attached to the cup, the handle will have to be "fettled," that is, the ridge where the two halves of the mold come together will have to be trimmed off. The little knobs at the ends will have to be trimmed off also. When this is done, attach the handle to the cup with slurry.

## Sprig molds

The great English potter, Josiah Wedgwood, devised a method of decorating ware by applying raised figures or ornaments of white clay to colored backgrounds. These ornaments were made in sprig molds. As you may imagine, a sprig mold is a block of plaster with a depression shaped like the ornament in reverse. Let's look at a sprig mold in use.

PLATE XIII

A ball of clay is flattened out.

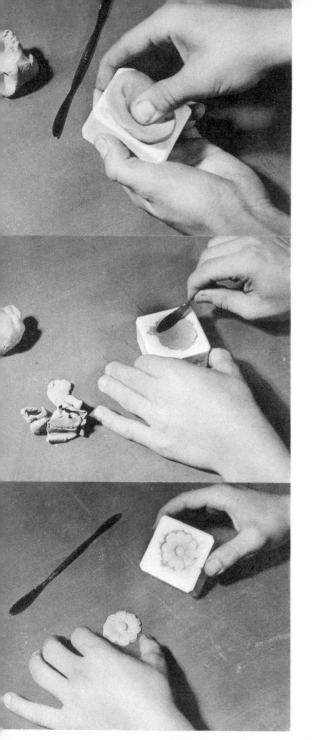

It is then pressed into the depression.

The back is smoothed with a spatula.

The pressing is carefully lifted out. The ornament can then be fastened to the side of a piece with slip.

Some of Wedgwood's sprig molds were made by the outstanding sculptors of his day. If you examine his Jasper ware, you will marvel at the dexterity of the craftsmen who were able to press these delicate figures and attach them without marring them.

A sprig mold is really a one-piece press mold which may be used for small pieces of jewelry, as well as decorations for ware. It is not difficult to make. Model the form in clay, making sure there are no undercuts, then

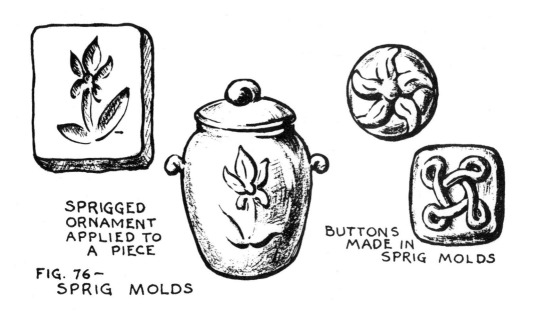

SPRIGGED
ORNAMENT
APPLIED TO
A PIECE

BUTTONS
MADE IN
SPRIG MOLDS

FIG. 76 —
SPRIG MOLDS

put it on a glass slab and cast a block of plaster over it. Moisten the clay and press it firmly against the glass before pouring the plaster; otherwise there is danger that your little ornament may float up into the plaster and be lost. When the plaster is dry, any slight irregularities may be removed by tooling. For very careful work, make a waste mold of the original form and cast the ornament in plaster; finish the surface with plaster tools, then size, and cast the final mold.

A sprig mold may be made without preliminary modeling, by cutting a hollow design in a plaster block with a gouge similar to that used for cutting linoleum block prints. This method gives a different quality to the ornament produced. It is especially suited to abstract decorations and plant forms.

Ceramic buttons may be made in sprig molds. The method is exactly the same, except that some way must be provided for sewing the button onto a garment. This may be a tiny tunnel of clay on the back or a number of openings going right through the button. Be careful not to make the openings so small that they close up when the button is glazed.

A word about casting small and delicate surfaces. Tiny air bubbles are apt to collect in the corners, and these, of course, will spoil the mold; so before the plaster mix begins to thicken, pour a tablespoon of the liquid plaster at the side of the model, then gently blow it over the form until the model is completely covered. This will get rid of the bubbles. After that, the rest of the plaster may be poured in the usual way.

*Jiggering*

We now come to a highly mechanical method of making tableware called "jiggering." In this process, a lump of clay is placed on a convex plaster bat and turned while a template is held against it. The bat shapes the inside of a plate and the template cuts the outside. When bowls are jiggered, the bat is concave, forming the outside surface, while the template cuts the inside. Jiggering is the most efficient method there is of making bowls and plates. Practically all commercial dinnerware is manufactured this way.

Factory equipment for jiggering is heavy and expensive, but a comparatively simple jiggering device can be built as shown in Fig. 77. This will work with any kick wheel, provided the wheel head has some provision for holding a bat in place.

A jigger arm made of wood, about 1¼" x 3", is hinged to the wall in back of the wheel or to an upright brace, so that it can be raised and lowered.

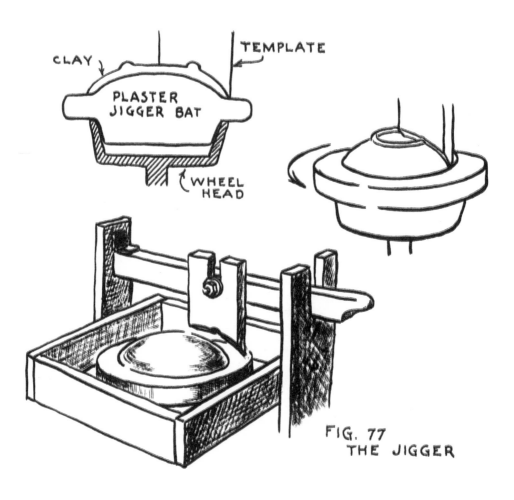

FIG. 77
THE JIGGER

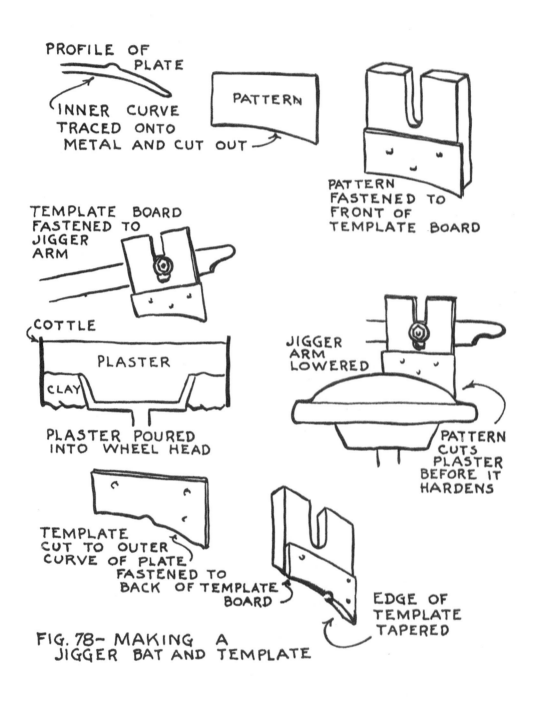

PROFILE OF PLATE

INNER CURVE TRACED ONTO METAL AND CUT OUT

PATTERN

PATTERN FASTENED TO FRONT OF TEMPLATE BOARD

TEMPLATE BOARD FASTENED TO JIGGER ARM

COTTLE

PLASTER

CLAY

PLASTER POURED INTO WHEEL HEAD

JIGGER ARM LOWERED

PATTERN CUTS PLASTER BEFORE IT HARDENS

TEMPLATE CUT TO OUTER CURVE OF PLATE FASTENED TO BACK OF TEMPLATE BOARD

EDGE OF TEMPLATE TAPERED

FIG. 78- MAKING A JIGGER BAT AND TEMPLATE

A piece of wood at the opposite side of the wheel has a slot to hold the jigger arm when it is in the cutting position. The jigger arm has an opening to permit the template board to be adjusted to the proper position—that is, just high enough above the bat to allow the thickness of a plate between them, and so placed that the corner of the template is directly over the center of the wheel. A bolt holds the template board to the arm.

## The jigger bat and template

The steps in making a jigger bat and template are shown in Fig. 78. Draw a cross section of one-half of the plate and trace the inside curve onto a piece of zinc; then cut it out with a pair of snips and file it as smooth as you can make it. (Snips are the scissors used by tinsmiths for cutting sheet metal.) This zinc profile must be screwed to a slotted template board and then fastened to the jigger arm in such a position that it will cut a block of plaster which is turning in the wheel, into the desired jigger bat. Be sure that the inside corner of the zinc profile is exactly over the center of the wheel.

The next step is casting the plaster out of which the bat is to be cut. If your wheel has a drop head, oil it thoroughly and build a collar of clay 3″ wide around the outside of the head. Tie a cottle of building paper around the outside of the clay, then mix and pour the plaster. If your wheel does not have a drop head, but has some notches to hold a bat in place, you may cast directly on the head. If the wheel has the flat type of head, it cannot be used for jiggering.

As soon as the plaster starts to set—but before it gets hard—remove the cottle and start the wheel; then bring the template down slowly and let the profile cut into the plaster. When the jigger arm is all the way down, the shape of the bat is finished. Allow the plaster to set, and hold the template against it once more while the wheel turns, to secure a good surface. Trim the outside edge of the bat with a turning tool, remove it from the wheel head, and set it aside to dry.

The template used in jiggering the plate should be made of heavier metal—steel if possible. The template can be made of wood alone without a metal facing, if hardwood is used. It must be cut to the shape of the outside curve of the plate and fastened to the back of the template board, which must be tapered as shown. Jiggering is more of a pressing process than a cutting one. This explains why the surface of the template must slope as it does. As the jigger bat turns, the clay is squeezed into shape, making a plate which is dense and strong.

## Using the jigger

Let's watch a potter while he jiggers a saucer.

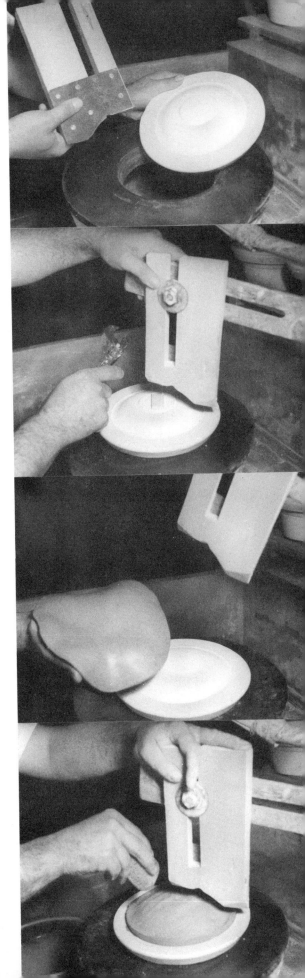

### PLATE XIV

He has a bat which fits into the drop head of his wheel and a template which will form the outside of the saucer.

To use the jigger, he sets the template in place so that it is the right height above the bat, using a little piece of wood as a thickness gauge.

He then takes a ball of clay the right size and flattens it on a board until he has a pancake of clay big enough to cover the jigger bat.

He has smoothed the top of this carefully with a steel spatula. The potter puts the clay on the jigger bat so that the smooth surface is next to the bat.

. . . 129 . . .

He rotates the wheel and presses the clay down firmly. Using a sponge, he wets the top surface of the clay and slowly lowers the template, keeping the wheel in motion all the time. The sponge is kept handy to wet the surface of the clay if it starts to get dry.

When the jigger arm is down all the way, he holds it there for several seconds to get a smooth surface, then raises it. The saucer is formed. He cuts off the excess clay at the rim.

Then he removes it. The bat can now be lifted out of the wheel and put aside to dry.

### A case mold

To get the full benefit from your jigger, you should have several identical bats for each plate form, because once the template is set in place, it is almost as easy to make six plates as one. To duplicate your jigger bat, make a case mold (a case mold is one from which other molds are made) by

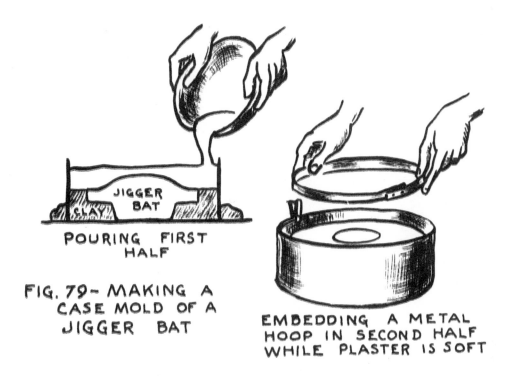

POURING FIRST
HALF

FIG. 79 – MAKING A
CASE MOLD OF A
JIGGER BAT

EMBEDDING A METAL
HOOP IN SECOND HALF
WHILE PLASTER IS SOFT

sizing it, setting it in clay as shown in Fig. 79, placing a cottle around it, and pouring plaster. This will form the bottom piece of the case mold. When this has set, turn it over, remove the clay (leaving the bat in place), and cut several notches in the rim. Size the piece of the mold just cast and size the bat; then set the cottle and pour the other half. This second half must not be poured any deeper than the height of the jigger bat, so that there will be an opening in the mold through which plaster may be poured to form additional jigger bats.

Plaster expands slightly as it sets. Therefore, unless the top piece of the case mold is reinforced, it will crack during use. A barrel hoop cut to a size slightly smaller than the outside circumference of the mold and fastened with a short nail, makes good reinforcing material. A heavy wire made into a circular loop, with the ends firmly twisted together, will serve also. Have the reinforcing ready before you pour; then after the plaster has started to set, but while it is still in the plastic state, press the hoop into the plaster until it goes halfway down but does not touch either the bat or the outer retaining wall.

As soon as the case mold has set, you may size it and begin to cast jigger bats; it is not necessary to wait until the mold dries. The jigger bats, however, must be thoroughly dry before they are used. Unfortunately, your original jigger bat, which you had to size, is no longer usable.

*Jiggering a bowl*

Bowls may also be made by jiggering, but a different type of bat and template are required. If the bat formed the inside of the bowl, it would need to be so sharply convex that the finished form would not lift off as it dried but would crack. For this reason, the jigger bat used in making bowls is concave, forming the outside of the bowl, while the template forms the inside.

The process of making the bat and the template for a bowl is similar to that used in the case of the plate. One-half of the bowl is drawn in cross section, and the curve of the outside is traced onto a piece of zinc which is then cut out and mounted on a piece of wood. This is used as a cutting tool to cut the jigger bat out of a block of plaster cast on the wheel head in the manner described for the plate. The template for jiggering the bowl is made in the same way, using the inside curve of the bowl for its profile.

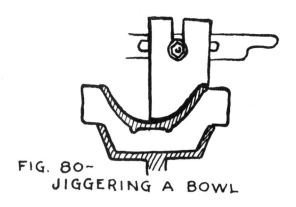

FIG. 80 -
JIGGERING A BOWL

*PLATE XV*

In making bowls on the jigger, the clay is not flattened into a pancake but is rolled into a ball.

This is pressed into the bottom of the jigger bat and worked up the sides with the fingers until a rough bowl shape is formed.

This rough shape is then moistened with the sponge, and the jigger arm is lowered, so that the template may cut the finished inside surface.

## A *flop-over mold*

A very simple type of mold, called the "flop-over," is sometimes used to make flat shapes—plates, platters, etc. This mold is a convex block of plaster shaped like the inside of the plate in reverse. It can be made in the same way as the bottom piece of the mold for the rectangular dish

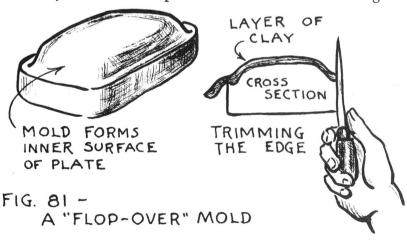

MOLD FORMS
INNER SURFACE
OF PLATE

LAYER OF
CLAY

CROSS
SECTION

TRIMMING
THE EDGE

FIG. 81 –
A "FLOP-OVER" MOLD

described on page 113, or, if the plate is round, it can be cut on the wheel. For ease in trimming, the outside edge of the mold is shaped like the plate itself.

When the flop-over mold is used, a thin layer of clay is rolled out, laid over the mold, and pressed into shape. The edges are then trimmed and the clay is allowed to dry on the mold. When dry, it has the form of the plate. The rectangular dish with a picture of Neptune shown on Plate XX was made this way.

This is an easy type of mold to use but it has one bad feature—the plates produced are perfectly flat on the bottom. If a foot is desired, it must be modeled and attached while the clay is still on the mold and before it has dried.

### "Running" plaster

Here is an entirely different method of making plaster models, new to potters, although plaster workers have used it for many years. The method makes use of the period of plasticity which plaster goes through before it sets hard; objects are shaped by running a template over the soft plaster—hence the name "running" (plaster workers call this "screed-ing").

Let's see how we can take advantage of this period of plasticity to shape a model for a bowl. Our first problem will be to rig up some device for running a template over the plaster while it is soft.

### A turning rig

To run a model for a bowl, we can borrow a trick from the pattern-makers and construct what they call a turning sled. We shall need a per-fectly smooth slab of plaster, about 14" x 14" x 1" thick, with a ¾" wooden dowel set in the center as a pivot post as shown in Fig. 82. The dowel must be slightly higher than the model will be and must be firmly held in place. Make a hole for it first, then cast a cone of plaster around it. A small nail driven into the end of the dowel will serve as a pivot for the sled. The sled is made of two pieces of wood nailed together, with a small piece of zinc or tin fastened on the end to serve as a socket for the pivot. The pieces of wood may be any convenient size, but the metal socket must rest on the top of the dowel when the sled stands flat on the plaster slab.

The next step is cutting the template for the shape. This should be drawn on paper first, then scribed on metal. A thin sheet of zinc may be used, or a piece of ordinary tin can, flattened. The template is cut out with a pair of tin snips and the edge carefully filed until it is perfectly smooth. If the model is to be any good, the template must be really smooth. In drawing the pattern for the template, remember to allow a waste rim. When the template is finished, nail it to the sled so that one end will just

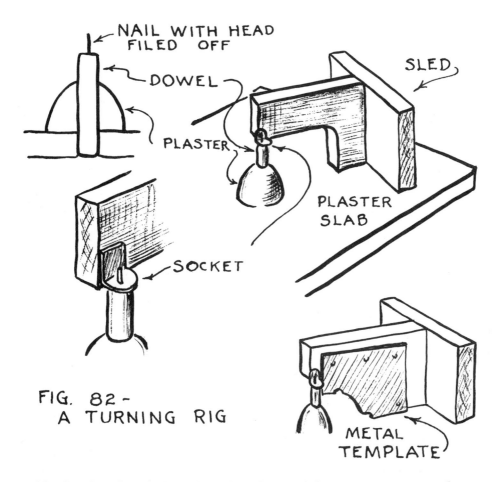

FIG. 82 -
A TURNING RIG

touch the dowel and the other the plaster slab. Now you are ready to begin turning.

### Sizing

The plaster slab must be either sized or shellacked and coated with stearine. Since the sled must slide freely on the slab, stearine is preferable because it makes a more slippery surface than size. Give the slab three coats of shellac, allowing about twenty minutes for each coat to dry; then brush stearine over the surface and wipe off the excess. The method of preparing stearine is described on page 70. Put a protective layer of clay around the dowel and the plaster cone which holds it, so that the model will come off easily.

### Tools

You will need a spoon, a flat steel scraper, a kidney-shaped scraper, a spatula, and two bowls. Have a pail of water handy in which to wash your hands, and a towel for drying.

*Mixing*

Put water in one of the bowls and add the plaster; allow it to slake in the usual fashion. When it has slaked, stir it once or twice, then dip out a cupful into the second bowl. The plaster in this second bowl will remain undisturbed while you stir the first bowlful. Plaster which is left alone does not set as rapidly as plaster which is stirred; so the cupful you dipped out will remain soft longer and be available for a finish coat after the other has set.

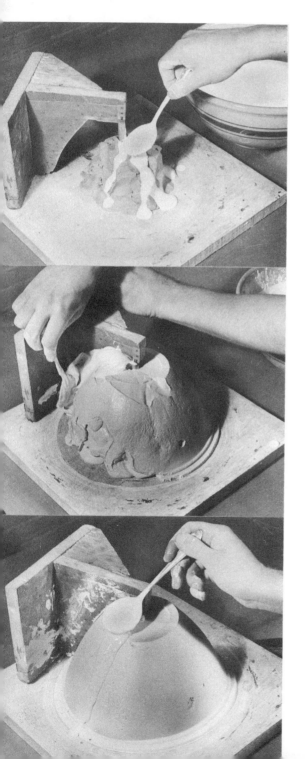

PLATE XVI

Stir the plaster in the first bowl until it starts to thicken. When it is thick enough so that one spoonful will stand on another, dip out some (using the spoon or your fingers if you prefer), and pile it on the clay which you have pressed around the pivot post and build up a shape which is roughly that of the model; then swing the sled around.

The first cut of the template will leave several voids in the model where the plaster was not built up high enough; so using the spoon, add more plaster at those points and run the template around again; repeat the operation until no hollows are left. Lift the sled off the pivot occasionally to clean off the excess plaster, and scrape the plaster slab. It is important that the sled run freely on the slab; keep both as clean as you can.

By this time the first bowlful of plaster will probably start to harden; set it aside and use the plaster in the second bowl to make a "splash coat" for a finishing run. This plaster will still be fairly liquid and you can cover the whole model with it quickly.

. . . 136 . . .

Then spin the template around for two or three turns to give the final surface. Now carefully lift off the sled without marking the model. In a few minutes the model will be ready to lift off the pivot post—the operation is finished. The model will have a hole in the bottom where the pivot projected through, but this can be plugged with clay and a mold made of the bowl in the usual way.

The turning sled should be cleaned and set aside until you are ready to run another shape. You will be able to use the same rig over and over to make circular plates, bowls, and cups, by merely changing the template.

### The turning box—a vase form

It is a simple matter to run plaster for vase shapes if you construct a turning box like the one shown in Plate XVII. The box has two bearings to hold a metal rod, one end of which is bent into a crank and a handle so that it can be turned. A removable piece of wood holds the metal template. As the plaster is piled up on the rod and the rod is turned, the template cuts the plaster to the desired shape. Let us see how the turning box is used.

### PLATE XVII

The potter has assembled his tools and the bowls for mixing plaster. A template to form a vase shape has been cut out of a piece of tin and fastened to the template board. The potter turns the rod and wraps a piece of heavy twine around it. This will give the plaster something to hold to.

The potter has mixed his plaster in the large bowl and dipped out a smaller bowlful to work with. The plaster in the larger bowl will be left undisturbed, to be used for the finishing coat. Using a spoon, he piles plaster on top of the cord tied around the rod.

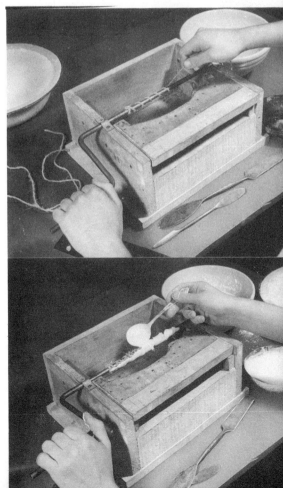

Continuing to pile plaster on the' rod.

More plaster piled on the rod. It is almost time for the first turn.

The potter has started to turn the rod and to cut the plaster with the template. A rough vase shape begins to appear.

More plaster has been piled on and the rod turned until the complete vase shape is formed. The potter has taken the template board out and is scraping plaster off the template.

Putting on the finishing coat.

The turning is finished—the potter removes the turning board.

The model completed. The potter has unfastened one of the metal strips which hold the rod in place and has pulled the rod out of the model.

Making the mold. A template has been cut out of heavy cardboard, shellacked and sized. The potter is now sizing the model.

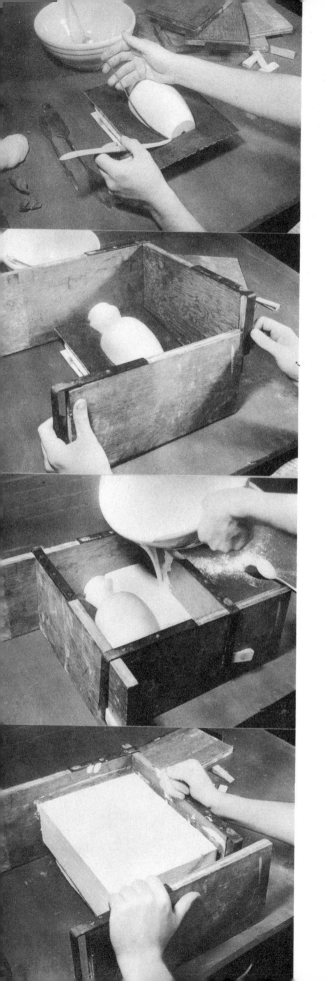

Setting the model in the template. A thin coil of clay seals the joint.

Putting the casting box in place.

Pouring the first half of the mold.

Removing the casting box after the first half of the mold has set.

. . . 140 . . .

Cutting notches in the first half of the mold.

Casting box in place, ready to pour the second half of the mold.

The finished mold. The plaster model ready to be removed.

Pouring slip into the mold. This picture was taken after the mold had been allowed to dry for several days. Note the piece of inner tube holding the two halves of the mold together.

. . . 141 . . .

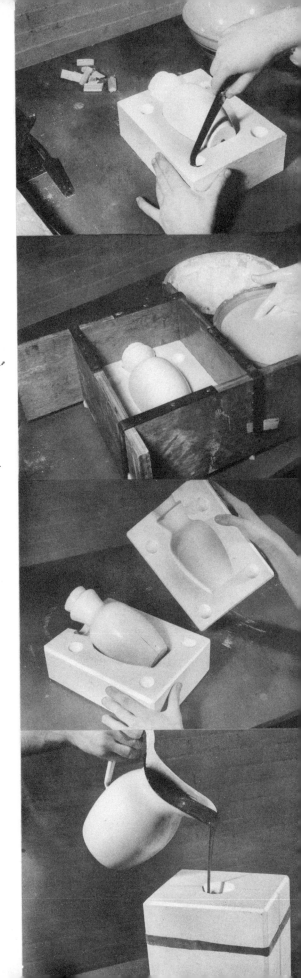

Pouring out the excess slip.

Removing the cast piece from the mold. The portion on top is a waste rim and will be trimmed off.

The finished vase.

*Running plaster for a rectangular plate*

Models for rectangular pottery forms as well as round ones can be made by running plaster, but a slightly different rig is needed. A bridge such as that shown in Fig. 83 is used to hold the template, and a pattern of the desired shape is cut out of a thin plaster slab or a piece of plywood. After plaster is piled on the pattern, the bridge holding the template is guided around the edge so that the plaster is cut to the desired shape.

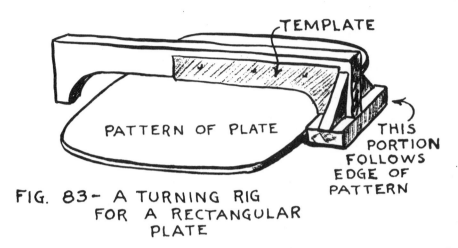

FIG. 83- A TURNING RIG FOR A RECTANGULAR PLATE

In the following series of pictures a potter uses this method to make a model of a large square plate. In this process he makes both surfaces of the plate, inside as well as outside, and so he needs two templates, one to form a mound which will have the shape of the inside of the plate, and a second to form the plate itself out of plaster cast over the mound.

*PLATE XVIII*

A pattern conforming to the outline of the plate has been cut out of plywood and is being nailed in place on a large table. The template has been cut and fastened to the bridge.

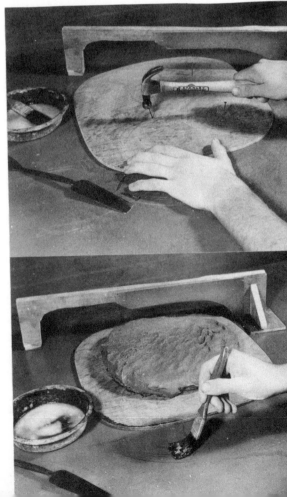

A mound of clay has been put on top of the pattern. The potter lubricates the surface of the table top with stearine so that the bridge will be able to move easily.

The potter builds a mound of plaster on top of the clay.

Running the template. The potter moves the bridge all the way around the pattern so that the flat portion of the bridge (at the right of the picture) is pressed tightly against the edge. The other leg of the bridge serves merely for support.

The rough shape of the mound is blocked out. The potter has cleaned the table and the template and is putting on plaster for the finishing coat.

The mound is finished. The surface has been smoothed with sandpaper; the potter sizes it preparatory to putting on plaster for the plate itself.

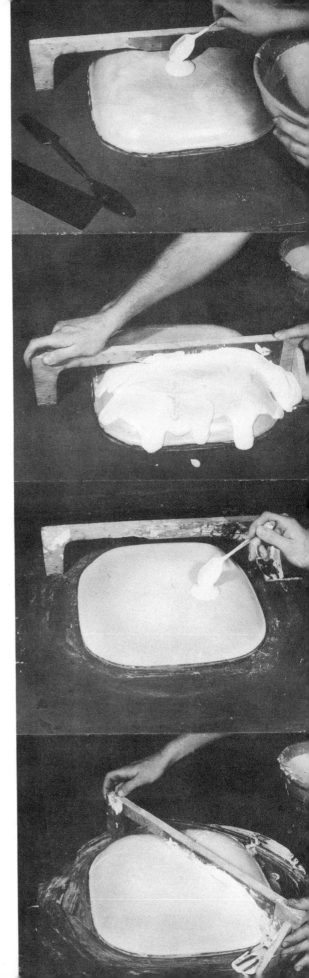

Starting to make the plate. The potter has his second template in readiness. The mound has been sized and plaster is put on top.

Running the plate.

The finish coat. The shape of the plate has been completed, and thinner plaster is put on for the final surface.

Running the finish coat.

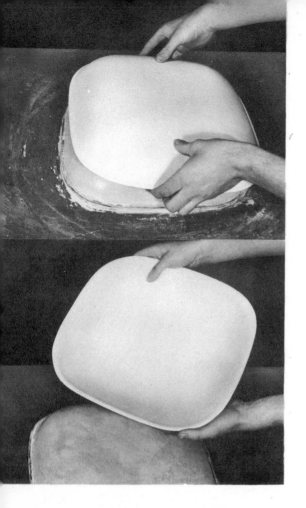

Lifting the plate off the mound.

The model of the plate completed. A solid casting mold for this can now be made by the method described earlier in this chapter.

### Molds for ceramic sculpture

Large pieces of terra cotta—that is, clay sculpture intended for firing—are usually pressed inside of molds. When sculptors make such molds they handle the plaster in a way quite different from any we have described so far. Instead of building a retaining wall and pouring plaster around the clay model, they throw plaster against the model, or paint it on with a soft brush. When the mix is fairly liquid, the model is completely covered with a thin plaster coating. As the plaster starts to set, more is piled on, until a layer an inch thick is built up over the entire model. To make the mold stronger, strips of burlap or heavy twine are sometimes pressed into the plaster while it is still soft, to serve as reinforcing. The places where the mold must separate are marked off first, and thin strips of brass, called "shims," are pressed into the clay along those lines. In this way a mold of several parts can be made in one operation.

### Pressing terra cotta

Pressing clay in a mold like the one just described is easy if the mold has an opening at the base large enough for the hand. It is merely necessary to tie the pieces of the mold together and brace them firmly; then press a layer of clay over the entire inner surface. The thickness of the layer will depend, of course, on the size of the piece. Unless the sculpture is more than 3 or 4 feet tall, a ¾" layer of clay should suffice.

Take care to make the layer uniform, and look out for folds or cracks. When you add clay to some which has been pressed in the mold, do not put the new clay along side of the old because that way you are almost certain to leave a little space where the two pieces join. Instead, put the new clay on top of that already in place, and press the two together so that they form a single mass. This will avoid creases in the surface of the piece. Make sure also that the clay is forced into every corner of the mold.

If, when the pieces of the mold are fastened together, the opening which remains is not big enough to get your hand into, you will have to press a layer of clay in each separate part of the mold, then tie them together and weld the joints on the inside with a long handled tool. A piece made this way will show cracks at the seams when it comes out of the mold. These will have to be worked over with modeling tools.

The clay used for terra cotta should contain a high percentage of grog. One part of 40-60 mesh grog to two of clay is about right. For large pieces use a coarser mesh.

As soon as the clay has hardened enough to hold its shape, take the mold apart and remove the piece. Trim off the ridges at the seams and do any necessary finishing.

The surface of terra cotta may have a rough texture or may be smooth. Rubbing with a wooden tool or a small steel spatula will give a polished surface with no sign of grog showing. For the opposite effect, use a damp sponge. This will bring the grog into sharp relief and give as rough a texture as you wish.

The following illustrations show the making and use of a terra-cotta mold.

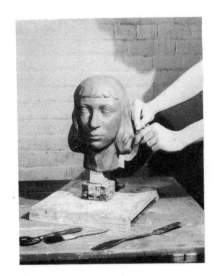

*PLATE XIX*

The sculptor is setting the shims in place.

Brushing a thin layer of plaster over the entire model.

Building the mold up to proper thickness.

Reinforcing the plaster with heavy twine.

Separating the two halves of the mold.

Removing the front half of the mold from the model.

Pressing a layer of clay into each half of the mold.

The two halves of the mold tied together.

Removing the pressed head from the mold.

. . . 149 . . .

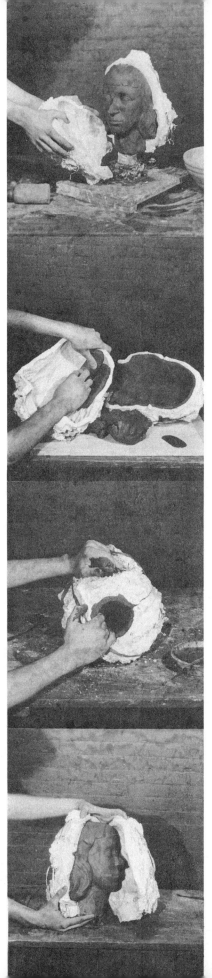

*Garden sculpture*

When made with good taste, terra-cotta figures can add much to the beauty of a house and its grounds.

The little fountain shown in the frontispiece stands against the rear wall of our own garden, and for a number of years it has splashed merrily away, giving us a lot of pleasure. It was made by a combination of methods. The girl and the fish were built by coils. The bowl was modeled in clay, a plaster mold was cast from the model, and the shell of the bowl was pressed in the mold. Holes were cut in the back so that the fountain could be bolted to a wall.

The fountain contains a tiny electric pump which circulates water up from the bowl through the fish's mouth from which it splashes back into the bowl again. Thus the fountain needs no piping whatsoever, for the same water is pumped over and over again. A wall at the back of the bowl, built by the slab method, conceals the pump from view. A cross section of the fountain would look like Fig. 84.

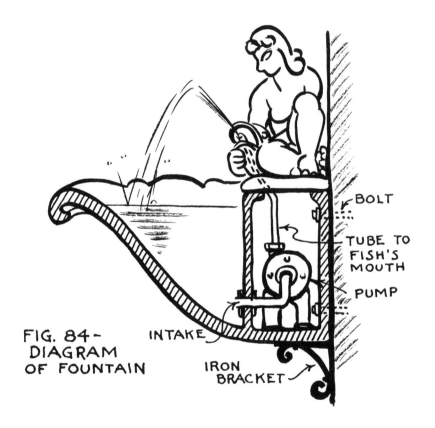

FIG. 84 –
DIAGRAM
OF FOUNTAIN

INTAKE

IRON
BRACKET

BOLT

TUBE TO
FISH'S
MOUTH

PUMP

This fountain was a lot of fun to make and was really much easier than it looks.

*Some principles of design in plaster work*

Pottery made in molds is different from pottery thrown on the wheel or that built by hand. It has its own style of beauty. It can be made smoother, thinner, lighter in weight, and walls may have a uniform thickness not obtainable in handmade ware. Don't ever try to make a mold produce something that looks handmade—not only is this artistically dishonest, it just won't work.

A mold can be made of any shape, but don't let that lead you astray into the production of over-elaborate forms. Plaster is best suited to clean surfaces, to the streamlined shapes of modern design. Don't make molds of cabbage leaves or rose petals.

Plaster molds make mass production of tableware possible, and this is a good thing. Remember, however, that you are an artist. Unless you plan a business enterprise, don't turn your studio into a factory. Use molds with restraint. When you have made one good pressing from a terra-cotta mold, break the mold.

Remember, in ceramic sculpture simplicity is best. Let your figures show their relationship with the earth they come from.

# chapter Eight

# Clay and Clay Bodies

What is clay? A number of different answers could be given to this question. The chemist would call it a hydrous silicate of alumina; the little boy, a nice sticky mud—and they would both be right. But only in part. Clay is not a single substance but a mixture of several substances; while aluminum silicate is the chief ingredient, impurities are always present. These impurities affect the working properties; hence no two clays dug from the ground are exactly alike. All clay, however, has two essential properties—when moist it is plastic, and when heated it becomes hard.

## A little chemistry

An exhaustive knowledge of chemistry is not necessary for ceramic work but you should be familiar enough with a few chemical elements to recognize their symbols and know something about their behavior. You should also know the chemical composition of a half-dozen or so minerals indispensable to the potter.

The earth's crust contains over ninety known elements, each of which has a letter or two as its symbol. When atoms of two or more elements combine to form a molecule of a new substance, the chemical formula of the new substance is made by grouping the symbols of the combining elements, with numbers written below the line to indicate how many atoms of each element are in the molecule of the new substance. Thus, two atoms of hydrogen (H) combine with one atom of oxygen (O) to form a molecule of water. The chemical formula of water is therefore $H_2O$.

Only a few of the chemical elements are important to us here. Surprisingly, one of these elements is present in such great quantities that it makes up more than one-half of the entire earth's rocky crust — about 58 per cent. That element is silicon (Si). The next most plentiful element, constituting about 15 per cent, is aluminum (Al). These elements are usually found in combination with oxygen, in which case we call them silica ($SiO_2$) and alumina ($Al_2O_3$).

Pure clay is composed of one part alumina and two parts silica, plus chemically combined water. Its formula is $Al_2O_3 \cdot 2SiO_2 \cdot 2H_2O$. That is why the chemist calls it a hydrous aluminum silicate. Note that the chemically combined water is not the water which gives clay its plasticity. If you allow clay to become bone dry, the chemically combined water will still be there.

## Feldspar

Feldspar is the parent of clay. There was no clay on our globe in the beginning, for all of our clay is a product of change, formed by the decomposition of feldspathic rock weathered by air and water during many thousands of years. Feldspar is an important material to the potter because it is used in most glazes and almost all clay bodies. It is the chief ingredient of granite and many other rocks. There are several different kinds of feldspar, but all of them contain alumina and silica plus something else. In the case of orthoclaze, the purest of the feldspars, the something else is potash ($K_2O$) and its formula is $K_2O \cdot Al_2O_3 \cdot 6SiO_2$. Other feldspars contain soda ($Na_2O$) instead of potash, some contain lime ($CaO$), and some contain several ingredients. During the weathering process, these substances are dissolved out of the feldspar, while alumina and silica remain to form clay. When you use a feldspar in a glaze, you should know its chemical formula so that you can tell what you are adding along with the alumina and the silica.

## Residual clay

Pure clay is composed of alumina, silica, and chemically combined water; but absolutely pure clay is almost non-existent. The clay most nearly pure is that which has remained in the same spot where it was formed. This is called residual clay. Kaolin, or china clay, is of this type. It is coarse in texture, difficult to work with (non-plastic), and highly refractory. (A refractory substance is one which resists heat, will not melt readily.) When kaolin is used in a clay body, feldspar or some other flux must be used with it, otherwise the kaolin would not mature in any ordinary kiln. It is white both before and after firing. Kaolin is the principal ingredient in china and porcelain.

## Sedimentary clay

Most clay has not remained where it was formed, but has moved great distances, carried by streams, by winds, by glaciers. Such clay is called sedimentary clay. As a result of its transportation it has been ground finer in grain and contains many impurities, hence it is more plastic and less refractory than residual clay. Its color in the natural state may be almost anything—blue, green, yellow, red, brown, gray, or even black. When fired it is usually some shade of red or buff.

Here are some different kinds of sedimentary clay you will have occasion to use.

### Plastic kaolin

Plastic kaolin is almost a contradiction, for actually no kaolin is really plastic. The term refers to certain clays which have been transported without becoming contaminated, and so burn white. Because of their finer grain size, they are a little more workable than regular kaolins and are therefore valuable as body ingredients. Florida lake kaolin is of this type.

### Ball clay

Ball clay is a sedimentary clay which, in most cases, has been carried in a stream and deposited on the bottom of some body of water. It is extremely fine in grain and usually has carbonaceous material mixed with it. As a result, it is highly plastic. When mined it is often dark in color, but if fires almost white. It is used in porcelain and white ware bodies to provide workability.

### Fire clay

Fire clay is a rough textured clay, usually dark in color, which will stand high temperatures. It is not plastic and is not ordinarily used for making ware, although you will find it an important ingredient if you make any stoneware bodies. Fire clays are used commercially in the manufacture of refractory brick.

### Stoneware clay

Like fire clay, stoneware clays will stand high temperatures, but they are smoother and more plastic and usually fire to a light buff color. In a reducing fire they become dark gray or brown. Monmouth and Jordan are stoneware clays.

### Common clay

Common clay is the material used to make bricks. It is abundant throughout the country, usually fires dark red or brown, and hardens at low temperatures. Common clays vary widely in their characteristics, but they have much to offer the potter who will take the trouble to learn their secrets.

### Digging your own

There is no thrill in pottery quite equal to that of digging your own clay from the ground, preparing it for use, and making something from it. This is an experience which many studio potters miss altogether when they rely entirely upon their dealers. Common clay is abundant, and the chances are that you are closer to a clay bed than you imagine. Try to find some and work with it.

As we said before, no two common clays are alike. They differ in color, they react differently to the fire, they have different degrees of plasticity. Some can be cast and some cannot. No matter what the clay is, however, there is some method by which it can be worked; it is up to you to discover that method.

You may find clay at the side of a stream or where a road has been cut through or where they are excavating for the cellar of a house not far away. It is often about five feet below the surface of the ground. You can recognize it by the fact that it will be plastic when wet, and can be modeled into shapes. Dig some and prepare it for use, then test its properties.

## Preparing the clay

You may be fortunate enough to find clay which can be used just as it comes from the ground, but this is rare. Natural clay almost always needs cleaning. The clay, after being dug, must be spread out to dry, preferably on wooden boards in the bright sun. When it is thoroughly dry, large lumps may be pounded with a mallet or a block of wood and broken up; then the clay can be made into slip by sifting it into a pail of water and allowing it to slake for an hour or two. It is advisable to use twice as much water as clay so that the resultant slip will be quite liquid and easier to screen. After the clay has slaked, stir it thoroughly and then pour it through a 40-mesh sieve. The clay would be better screened through a sieve of finer mesh than this, say 80 or 100, but it would be difficult to get it through. If trouble is experienced in screening through a 40-mesh sieve, you may have to pour the clay through a coarser sieve first.

After screening, allow the liquid slip to settle for three or four hours, then pour the excess water off the top. The remaining clay slip can then be poured into plaster drying bats and allowed to harden until it is the right consistency for wedging.

## Testing the physical properties of a clay

Your pottery work will be better if you know the characteristics of the clay you use. A great deal can be learned about a clay by feeling it when it is moist. Plasticity and working quality can be judged that way, but until you try it out, you will not be sure at just what temperature your clay matures. There are other properties which you should measure, also— density, porosity, and degree of shrinkage. Usually when you use a natural clay, you can alter its characteristics by adding something to make it work better (when you do this you will be making a clay body). Let us consider some of these physical properties to see how they may be tested, and how, if necessary, they can be changed.

### Plasticity

Plasticity is the property which makes clay workable. It is difficult to measure, for it is largely a matter of opinion; the same clay may seem extremely plastic to one potter and only moderately so to another. In general, we can say that if a small piece can be pulled into a thin cylinder about the size and shape of a lead pencil, the clay is quite plastic or "long." If it refuses to take such a shape, but breaks and crumbles instead, the clay is less plastic, or "short."

It is not known for sure what makes clay plastic. Fineness of grain has something to do with it, since those clays which have been ground fine are usually more plastic than others. Organic matter has a lot to do with it, also. It is said that the old Chinese potters used to throw the carcasses of dead animals into their clay pits so that the products of decomposition would improve the clay. For a similar reason, aging the clay—that is, keeping it moist in a container for several months—makes it better to work with. (Don't worry if your clay begins to smell bad—that's really a good sign.) Sometimes inoculating a fresh batch of clay with some of an old batch promotes the growth of bacteria and so helps plasticity. Adding a spoonful of weak hydrochloric acid or a little vinegar helps, also.

It is much easier to make a clay less plastic than more so. If you have a clay which is not plastic enough and the methods of aging described above do not help, try adding about 10 per cent of ball clay. You can also try the addition of 1 or 2 per cent of bentonite. Bentonite is a clay of volcanic origin, about the most plastic material known.

### Water of plasticity

You may wish to measure the percentage of water needed to make your clay plastic. To do this, weigh out 100 grams of dry clay powder and put it on a glass slab. Then put 50 grams of water into a graduate from which you can pour it, drop by drop, onto the clay, meanwhile working the clay with a spatula until just the right amount of water has been added to make the clay plastic. The reading on the graduate will show the number of grams of water you have used. Since you started with 100 grams of clay, this number of grams is the percentage of water of plasticity. In most clays, the percentage is between 30 and 45. Usually the higher the percentage, the more plastic the clay.

### Firing range

The second essential property of clay is that of becoming hard and dense when fired. Since clays differ in the temperature they require to mature, you will have to fire some test bars to learn the firing range of the clay with which you work. The ideal temperature to which to fire a clay is the one at which it will achieve maximum hardness and density without slumping or changing shape. One way to find this point would be to have a series of firings of the kiln at different temperatures and see which one produced the best results. An easier and quicker way, however, is to make a test tile 6″ long, 1½″ wide, and ¼″ thick. Put this in the kiln so that the ends of the tile rest upon two kiln props as shown in Fig. 85, choosing a spot where you can watch the tile through the peep hole during the firing.

TEST BAR

FIG. 85 –
FINDING THE
MATURING POINT
OF CLAY

CONES
INDICATE
TEMPERATURE
AT WHICH
BAR BENDS

Make a cone pat with a series of four or five cones as described in Chapter Nine and put it in the kiln near the test bar so that you can see it through the peep hole. When your test tile begins to bend in the middle, the kiln has reached the maximum temperature which the clay will stand without deforming. The cones will tell you what this temperature is.

Suppose, however, you find that the maturing point of your clay is higher than your kiln will fire, what then? This is apt to happen if you use a kiln which cannot go above cone 04. In that case it will be necessary to lower the maturing point of the clay by adding a flux. A good material to use for this purpose is a frit, such as one of the special body frits sold by ceramic dealers. If you use a flux, make a series of test bars of the clay with different percentages of the flux added, ranging from 2 per cent to 5 per cent, and fire them resting on props as described above. If a bar bends in the firing, the percentage of flux is too great. The percentage to use will be the highest the clay can take without slumping. Glass cullet (ground-up bottles) can also be used as a clay flux.

Common clays usually mature at a low temperature, but they are apt to have an abrupt end point in their firing range. That is, if a clay matures at cone 04 it may be seriously overfired two cones higher at cone 02. Stoneware and higher fire clays, on the other hand, are usually more flexible. Monmouth clay, for example, may be safely fired anywhere between cone 1 and cone 10.

It is important to have the clay mature. If it is underfired, the ware will be soft and glazes will always develop fine cracks or "craze." Studio potters whose kilns have a top temperature of cone 04 have often tried to use Monmouth clay and been disappointed in the results, blaming their failures on the glazes, when underfiring was the real fault. Even Monmouth clay, however, can be made to mature at cone 04 by the addition of frit as a flux.

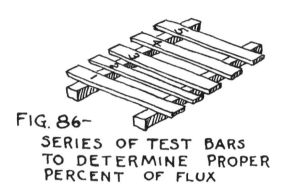

FIG. 86–

SERIES OF TEST BARS
TO DETERMINE PROPER
PERCENT OF FLUX

### Density

When you have determined the best temperature at which to fire the clay, test its density at that point. You can judge this quality in your ware by tapping it and listening to the ring. The denser it is, the clearer the tone. A more accurate measure, however, is the absorption test. Weigh a piece of fired clay (bisque), then let the piece stand in water overnight. After it has soaked for twelve hours, take it out of the water, remove any surface moisture and weigh the piece again. Its percentage of absorption will be indicated by the following formula:

$$\frac{\text{weight wet minus weight dry}}{\text{weight dry}} \times 100 = \% \text{ absorption}$$

In general, an absorption of 5 to 10 per cent is all right. Above 10 per cent, the ware will be too absorbent for use. Glazes will craze and liquids will be absorbed into the body, eventually seeping through.

Density can be increased and absorption reduced by using fluxes as described above or by adding flint. Try various amounts from 5 per cent to 20 per cent, making a number of test tiles and firing them to find out which percentage gives the best results.

### Porosity

A clay may be extremely plastic and easy to work with and yet be unsuitable for making ware because every piece comes out of the kiln warped or cracked. The clay is not porous enough. There is no way for the water to leave, and so in drying and during firing distortion takes place. Something must be added to the clay to "open it up," to give it porosity. Your problem will be to do this without destroying its plasticity to the point where the clay becomes unworkable, for plasticity and porosity do not often go together. You may have to sacrifice some of one in order to increase the other.

Try adding flint in various proportions. (Flint seems to be the answer to many of the potter's problems.) Make a test tile with 5 per cent flint added, another with 10 per cent, another with 15 per cent, and another with 20 per cent. See how they work.

If additions of flint do not solve your problem, try using a coarser screen in preparing the clay, for frequently a natural clay contains enough sand to make it porous. Thus a clay which warps badly when screened through a 60-mesh sieve may work satisfactorily if screened through a 30-mesh sieve. You may run into trouble here if refractory particles of stone remain in the clay and "dunt" during the firing—that is, force out pieces on the surface, leaving little craters; but this does not always happen. Some potters who use native clay don't screen it at all, preferring the coarse, rough surface obtained that way.

In heavy pieces or where coarse texture is desirable, porosity can be obtained by the use of grog. Use 40-60 mesh and add from 10 to 20 per cent.

## Shrinkage

Clay shrinks as it dries and it shrinks some more when it is fired. Different clays shrink different amounts; in some cases the final piece that comes out of the kiln will be one-fifth shorter than the original clay shape.

To measure shrinkage, make a tile out of the clay, about 6" long, 1" wide, ¼" thick, as shown in Fig. 87. On this, score a line with a knife and measure two points exactly ten centimeters apart. (We use centimeters because it is easier to measure tenths that way.) Allow the tile to dry, and then measure the distance between the two points. This will show you the dry shrinkage of the clay. Next fire the tile to the maturing point and measure the distance again. This will give you the fired shrinkage. This shrinkage may be expressed as a percentage as follows:

$$\frac{\text{original length minus fired length}}{\text{original length}} \times 100 = \% \text{ shrinkage}$$

For example, if the distance between the two points after the tile is fired is 8.4 centimeters, the percentage would be

$$\frac{10\text{-}8.4}{10} \times 100 = 16\% \text{ shrinkage}$$

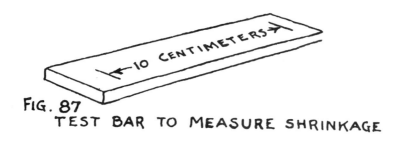

**FIG. 87**

TEST BAR TO MEASURE SHRINKAGE

It is necessary to know the shrinkage of any clay you work with if you want to make ware which will be a particular size when fired. When you have fired the test tile, you can make a shrinkage rule for yourself, like that shown in Fig. 88. Draw a line, *AB*, equal to the unfired length. Draw another line, *CD*, parallel to *AB* and equal to the fired length. Draw lines through *AC* and *BD*, prolonging them until they meet at the point *O*. On *CD*, lay off points 1, 2, 3, etc., 1″ apart. Draw lines from the point *O* through the points laid off on *CD* and extend them until they cut the line *AB* at 1′, 2′, 3′, etc. The distances between the points on line *AB* show how long a piece of clay must be when wet in order to be one inch long when fired. Make a ruler out of a strip of thin wood or a piece of cardboard and on it mark off spaces equal to those on the line *AB*, numbering them 1, 2, 3, etc. Now you have a shrinkage rule. When you measure a piece of plastic clay with it, the reading on your rule will show how long in inches the piece of clay will be when it comes out of the kiln.

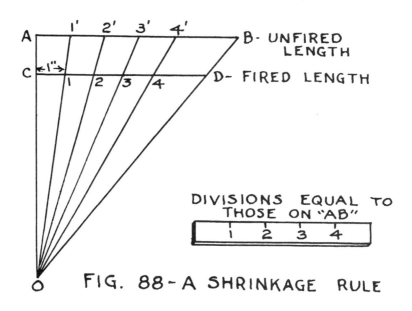

FIG. 88 - A SHRINKAGE RULE

*Clay bodies*

In the manufacture of heavy clay products, brick, building tile, etc., clay is used just as it comes from the ground. This is also true of earthenware. In the production of finer wares, however, clay bodies are usually prepared through blending.

A clay body must have enough plasticity to be workable, it must be porous enough so that shrinkage can be controlled and so that warping does not deform the ware; it must reach density at practicable temperatures. and if the ware is to be cast, it must be able to be deflocculated.

White ware bodies usually contain at least four different ingredients—ball clay for plasticity, china clay for whiteness, flint as a filler, and feldspar as a flux. Frits are also used as fluxes, especially in the low-temperature range. Talc has been used as a flux, but it produces some unpredictable results, and research workers are experimenting further with it. Whiting in small quantities is also used as a flux.

In industrial work, clay bodies are prepared by weighing out the ingredients dry, then putting them in water and allowing them to slake, after which the mixture is put through a blunger. This is a stirring machine which thoroughly mixes the slip for several hours. After this, in the case of white ware bodies, the slip is passed over magnets to remove iron particles. The slip then goes to the filter press where moisture is pressed out and it becomes layers of plastic clay. These are put into a pugmill for further mixing, after which the clay is ready for forming on the jigger. If the ware is to be cast, the clay which comes from the filter press is allowed to dry, then made into a casting slip and deflocculated.

You can prepare clay bodies with much less elaborate equipment than this, however. After the ingredients have been weighed out and allowed to slake, the slip may be stirred with a stick, then screened and poured into plaster drying bats where it can remain until it is hard enough to be wedged. Remember that aging helps plasticity. If you keep the clay moist in a tightly covered container for several weeks before you use it, you will find it easier to work with.

Working out a body formula of your own is an interesting experience, well worth experimentation. Different clays may be used for their special qualities of texture or color; plasticity may be obtained by adding ball clay or bentonite, and density may be secured with flint. If you have trouble getting a body which will mature within the temperature range of your kiln, try adding a flux such as body frit or glass cullet.

## Some clay body recipes

Here are a few body recipes. Quantities given refer to parts by weight. A cone 04 white body, good for throwing.

| | |
|---|---|
| Florida lake clay | 50 |
| Feldspar | 10 |
| Flint | 27 |
| Ball clay | 10 |
| Cryolite | 3 |
| Bentonite ½% | 0.5 |

Another cone 04 white body for throwing or jiggering.

| | |
|---|---|
| North Carolina kaolin | 15 |
| Ball clay | 30 |
| Feldspar | 8.75 |
| Talc | 25 |
| Flint | 15 |
| Ferro Enamel Co. Frit 3195 | 6.25 |
| Bentonite 2% | 2 |

This body makes an excellent casting slip if the bentonite is left out. It can be deflocculated according to the following formula.

| | |
|---|---|
| White body | 1000 |
| Water | 480 |
| Sodium silicate | 1.5 |
| Soda ash | 1.5 |
| Sodium tannate | 2 |

A cone 04 terra-cotta body for ceramic sculpture.

| | |
|---|---|
| Monmouth or Jordan clay | 30 |
| Campbell's or Dalton red clay | 25 |
| Grog 20-40 mesh | 30 |
| Flint | 15 |

This body is difficult to throw with but is excellent for modeling. It will fire a pale red. For a richer color, add 2 per cent of red iron oxide.

## High fire bodies

As we said in Chapter One, earthenware is just as worthy of respect as porcelain. There are some advantages, however, to high temperature ware. At cone 8 and above, many technical problems disappear. Clay becomes hard and vitreous and is serviceable even without a glaze. Pieces are stronger. Colors are more subtle, approaching the natural colors of rocks. The longer you look at high fired ware, the more you will like it.

At high temperatures, impurities melt and produce specks of color and interesting textures in clay. Not all clays will stand high firing, but those that will are better for it. Monmouth clay, for example, fired to cone 04, is a sickly yellow. It is porous, glazes won't fit, it cannot be used to hold liquids. Fired to cone 9, however, it is quite different—hard and dense with a beautiful silvery gray color.

You may not have an opportunity to do high fire work, but if you ever have access to a high fire kiln, take advantage of it and make some pieces of stoneware or porcelain. Here are some recipes for high fire bodies.

A cone 8 stoneware body, good for throwing.

| Monmouth or Jordan clay | 20 |
| XX sagger clay | 55 |
| North American fire clay | 10 |
| Nepheline syenite | 5 |
| Flint | 5 |
| Grog 40-60 mesh | 5 |
| Iron chromate | 2 |

The iron chromate gives this a warm gray tone.
Another stoneware body, cone 2 to cone 8, good for throwing or casting.

| Monmouth or Jordan clay | 20 |
| Campbell's or Dalton red clay | 25 |
| XX sagger clay | 20 |
| North American fire clay | 10 |
| Nepheline syenite | 10 |
| Flint | 5 |
| Grog 40-60 mesh | 12 |

This body will fire a warm red. To use it for casting, make a deflocculated slip as follows.

| Clay body | 1000 |
| Water | 400 |
| Sodium silicate | 1.5 |
| Soda ash | 1.0 |

A porcelain body for cone 10 to cone 15.

| English china clay | 17 |
| Florida lake clay | 8 |
| Ball clay | 25 |
| Feldspar | 25 |
| Flint | 25 |

This body follows the usual porcelain formula of one part each of kaolin, ball clay, feldspar, and flint. For casting make a deflocculated slip as described for the stoneware body above.

### Color in clay bodies

Clay bodies can be colored in the way that glazes are, by the addition of metal oxides; but if you plan to do any quantity of work with colored bodies, you will find it cheaper to use the prepared body stains. Red iron oxide and iron chromate are good, inexpensive body colorants. For small pieces of sculpture, you may find it interesting to experiment with oxides of copper, cobalt, and manganese.

Grog adds much to the beauty of clay bodies, especially when it is of a contrasting color. Buff grog looks good in red clay and, similarly, red grog gives an interesting effect in buff clay. I have never been able to buy red grog, but have made it by pounding up a common brick and screening the result. An easier way to make colored grog is to add the desired color to some plastic clay, then let it dry, crush it with a rolling pin and screen it to the proper size. After this, put it in an unglazed bisque dish and fire it in your kiln. When it has been fired it will need crushing and screening again, but this will be much easier than crushing hard fired clay.

Ground-up porcelain, of course, produces a white grog. For some queer reason, this is called "pitchers."

SOME POINTS ON CLAY BODIES:

*1. The steps in testing clay sound like a tough job, but don't be discouraged. A satisfying feeling of accomplishment awaits you when you have mastered them.*

*2. Work with several different kinds of clay to become familiar with them. Use kaolin and ball clay, as well as your regular working clay.*

*3. Compose a clay body according to your own formula.*

*4. There is a real thrill to working with clay you have dug from the ground. There is lots of it around. Try to find some and use it.*

*5. Color can be added to a clay body, but don't overdo it. Often bright colors which attract at first soon lose their appeal. The subtle natural colors of clay are more pleasing in the long run.*

# chapter Nine

# The Fire

*D*on't imagine that when you have learned how to form ware your education as a potter is complete. Far from it! The fire is just as important as the clay and it has secrets of its own which you must learn.

We know that a remarkable change takes place in clay when it is heated. What was formerly a soft plastic material becomes hard and brittle, changes color, and even becomes waterproof if the fire is hot enough. To bring about this change, the potter must supply heat and must control it so that the right temperature, the "maturing temperature," of the clay is reached.

Applying heat to an object raises its temperature. How much, depends not only upon the amount of heat, but how it is applied and how it is confined. A lighted match, for example, held under a teaspoon filled with water will raise the temperature of the water several degrees. The same amount of heat, however, would have little effect in raising the temperature of a room. In the first case the heat is confined within a small space, in the latter it is dissipated. In firing his ware, the potter must produce heat and keep it confined within his kiln so that the clay reaches maturing temperature without the loss of time or fuel.

## Pyrometric cones

The temperatures at which kilns are fired are much too high to be measured by ordinary thermometers; hence, other pyrometric or heat measuring devices must be used. The most popular of these is the pyrometric cone. A cone is a little pyramid made of clay with fluxes added so that it will melt at a known temperature. A number, indicating its temperature, is stamped in the side. When the potter fires his kiln, he sets a series of cones in a lump of clay called a "cone pat" and places it in the kiln in such a way that he can see it through the peephole. The series always includes at least three cones, one of the temperature needed, one lower, and one higher. Thus if the kiln is to be fired to cone 4, the cone pat will hold cones 3, 4, and 5. The cones are set at a slant as shown in Fig. 89, tipping in the direction of the cone which will bend first. This is done to allow each cone to bend freely without falling against another. The clay out of which the cone pat is made should contain a lot of grog so that it does not crack during the firing and drop the cones.

As the temperature of the kiln rises and approaches the desired point, cone 3 will start to bend. This is a warning signal to the potter. He continues the firing until cone 4 bends and then shuts off the kiln before cone 5 has begun to bend. This shows that the kiln has reached the temperature of cone 4 but has not gone beyond it.

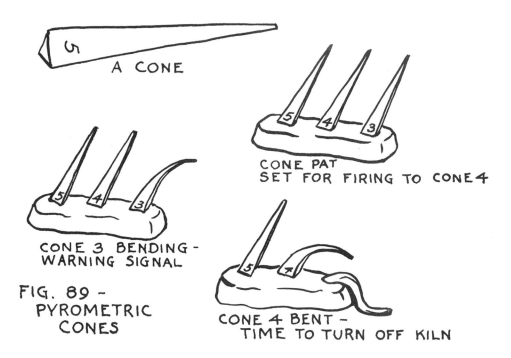

A CONE

CONE PAT
SET FOR FIRING TO CONE 4

CONE 3 BENDING -
WARNING SIGNAL

FIG. 89 -
PYROMETRIC
CONES

CONE 4 BENT -
TIME TO TURN OFF KILN

In a rapid fire, a cone requires a slightly higher temperature to bend than it does when the fire is slower and the heat has more time to "soak" the ware. Thus the cone is not merely a measure of temperature; it is also an indication of the effect of the fire upon a piece of clay. This is what makes cones so valuable to the potter.

The following table gives the temperatures of cones from 022 to 15. These temperatures apply only if the rate of firing is comparatively rapid (about 170° C. per hour). At a slower rate, the cones would bend at slightly lower temperatures.

The color of the kiln at each point in the firing can be described only approximately and the same is true of what happens to clay. Don't interpret this table as indicating that the maturing point of all native red clays is cone 06 but rather that most red clays mature somewhere in that neighborhood.

## TABLE OF CONE TEMPERATURES

| Cone | Centigrade | Fahrenheit | Color of Fire | What Happens to Clay | Type of Ware and Glazes |
|------|------------|------------|---------------|----------------------|-------------------------|
| 15 | 1435 | 2615 | | | |
| 14 | 1400 | 2552 | | | |
| 13 | 1350 | 2462 | | porcelain | porcelain |
| 12 | 1335 | 2435 | | matures | |
| 11 | 1325 | 2417 | white | | |
| 10 | 1305 | 2381 | | | china bodies |
| 9 | 1285 | 2345 | | stoneware clays | stoneware |
| 8 | 1260 | 2300 | | mature | salt glazes |
| 7 | 1250 | 2282 | | | |
| 6 | 1230 | 2246 | | | |
| 5 | 1205 | 2201 | | | |
| 4 | 1190 | 2174 | | red clays melt | china glazes |
| 3 | 1170 | 2138 | | | |
| 2 | 1165 | 2129 | | | semi-vitreous ware |
| 1 | 1160 | 2120 | | | |
| 01 | 1145 | 2093 | yellow | | |
| 02 | 1125 | 2057 | | buff clays | earthenware |
| 03 | 1115 | 2039 | | mature | |
| 04 | 1060 | 1940 | | | |
| 05 | 1040 | 1904 | | | |
| 06 | 1015 | 1859 | | red clays mature | |
| 07 | 990 | 1814 | | | low fire earthenware |
| 08 | 950 | 1742 | orange | | |
| 09 | 930 | 1706 | | | low fire lead glazes |
| 010 | 905 | 1661 | | | |
| 011 | 895 | 1643 | cherry red | | |
| 012 | 875 | 1607 | | | lustre glazes |
| 013 | 860 | 1580 | | | |
| 014 | 830 | 1526 | | | |
| 015 | 805 | 1481 | | organic matter in | chrome red glazes |
| 016 | 795 | 1463 | | clay burns out | |
| 017 | 770 | 1418 | dull red | | |
| 018 | 720 | 1328 | | | overglaze colors |
| 019 | 660 | 1220 | | | enamels |
| 020 | 650 | 1202 | | | |
| 021 | 615 | 1139 | | | |
| 022 | 605 | 1121 | | dehydration begins | |

### Pyrometers

Another device used to measure kiln temperatures is the electric pyrometer with a thermo-couple. This is a metal bead made by soldering together two different elements, usually platinum and rhodium. When such a bead is heated, a tiny electric current is generated. If the bead is attached to an ammeter, the current can be measured and translated into degrees of temperature. This type of pyrometer is especially useful with studio electric kilns.

In the operation of big furnaces, a telescope type of pyrometer is often used. This has a small wire which can be made to glow by an electric current passing through it. The wire is mounted in a tube through which the operator looks into the kiln. The wire cuts across his line of vision so that it makes a black line against the glowing background of the kiln. As current is passed through the wire, it starts to glow until, as the current increases, a point is reached at which the wire disappears because it is glowing just as brightly as the kiln itself. By reading the amount of current passing through the wire at that moment, the operator can tell the temperature of the kiln.

### Fuels

Your choice of kiln will depend upon the kind and amount of ware you plan to make, the space at your disposal, and the kind of fuel you intend to use. If natural gas is available and there is a good sized chimney in existence to which the flue of your kiln may be attached, a gas-fired kiln may be the best type to buy. Manufactured gas does not do as good a job of heating as natural gas. If you plan to use manufactured gas as a fuel, your kiln burners should be equipped with blowers.

Oil is an efficient fuel. It must be used with a blower and it needs a flue, although not as big a one as a gas kiln. Coal is out of the question for the average potter and so is wood, although occasionally wood may be used to fire some pieces of camp craft work in an outdoor kiln.

If you do not have a large amount of work to be fired, an electric kiln may be the best buy. Electric kilns are easy to fire, inexpensive to operate, and do not require flues. Many are now on the market, ranging in size from 3" x 4" x 4" (inside dimensions) upward. The smallest and cheapest electric kiln is really too tiny to be much good for anything other than testing, but one with a firing chamber 12" x 14" x 14" is big enough for the average studio. (See the illustration on page 103.)

Electric kilns are heated by elements which get hot when an electric current passes through them. Most electric elements are made of Nichrome wire, which melts when it reaches a temperature above cone 02. A kiln with elements of this type, therefore, is useful only for comparatively low fired earthenware; in that temperature range it is entirely satisfactory. Recently two other types of elements have been developed, the Globar and Kanthal. The former is a ceramic product (silicon carbide) containing no metal. It can reach temperatures up to cone 15; so a kiln with such elements will fire stoneware and porcelain. Kanthal, a metal alloy made in Sweden, cannot equal the temperature of Globar elements but it will stand much higher temperatures than Nichrome. Stoneware and low-temperature porcelain can be fired in a kiln with Kanthal wire elements.

The big disadvantage of electric kilns is that the elements burn out. They will last longer with proper care, of course, but eventually they will go in spite of all precautions. Be sure to find out how much replacement elements cost before you buy any type of electric kiln.

## Types of kiln

One of the simplest kilns I ever saw was a homemade box made of insulating refractory brick, with four holes at the bottom for bunsen burners, and an opening at the top which could be closed by laying two bricks over it. It had no chimney. A layer of asbestos millboard fastened with iron rods enclosed the whole kiln and held the bricks together. This little kiln fired to cone 04 with ease. A cross section of it is shown in Fig. 90.

## Muffle kilns

A muffle is a chamber made of refractory material in which ware is placed for firing. Between the muffle and the outer wall of the kiln is a space through which flames circulate, entering at the bottom, passing all around the muffle and leaving through a flue at the top. In some muffle kilns the wall of the muffle contains passages for the flames; in others, the flames travel in tubes just inside the muffle itself. The latter type provides more even heat because tubes are placed at the front and rear as well as the sides (the tubes at the front are removed when the kiln is loaded or unloaded). Muffle kilns without a passage for the flames inside the door are apt to be cooler at that portion.

Muffle kilns protect the ware from contact with the flame—an important factor in glazed work. They are not economical of fuel, however, as too much heat escapes up the chimney.

## Portable kilns

Portable kilns are usually of the muffle type. The term *portable* does not mean that you can pick the kiln up and carry it around, but merely that it was manufactured in a factory and shipped in one piece. Non-portable kilns are built on the spot.

## Down draft kilns

A down draft kiln has no muffle. The flames enter from the front or sides, pass over a baffle wall, and reach the ware at the top. They are then drawn down through openings in the floor into a flue connected to a chimney. In their passage through the kiln, the flames come in direct contact with everything in it. This is all right for bisque firing but no good for glazed pieces, so these are stacked in saggers or boxes made of refractory materials which act as separate muffles (Fig. 91).

Down draft kilns are more economical of fuel than muffle kilns. For high fire work a down draft kiln is essential.

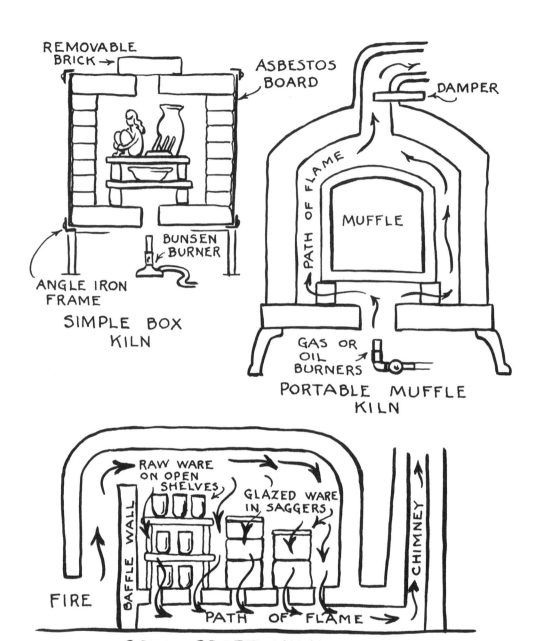

REMOVABLE BRICK →

ASBESTOS BOARD

DAMPER

PATH OF FLAME

MUFFLE

BUNSEN BURNER

ANGLE IRON FRAME

SIMPLE BOX KILN

GAS OR OIL BURNERS

PORTABLE MUFFLE KILN

RAW WARE ON OPEN SHELVES

GLAZED WARE IN SAGGERS

CHIMNEY

BAFFLE WALL

FIRE

PATH OF FLAME

DOWN DRAFT KILN

FIG. 90 - DIAGRAMS OF KILNS

## Tunnel kilns

The kilns previously described are "periodic," that is, they must be fired, allowed to cool, unloaded, then loaded and fired again. A more efficient type of kiln for industrial use is the continuous or tunnel kiln in which ware travels slowly on a moving platform through a tunnel where it encounters successively increasing temperatures, until, at the center of the tunnel, full maturing temperature is reached. Continuing on its way, the ware cools slowly until at the end of the tunnel it is ready to be lifted off the platform and sent to the shipping room. A tunnel kiln operates twenty-four hours a day, seven days a week and requires a constant staff of operators—not the kiln for the studio potter. It is an interesting machine—if you have never seen one, visit a pottery plant where you can watch one in operation.

## Kiln construction

Many potters have built their own kilns and so can you—but don't try it until you have had considerable experience in firing kilns of different types and have had an opportunity to study their construction. No attempt will be made in this book to furnish plans for kiln building. You can get such plans, however, from the manufacturers of refractory brick, along with helpful advice to suit your special needs.

The main problems in building a kiln are providing proper circulation of heat, and adequate insulation. The portions of the kiln which come in contact with the flame must be refractory, able to stand intense heat. On the outside of these there must be insulating materials to hold heat. The best insulator is dead air space. Other insulators are fuller's earth, asbestos, glass fibre, and vermiculite (bloated mica). Ordinary clay, mixed with 60 per cent of coarse sawdust, and burned slowly, produces a porous brick with good insulating properties.

COVER FOR TOP SAGGER

EACH SAGGER SERVES AS A COVER FOR THE ONE BENEATH

FIG. 91 ~ SAGGERS

Refractory insulating bricks are made by a number of different manufacturers. These will stand high temperatures and act as non-conductors of
heat at the same time. Such bricks are labeled K20, K26, K28, and so on.
The number indicates the hundreds of degrees Fahrenheit the brick can
stand. Thus K20 is good for 2000° Fahrenheit, K26 for 2600° F. K26, K28,
and K30 are suitable for almost any kiln work. K20 is good for low fire kilns,
especially electric kilns, while bricks numbered below K20 will not stand
direct contact with the fire but must be used in back of a refractory layer.

To simplify kiln construction, manufacturers of refractory insulating
brick make them in a number of different shapes and sizes adaptable to all
sorts of arches and walls. You will find these fully illustrated in their catalogues. Some firms also produce high-temperature mortars suitable for
casting roof slabs or floors.

*Firing*

A few simple precautions followed in stacking and firing your kiln will
save heartaches when you open it. Where production is large, raw ware and
glazed pieces are fired separately, but the studio potter usually fires both at
the same time. There is no harm in doing this if the firing schedule is controlled so that both types of ware are matured properly.

Too often impatience leads us to put raw pieces into the kiln before they
are bone-dry. Result—moisture cannot get out and the pieces blow up. One
such explosion can ruin everything else in the kiln. Remember, clay needs
several days to dry out—for safety's sake, allow too much time for drying
rather than too little. If in doubt, hold the piece against your cheek. The
least sensation of coolness means that the piece is not dry enough to put
into the kiln. Don't fire a piece of pottery if any part of it is an inch thick
or more, unless it contains grog.

*Stacking*

When clay matures, the fluxes in it melt and soften. Any unequal strains
on a piece at this time will cause it to warp. Be careful that pieces have level
surfaces to stand on. Grind off any bumps from kiln shelves to make them
even, and if necessary put a little flint under pieces to give them uniform
support.

Unglazed raw ware can be stacked quite close, one piece inside another,
without ill effects; but watch the distribution of weight. Do not commit the
sins shown in Fig. 92.

Glazed ware will stick fast to anything it touches during the fire. This
means that special attention must be paid to the foot. The safest way to fire
a glazed piece is by "dry footing," or removing all of the glaze from the ring
on which the piece stands, so that the portion resting on the kiln shelf is
bare. This prevents the piece from sticking and also gives it better support.
The glaze, of course, must not flow too freely; otherwise, it will run down

BAD—

THE BOWL WILL
CRACK THE PLATE

THESE PIECES
WILL WARP

FIG. 92 – STACKING
RAW WARE

GOOD—

CUPS MAY
BE "BOXED"

THIS IS GOOD
IF FOOTINGS
ARE STRONG

PLATES MAY BE
STACKED THIS
WAY IF FOOT IS
OVER FOOT,

(BUT NEVER
MORE THAN
THREE HIGH)

the side of the piece and glue it fast to the kiln shelf, in spite of the dry footing.

*Stilts*

There are a number of different kinds of supports on which glazed pieces can be stood in the kiln during the fire. The most widely used are stilts. They hold up the piece on points, making it unnecessary to clean the glaze off the foot. The point makes a slight mark in the glaze, but this does not affect the appearance or serviceability of the ware. It is important when using stilts to place the piece so that the points support the rim of the foot, as shown in Fig. 93. If the points are placed inside the rim, the piece may break when it contracts during the cooling period.

Ware which is to be fired on stilts should be bisqued at a temperature two or three cones higher than the temperature of the glaze firing, otherwise there is danger that the stilts will push it out of shape. Raw ware on which glaze has been applied without bisque firing first should not be stood on stilts. Such pieces must be dry footed and placed flat on the kiln shelf.

Before you put a glazed piece in the kiln, examine it to see if the glaze is apt to cause trouble. If it is unevenly applied, thick in some places and thin in others, the piece should not be fired. Glaze which is too thick will run off the piece or crawl. Glaze which is too thin will not flow and form the desired surface.

Glazed pieces must be thoroughly dry. Apply the same test that you use for raw ware, namely, hold it against your cheek. If it feels cool, do not put it in the kiln.

. . . 173 . . .

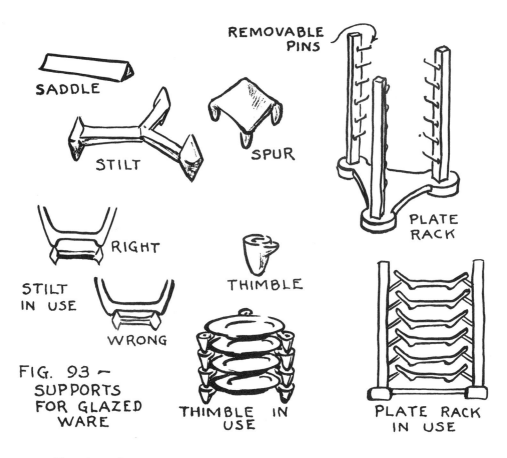

FIG. 93 —
SUPPORTS
FOR GLAZED
WARE

Examine the surface of the glaze. If there are cracks, the glaze will probably crawl. Try rubbing the cracks gently with your fingertip to remove them and produce a smooth, even surface. This will sometimes correct the difficulty; but if sections of the glaze flake off, the piece should be washed and reglazed.

Place glazed pieces in the kiln so that they are protected from each other. Every new batch of glaze is to be regarded with suspicion—you might have forgotten to put in the alumina or made a mistake in weighing the flux, and the glaze may be much more fluid than you suspect. Guard against this possibility by placing the ware in such a way that if the glaze should run, it will not ruin other pieces. A good potter will never use any glaze until he has fired a test sample first.

Some glazes affect others during the fire. Chrome is a bad actor in this respect, for a glaze containing it will give a pinkish tinge to any tin glazes which stand near it. Lead will sometimes volatilize and settle on near-by pieces. With bright glazes this won't matter, but mat pieces will become glossy when you don't want them that way. You will learn by experience which glazes need to be kept to themselves and will be able to take the necessary precautions when stacking.

. . . 174 . . .

### Kiln wash

To protect kiln shelves from bits of glaze which will fall on them, paint them before each firing with a coat of kiln wash made of equal parts of flint and china clay mixed with water to the consistency of cream. Brush this mixture on the shelves with a varnish brush. Kiln wash does not fuse during the firing; any glaze which falls on it can be easily chipped off.

Kiln wash should be applied to the floor of the kiln but not to the top or the sides, and it should be used only on the top surface of kiln shelves. If you put it on the under side of a shelf, it will flake off during the firing and fall into glazed pieces making ugly blemishes almost impossible to remove.

### Kiln dirt

Too many pieces of pottery are marred by kiln dirt. Shelves and walls constantly shed particles, hard to notice when the kiln is stacked but big enough to ruin the beauty of a glazed bowl when they land in its center. Stack your glazed pieces with care to avoid this. Just before the final placing, take them out of the kiln and blow gently on the inside surface to remove any specks.

### Placement in the kiln

Some parts of your kiln will fire hotter than others. Consider this variation when you place the ware, so that those glazes which require the highest temperature will be in the hottest part. As a rule, in a muffle kiln the hottest part is on the floor in the back, and the coolest is in the top front section. In down draft kilns, the reverse is true; the hottest part is at the top. Until you know your kiln thoroughly, place cone pats in different parts of the kiln during each firing, to gain an accurate picture of the temperature of each portion.

Uneven heating causes warping. Try to place large bowls in a portion of the kiln where they will receive the same degree of heat from all sides. Kilns which are heated at the front and back as well as the sides are a big advantage in this respect.

### The firing schedule

The best word of advice here is go slowly. This applies not only to the firing process but to the cooling as well. It should take at least eight hours for a small kiln to reach the temperature of cone 04. Larger kilns require more time. There are parts of the firing cycle where the rate may be increased, but these differ for bisque and glazed ware.

The first portion of the firing is the "water smoking" period, during which atmospheric water is driven out of the clay. This must be slow for raw ware, especially if there are any large pieces in the kiln. If, however, everything in the kiln has been fired once before, the kiln may go up more quickly.

Between 350° C. and 400° C., organic matter in the clay burns out; go slowly during this period if you have any native red clays in the kiln. At 500° C., the water smoking period is ended and densification begins.

At 573° C. the kiln begins to get red hot, and a physical change takes place in the silica, making it expand. Go slowly here, for big pieces are apt to break at this point. This is a critical point in the cooling period, as well as the heating period, for the silica changes back again and contracts. If a piece comes out split, you can tell if the trouble occurred during the heating or the cooling by examining the edge of the break. When the glaze has flowed over the edge of the crack, it indicates that the piece broke while being heated. If the edge of the break is hard and sharp, the piece broke while cooling.

Beyond 600° C., when the kiln is cherry red, the firing rate of bisque ware can be speeded up. Glazed pieces must be fired a little more slowly because too rapid firing of a glaze causes pin holes.

When the kiln has reached maturing temperature, shut off the fire and allow the damper to remain open for ten minutes so that any products of combustion may escape; then close the damper and allow the kiln to cool slowly, and wait at least twenty-four hours before opening it.

Don't be in a hurry to take pieces out of the kiln. A good rule to follow is never to remove ware until you can lift it with your bare hands. Frankly, however, I don't know many potters who obey this rule. Even though we all know better, we violate it constantly. More than once I have put on a pair of asbestos gloves and snatched from the kiln a piece I was eager to examine, only to have it go "ping" and fall apart in my hands. Don't be as foolish as that.

### The flame

In all kilns except the electric, the heat comes from the combustion of fuel. Combustion is the union of carbon with oxygen. Fuels are largely organic matter, combinations of carbon, oxygen, hydrogen, and nitrogen. When the flame gets all the oxygen it needs and burns with maximum efficiency, you have an *oxidizing* fire. In this case, the combustion produces carbon dioxide ($CO_2$), water, and nitrogen which escape up the flue. If there is not enough oxygen for the flame or too much carbon, the combustion will produce carbon monoxide (CO) plus free carbon. Carbon monoxide is hungry for oxygen and will steal it from other substances. When this happens, you have a *reducing* fire.

Except under special circumstances which will be described in the next section, the potter always wants an oxidizing atmosphere in his kiln.

### Reduction

There is an old Chinese legend which tells of a potter who lived many centuries ago. One day he was firing his kiln and was having a lot of trouble. It was one of those days when everything goes wrong. The fire wouldn't burn properly, the chimney wouldn't draw, the place was full of smoke and the air was filled with a horrible odor. The potter was afraid that most of the ware which he had glazed with a lovely green copper glaze would be ruined.

When he opened the kiln he found his fears were justified, for piece after piece came out blistered, blackened, and dull. But in the very center of the kiln, there was one vase which was a beautiful blood red. Such a color had never been seen before on any piece of pottery. The potter's neighbors and co-workers marvelled at it. It was so beautiful that it was sent to the Emperor as a gift. The Emperor in turn admired the color so much that he had the vase broken and the fragments set in rings as though they were precious stones. Then he sent the potter an order for a dozen more red vases.

There the potter's troubles began. He tried again and again but he could not reproduce that red color. He checked his glaze formulas carefully and used exactly the same ingredients that he used that day, but all the pots came out green. The Emperor grew impatient. Messengers arrived from the palace saying—produce or else. Finally our potter was in despair. He decided to fire one last kiln and loaded it with vases covered with glazes as before. But during the height of the fire, his courage failed him. He opened the door of his kiln and jumped in.

His assistants ran up quickly. The kiln fire was smoky and there was a bad smell in the air. They shut down the flames and allowed the kiln to cool, and when they opened it, what did they find? No trace of our poor potter, but—yes, you've guessed it—the kiln was full of beautiful red pots.

And there, according to the legend, was discovered the secret of reduction. The potter's assistants reasoned that if a human body produced such results, maybe a dead pig would work and they tossed a pig into the next fire. Again they got beautiful red pieces. Then they tried substituting such things as wood and straw and still the trick worked.

Reduction, as we said before, results when the fire is overloaded with carbon. When this happens, green oxide of copper loses some of its oxygen and becomes a red oxide. Likewise, red oxide of iron loses some of its oxygen and becomes a black oxide. Red oxide of copper produces the "sang-de-boeuf" or ox blood color, while the black oxide of iron produces the gray green color known as "celadon." (These two colors are illustrated on Color Plate 2.)

Ordinarily the use of reduction is reserved for high fire work with porcelain or stoneware (as a matter of fact, it is difficult to control a high fire without getting some reduction in spite of all precautions). At low temperatures, reduction is something the potter tries to avoid at all costs, for it ruins any glazes which have lead in them. However, there are times when you will want to produce reduction deliberately for special color effects with leadless glazes or for making lustres.

Reduction is obtained in the down draft type of kiln by closing the damper and adjusting the burners so that the flame does not get enough air and burns yellow. This sends free carbon into the kiln. There is loss of heat during this proces, so in high fire work the potter has to alternate periods of oxidation and reduction. With the muffle type of kiln, it is not so easy to produce controlled reduction, for the flames do not touch the ware; and, if the muffle is tight, even though the flame releases free carbon it will not get a chance to act on the pieces. Reduction can be produced, however, by putting some organic material, such as pine splinters, inside the muffle. In the case of some low fire lustre glazes, organic material is actually mixed in with the glaze itself.

One advantage of the electric kiln is that it will never reduce when you don't want it to. There is no flame to release carbon—the heat is always neutral. Yet it is possible to create a reducing atmosphere in such a kiln by introducing organic matter, as mentioned above. A friend of mine has made some remarkable lustres and copper reds in a small electric kiln by using moth balls. He fires the kiln to cone 04, then allows it to cool down to cone 016 or 780° centigrade (a pyrometer is necessary for this operation—cones won't tell you how much a kiln has cooled). At this point he puts in the moth balls, inserting one every five minutes until he has put in about a dozen, then he closes the door tightly and allows the kiln to cool as usual.

Look out if you plan to try this—it is a tricky operation. The first time my friend did it he burned off his eyebrows, for when he opened the kiln door and tossed a moth ball into the hot chamber, a burst of flame leaped out. Now he has made a tiny opening in the kiln door with a plug to fit it. As a moth ball is popped in, the plug closes the opening immediately after it.

Usually the problem is not to create reduction but to avoid it. If your kiln reduces when you want an oxidizing fire, check the flue to see that it is not obstructed, check the dampers to see that they open fully, check the adjustment of the burners to make sure you are getting proper combustion, and seal up any cracks in the muffle. These precautions should remedy the trouble.

SOME POINTS ABOUT THE FIRE:

*1. Pottery is a product of earth and heat. The beauty of a finished piece may be due as much to the firing as to the forming; hence the potter must know his kiln as well as he knows his clay.*

*2. Learn as much as you can about kilns of different types. Whenever you have a chance to examine a kiln, do so.*

*3. Take care in loading your kiln. Bad stacking can ruin beautiful work.*

*4. Paint the kiln floor and shelves with kiln wash before firing glazed ware.*

*5. Don't put anything into your kilns unless it is thoroughly dry. Examine heavy pieces to make sure they contain grog.*

*6. Stay with your kiln while it is firing.*

*7. Fire your kiln slowly and allow ample time for cooling before you open it.*

# chapter Ten

# Glazes

One could write a lengthy book on glazes alone and still not cover the subject fully. There is so much to know! This chapter will give the rudiments of glaze theory—technical information about the chemistry of glazes and glaze calculation. The chapter which follows will tell how to mix and apply glazes and will give a number of recipes for glazes of various types.

It is thrilling to open your kiln and take out a piece covered with a beautiful glaze which you have made yourself out of ingredients combined according to your own formula. Then you really taste the joys of creating. There are failures along the way, it is true, but the successes make up for the disappointments.

Prepared glazes can be bought from dealers, but you will probably prefer to make your own. Not only will you have the pleasure of creation that way but you will find it much less expensive; glazes which you buy usually cost $1.25 per pound or more, while those you make yourself will be closer to 25 cents per pound. A knowledge of chemistry will help, but it is not absolutely necessary. As long as you know something about the three main ingredients of glazes and are willing to do some experimenting, you should have no difficulty.

## What is a glaze?

We know that clay contains glass-forming oxides which liquefy when subjected to extreme heat. We know also that some clays have a greater proportion of these than others and hence vitrify at lower temperatures. Let us suppose that we have two different clays, one a stoneware clay which needs to be fired very high in order to mature, and the other a common red clay which matures at cone 04. Let us suppose further that we made two bowls, one out of each clay, and put them in a kiln together. As the temperature of the kiln rose, the red clay bowl would mature first while the other would still be much underfired; but as the temperature continued to rise, the red bowl would start to soften and would finally melt. When the temperature of the kiln reached cone 10, our stoneware bowl would be fully matured and the other just a pool of liquid. When the kiln cooled the pool which started out as a red bowl would harden into something looking like dark brown glass.

This suggests something. Suppose we were to make a slip out of the red clay and paint it on the stoneware bowl, then fire the bowl again to cone 10. This time, instead of being on the floor of the kiln, the melted red clay will have formed a glossy dark coating on the bowl itself—will be, in fact, a glaze. Not a very good glaze to be sure, for it will be rough in spots, but a glaze nonetheless. Take a look at the pitcher and mug shown on Plate IX. They were glazed in just this way.

Can we make this method work at lower temperatures? We know that adding a flux to clay will lower its maturing point. If enough flux is added, the clay will melt at the temperature where it would ordinarily mature. Lead is the most active low-temperature flux we know of; so let us mix equal parts of white lead and red clay into a slip and paint it on a small test tile. Then let's try two parts of lead and one of clay on another tile. If we now fire both tiles to cone 04 and examine the results, we will probably find that the first tile has a dull rough surface (not enough flux), while the second is bright and glossy. We have made a glaze.

A glaze, then, is a glass—that is, something which has melted into a liquid and on cooling has hardened into a glossy coating on a piece of ceramic ware. It serves to make the ware waterproof and at the same time to give it a more pleasing appearance. It is always produced on the ware itself by the action of heat.

Glass is mainly melted sand or silica, but silica will not melt at the temperatures reached in an ordinary kiln, so fluxes must be added. For pottery glazes, a third ingredient is necessary; silica and flux alone would make a glaze but it would be so liquid during the firing that it would drain completely off the ware. Something must be added to slow up this running action, to give the glaze viscosity. That is alumina.

And there we have the three essential ingredients of all glazes—*flux, alumina,* and *silica*.

Clay itself contains these three ingredients and so does feldspar. Either would make a glaze all by itself if we could get it hot enough; but since our work will be done at much lower temperatures, we will have to compound our glazes and use fluxes which melt within our temperature range.

The alumina and silica in glazes are obtained from feldspar, clay, and flint. The fluxes, however, come from many different sources. According to the kind of flux used, glazes may be classified as lead, alkaline, borosilicate, leadless, or feldspathic. Glazes may also be classified as raw or fritted, depending on whether or not the ingredients are fused into a glass and then pulverized before being used in the glaze. In addition to these, there are

## COLOR PLATE No. 3
Fired samples of glazes with various coloring oxides. (Numbers refer
to recipes in Chapter Eleven)

Top row, left to right:
  Glaze No. 1 with manganese carbonate; glaze No. 11, mirror black; mottled effect
  obtained by putting glaze No. 2 over brown lustre glaze No. 12; glaze No. 1 with
  chromium oxide; glaze No. 3 with red iron oxide.

Middle row, left to right:
  Glaze No. 1 with cobalt oxide over a red clay body; glaze No. 1 with cobalt oxide
  over a white clay body; glaze No. 2 with cobalt oxide over a red clay body; glaze
  No. 4 over a red clay body; glaze No. 2 with antimony oxide.

Bottom row, left to right:
  Glaze No. 1 with pink oxide over a white clay body; glaze No. 1 with copper oxide
  over a red clay body; glaze No. 17, rutile with copper oxide over a red clay body;
  glaze No. 15, borosilicate with copper oxide; glaze No. 14, alkaline with copper oxide.

a number of special types of glazes such as slip glazes, salt glazes, and lustres.

## Lead glazes

The most widely used flux in low temperature glazes is lead which the potter obtains by using either red lead or white lead. Red lead is cheaper but it is harder to handle. Otherwise there is not much difference, except that it is necessary to use a trifle more white lead. We shall explain why when we come to molecular weights. Red lead alone will make a glaze; some of the native potters of North Carolina use it mixed with molasses to hold it on the ware. This seems to contradict what we said about the three essential ingredients of glazes, but actually it does not, for during the fire the lead dissolves some of the clay of the pot it is on and the glaze gets its alumina and silica that way.

Lead glazes are soft, brilliant, slightly yellow in color. This yellow tinge affects other colors which are added to lead glazes, sometimes spoiling their effect. Aside from this difficulty, lead is a quite satisfactory flux, easy to handle, with a temperature range from cone 010 to about cone 5. At the lowest temperature, cone 010, lead could be the only flux used in a glaze; but from cone 07 upward, other fluxes, such as calcium, zinc, magnesium, are used along with it.

A special word of caution. Many of the materials used in preparing glazes are poisonous—lead particularly so. Be careful to wash your hands thoroughly after working with glazes.

## Alkaline glazes

Soda and potash are excellent low-temperature fluxes which produce bright colors, but since they are ordinarily soluble in water, they are difficult to use. Both soda and potash are found in insoluble form in feldspar, but feldspar contains large proportions of alumina and silica, so only small amounts of it may be added to a glaze. The potter who wishes to use more soda and potash must add them to the glaze as borax, sal soda, soda ash, sodium bicarbonate, pearl ash, or potassium bichromate. All of these substances are water soluble. A glaze which contains them must be ground by hand in a small amount of water and applied immediately. Results are never certain. The ware on which the glaze is applied absorbs some of the soluble ingredients; it is best, therefore, to use a hard fired bisque, although even then it is almost impossible to avoid crazing. The Egyptians, who were the first to use this type of glaze, often applied it to bowls which had been carved out of steatite rock (talc).

Alkaline glazes are brilliant in color. When copper is added they produce a beautiful turquoise which cannot be obtained in any other way (copper in a lead glaze is a harsh, grassy green). Potters who seek the colors made by soda and potash without the disadvantages of raw alkaline glazes, find a solution of their problem in fritting.

. . . 181 . . .

*Fritted glazes*

A frit is a glaze which has been fired in a crucible to form a glass and upon cooling has been ground into a powder. This material may be used alone as a glaze or may be combined with other ingredients. The advantages of using a frit are many. Soluble materials become insoluble in fritted form. Furthermore fritting gets rid of things we don't need. Many of the raw materials used in glazes contain organic matter, carbon dioxide, nitrates, and other things which must be burned out during the firing process. When these leave as gases they must bubble through the glaze; this often causes blisters. When a glaze has been fritted, all of this is done before the glaze is applied to the ware; hence a fritted glaze is less apt to crawl.

Formerly, studio potters had to make their own frits—a long and tedious process that required a special frit kiln. The raw ingredients were mixed together dry and placed in a crucible with an opening at the bottom, as shown in Fig. 94. Flames directed against the sides of the crucible melted the mixture which ran in molten form out of the bottom and dropped into a pail of water. The sudden change of temperature shattered the drops of liquid glass into tiny fragments which then had to be pulverized for use in glazes.

Within the last few years commercial frits have begun to be produced

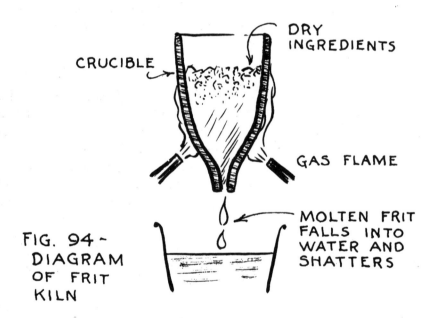

CRUCIBLE

DRY INGREDIENTS

GAS FLAME

MOLTEN FRIT FALLS INTO WATER AND SHATTERS

FIG. 94 - DIAGRAM OF FRIT KILN

on a large scale, and the studio potter is now able to purchase, quite inexpensively, frits of many different compositions. The Ferro-Enamel Company of Cleveland, Ohio, for example, makes a number of different frits, some of them containing soda and no lead, others with high lead content. The convenience of these frits is so great and the results are so uniform that the studio potter would be wise not to attempt making his own frits but to purchase those already prepared.

### Ground glass

Ground glass or glass cullet is really a frit, but since the chemical ingredients of the scrap are usually unknown, its use is a matter of trial and error. With enough clay added to slow down its running, glass can make a highly satisfactory glaze and you may wish to do some experimenting with it. Don't attempt to grind up your own bottles, however—it's not only hard work but extremely dangerous. Buy your glass already ground from one of the ceramic dealers.

### Borosilicate glazes

Borosilicate glazes contain boric oxide ($B_2O_3$) which unites with silica during the fire. Lead may or may not be present also. Boric oxide can be obtained from boric acid or borax which are water soluble and so give all the troubles of alkaline glazes; fortunately for the potter, however, boric oxide is also found in insoluble form in calcium borate ($2CaO \cdot 3BO_3 \cdot 5H_2O$) or colemanite. This is a byproduct in the manufacture of borax. It is a highly satisfactory material which produces beautiful effects in glazes. Combined with copper, it makes a rich greenish blue, not quite turquoise but close to it.

### Leadless glazes

Leadless glazes are used at cone 4 and above. At that temperature we can get plenty of fluxing action from calcium and zinc and no longer need to use lead. As a matter of fact, at cone 7 lead volatilizes and leaves a glaze anyway. Bristol glazes which fire from cone 4 to cone 8 use zinc as a flux, while stoneware and porcelain glazes, firing from cone 8 to cone 12, make use of feldspar, calcium, and magnesium.

### Salt glaze

Salt glazing is done by throwing salt into the chamber of the kiln when the temperature has reached its highest point. The salt volatilizes and forms a mist which settles on all surfaces of the ware. The soda in the salt combines with the clay to form an extremely hard glaze. Salt glazing is particularly suited to stoneware for it works best at temperatures from cone 4 to cone 9. It is good for carved or decorated surfaces. On flat surfaces salt glazing produces an "orange peel" texture (see the illustrations on Plate VIII).

Salt glazing requires a special kiln reserved for that purpose, because the salt glazes the inside of the kiln as well as the ware. Most of the heavy terra-cotta pipe used to carry water under our streets is salt glazed. A sculptor friend of mine who lives not far from a terra-cotta plant has occasionally been able to prevail upon the foreman to put a piece or two of clay sculpture into the big salt glazing kiln in odd corners where there was room to spare.

. . . 183 . . .

As a result some of his sculpture has come out fired, with a mottled salt glaze beautiful to behold.

## Slip glaze

Slip glazes are made by using a low firing clay as a glaze on a higher firing clay, as described earlier in this chapter. Albany slip is excellent for this purpose. It makes such a good glaze at high temperatures that it is widely used on stoneware crocks and porcelain insulators.

## Lustre

If you have seen some of the large decorated plates made in Spain during the fifteenth century, you know the beautiful iridescence which lights their surfaces. This lustre is obtained by depositing a thin film of metal on top of the glaze so that it refracts light in the same way as a layer of oil on top of water.

Lustres require reduction. Sometimes this is secured by manipulating the fire, sometimes by the introduction of organic matter into the glaze itself.

## GLAZE CALCULATION

You don't need to read this section if you don't want to. Many potters develop their glazes by experimenting, varying the ingredients until they arrive at satisfactory results through a method of trial and error. So skip to the next chapter if you wish. But if you are good at mathematics and have a scientific desire to know the why as well as the how, this is the way molecular glaze formulas are developed.

## The molecular glaze formula

The materials which go into glazes are all inorganic substances which combine in some manner with oxygen. It is as oxides, therefore, that they are of value to the potter although they may or may not be oxides before firing. White lead, for example, is a carbonate, but after it is fired it becomes lead oxide ($PbO$). Some materials used in glazes provide several oxides. Feldspar, for example, adds oxides of potassium ($K_2O$), sodium ($Na_2O$), aluminum ($Al_2O_3$), and silicon ($SiO_2$).

In order to see at a glance what the active ingredients of a glaze are and in what proportion they are present, the molecular glaze formula was devised. This lists molecules of all the glaze oxides in three different columns. In the first column are placed those elements which combine with oxygen in a one-to-one ratio (example $PbO$) and those which combine with oxygen in a two-to-one ratio ($Na_2O$). This column is called the RO or $R_2O$ column. In the second column are placed those elements which combine with oxygen in a two-to-three ratio ($Al_2O_3$), and in the last column, those which combine with oxygen in a one-to-two ratio ($SiO_2$). These last two columns are called the $R_2O_3$ and $RO_2$ columns, respectively. Here is a tabulation which shows most of the oxides ordinarily used in glazes arranged in these three columns.

| RO or R₂O | | R₂O₃ | | RO₂ | |
|---|---|---|---|---|---|
| Lead Oxide | PbO | Alumina | $Al_2O_3$ | Silica | $SiO_2$ |
| Zinc Oxide | ZnO | Boric Oxide | $B_2O_3$ | Rutile (Titanium Oxide) | $TiO_2$ |
| Potash | $K_2O$ | | | Tin Oxide | $SnO_2$ |
| Soda | $Na_2O$ | | | Zirconium Oxide | $ZrO_2$ |
| Lime | CaO | | | | |
| Barium Oxide | BaO | | | | |
| Magnesia | MgO | | | | |
| Strontia | SrO | | | | |

All of the substances in the first column are fluxes. The other two essential ingredients of glazes, alumina and silica, come in columns 2 and 3, respectively. Boric oxide which acts as a flux is an exception, for it comes in column 2. In column 3, in addition to silica, we find titanium, tin, and zirconium. These do not affect a glaze formula, but they change the appearance of a glaze considerably. Titanium oxide forms crystals which produce interesting effects, and both tin and zirconium make glazes white and opaque.

Remember that the quantities in molecular formulas show relationships of molecules. By changing the proportions of flux to alumina and silica and by using different substances as fluxes, we are able to suit glazes to different purposes, making some fire at low temperatures, others at high, making some glossy, others mat, and so on. Slight changes in the ratio of silica will change the expansion of a glaze, making it fit on different bodies.

Quantities are always chosen so that the first column adds up to one (this makes comparison of different formulas possible). The alumina is always less than one, ranging from .05 for low-temperature glazes to .6 for high fire glazes, and the silica is usually three times the alumina plus one. This is not a hard and fast rule, however—the proportions are frequently changed to secure a better fit on the body used.

You will have to do some experimenting to work out glaze formulas suited to your clay and your kiln. Here are some general directions for glazes at different temperatures.

At the lowest temperatures (from cone 015 to cone 012), lead can be used all alone as a flux. The formula for a cone 015 lead glaze might read:

$$PbO \quad 1.0\} \; Al_2O_3 \quad .05 \; \{SiO_2 \quad 1.15$$

Here PbO is the only ingredient in column 1, the alumina content is at its lowest limit, .05, and the silica is three times .05 plus 1, or 1.15.

For temperatures from cone 010 to cone 07, small quantities of whiting and feldspar can be added as fluxes and the alumina and silica can be increased slightly. In this temperature range the formula for a lead glaze would come within these limits:

$$\left. \begin{array}{l} PbO \; - .7 \text{ to } 1.0 \\ CaO \; - .0 \text{ to } \;\; .3 \\ K_2O \; - .0 \text{ to } \;\; .2 \\ Na_2O \; - .0 \text{ to } \;\; .2 \end{array} \right\} Al_2O_3 - .05 \text{ to } .2 \left\{ SiO_2 - 1.0 \text{ to } 1.6 \right.$$

NOTE. The $K_2O$ or $Na_2O$ in this formula would be obtained from feldspar.

Most commercial spars contain both potassium and sodium; hence, in formulas these are often computed as a single ingredient, written KNaO.

Here are two cone 07 lead glazes:

$$\left.\begin{array}{ll} PbO & - .7 \\ CaO & - .3 \end{array}\right\} Al_2O_3 - .08 \left\{ SiO_2 - 1.25 \right.$$

$$\left.\begin{array}{ll} PbO & - .6 \\ CaO & - .25 \\ KNaO & - .15 \end{array}\right\} Al_2O_3 - .1 \left\{ SiO_2 - 1.5 \right.$$

Observe that as quantities in column 1 change, they still add up to one.

For the same temperature range, cone 010 to cone 07, we might prepare an alkaline glaze, either raw or fritted, in which potassium and sodium are used as fluxes. In this case they will be obtained not from feldspar but from borax, soda ash, or other soluble substances. The formula of such an alkaline glaze would come within these limits:

$$\left.\begin{array}{ll} KNaO & - .5 \text{ to } .7 \\ CaO & - .3 \text{ to } .5 \end{array}\right) \left.\begin{array}{ll} Al_2O_3 & - .05 \text{ to } .15 \\ B_2O_3 & - .0 \text{ to } 1.0 \end{array}\right\} SiO_2 - 1.5 \text{ to } 2.5$$

Here is a formula for an alkaline glaze for cone 08:

$$\left.\begin{array}{ll} K_2O & - .2 \\ Na_2O & - .6 \\ CaO & - .2 \end{array}\right) \left.\begin{array}{ll} Al_2O_3 & - .15 \\ B_2O_3 & - .5 \end{array}\right\} SiO_2 - 1.6$$

For temperatures from cone 04 to cone 1 or 2, zinc and magnesium may be added to the list of fluxes. Here are the formula limits for this range:

$$\left.\begin{array}{ll} PbO & - .1 \text{ to } .7 \\ CaO & - .1 \text{ to } .4 \\ KNaO & - .1 \text{ to } .3 \\ ZnO & - .0 \text{ to } .1 \\ MgO & - .0 \text{ to } .1 \end{array}\right) \left.\begin{array}{ll} Al_2O_3 & - .15 \text{ to } .35 \\ B_2O_3 & - .0 \text{ to } .3 \end{array}\right\} SiO_2 - 1.5 \text{ to } 2.5$$

Here is a cone 04 lead glaze:

$$\left.\begin{array}{ll} PbO & - .55 \\ CaO & - .35 \\ KNaO & - .1 \end{array}\right\} Al_2O_3 - .2 \left\{ SiO_2 - 1.6 \right.$$

All of the glazes listed so far have been bright or glossy. A mat surface can be achieved by introducing barium among the fluxes, along with some zinc, or by increasing the alumina. The cone 04 lead glaze above can be made mat by reducing the lead and the calcium, replacing the quantities taken out with barium and zinc. The formula would now read:

$$\left.\begin{array}{ll} PbO & - .45 \\ CaO & - .15 \\ KNaO & - .1 \\ BaO & - .2 \\ ZnO & - .1 \end{array}\right\} Al_2O_3 - .2 \left\{ SiO_2 - 1.6 \right.$$

To alter the same glaze to an alumina mat, leave the first column unchanged but increase the second and slightly reduce the third. The formula would now read:

$$\left.\begin{array}{l} \text{PbO} \quad - .55 \\ \text{CaO} \quad - .35 \\ \text{KNaO} - .1 \end{array}\right\} Al_2O_3 - .3 \left\{ SiO_2 - 1.4 \right.$$

White ware and china glazes for temperatures from cone 1 to cone 5 would come within the following limits:

$$\left.\begin{array}{l} \text{PbO} \quad - .2 \text{ to } .35 \\ \text{CaO} \quad - .35 \text{ to } .50 \\ \text{KNaO} - .2 \text{ to } .35 \\ \text{ZnO} \quad - .0 \text{ to } .10 \end{array}\right\} \begin{array}{l} Al_2O_3 \ - .2 \text{ to } .35 \\ B_2O_3 \ \ - .3 \text{ to } .7 \end{array} \left\{ SiO_2 - 2.0 \text{ to } 3.5 \right.$$

In these glazes, the KNaO is obtained from borax and soda ash, hence the glazes are usually fritted.

Bristol (leadless) glazes for cone 4 to cone 8 have these limits:

$$\left.\begin{array}{l} \text{KNaO} - .25 \text{ to } .5 \\ \text{CaO} \quad - .10 \text{ to } .3 \\ \text{ZnO} \quad - .15 \text{ to } .4 \\ \text{MgO} \quad - .0 \text{ to } .2 \end{array}\right\} Al_2O_3 - .35 \text{ to } .6 \left\{ SiO_2 - 2.5 \text{ to } 4.0 \right.$$

In Bristol glazes the KNaO is obtained from feldspar.

Feldspathic glazes for stoneware and porcelain for temperatures from cone 8 to cone 15 fall within the following limits:

$$\left.\begin{array}{l} \text{KNaO} - .2 \text{ to } .4 \\ \text{CaO} \quad - .4 \text{ to } .7 \\ \text{MgO} \quad - .0 \text{ to } .3 \\ \text{ZnO} \quad - .0 \text{ to } .2 \end{array}\right\} Al_2O_3 - .4 \text{ to } .6 \left\{ SiO_2 - 3.0 \text{ to } 5.0 \right.$$

$K_2O$ and $Na_2O$ in the above glazes are obtained from feldspar.

## TABLE OF CERAMIC RAW MATERIALS

| Substance | Formula | Molecular Weight | Equivalent Weight | Fired Formula | Fired Weight |
|---|---|---|---|---|---|
| Barium Carbonate | $BaCO_3$ | 197 | 197 | $BaO$ | 153 |
| Bone Ash | $Ca_3(PO_4)_2$ | 310 | 103 | $CaO$ | 56 |
| Borax | $Na_2O \cdot 2B_2O_3 \cdot 10H_2O$ | 382 | 382 | $Na_2O \cdot 2B_2O_3$ | 202 |
| Boric Acid | $B_2O_3 \cdot 3H_2O$ | 124 | 124 | $B_2O_3$ | 70 |
| Calcium Borate (Colemanite) | $2CaO \cdot 3B_2O_3 \cdot 5H_2O$ | 412 | 206 | $CaO \cdot 1.5B_2O_3$ | 161 |
| China Clay | $Al_2O_3 \cdot 2SiO_2 \cdot 2H_2O$ | 258 | 258 | $Al_2O_3 \cdot 2SiO_2$ | 222 |
| Cryolite | $Na_3AlF_6$ | 210 | 420 | $3Na_2O \cdot Al_2O_3$ | 288 |
| Dolomite | $CaCO_3 \cdot MgCO_3$ | 184 | 184 | $CaO \cdot MgO$ | 96 |
| Feldspars | | | | | |
|   Albite | $Na_2O \cdot Al_2O_3 \cdot 6SiO_2$ | 524 | 524 | Unchanged | 524 |
|   Anorthite | $CaO \cdot Al_2O_3 \cdot 2SiO_2$ | 278 | 278 | Unchanged | 278 |
|   Buckingham Spar | $K_2O \cdot 1.13Al_2O_3 \cdot 6.45SiO_2$ | 596 | 596 | Unchanged | 596 |

| Substance | Formula | Molecular Weight | Equivalent Weight | Fired Formula | Fired Weight |
|---|---|---|---|---|---|
| Cornwall Stone | CaO .304 / Na$_2$O .340 / K$_2$O .356 } Al$_2$O$_3$ 1.075 {SiO$_2$ 8.10 | 667 | 667 | Unchanged | 667 |
| Godfrey Spar | K$_2$O .36 / Na$_2$O .64 } Al$_2$O$_3$ 1.18 {SiO$_2$ 8.80 | 722 | 722 | Unchanged | 722 |
| Nepheline Syenite | K$_2$O .25 / Na$_2$O .75 } Al$_2$O$_3$ 1.11 {SiO$_2$ 4.65 | 462 | 462 | Unchanged | 462 |
| Orthoclase | K$_2$O·Al$_2$O$_3$·6SiO$_2$ | 556 | 556 | Unchanged | 556 |
| Oxford Spar | CaO .028 / Na$_2$O .256 / K$_2$O .716 } Al$_2$O$_3$ 1.105 {SiO$_2$ 6.38 | 581 | 581 | Unchanged | 581 |
| Plastic Vitrox | CaO .053 / Na$_2$O .334 / K$_2$O .613 } Al$_2$O$_3$ 1.33 {SiO$_2$ 13.9 | 1051 | 1051 | Unchanged | 1051 |
| Flint | SiO$_2$ | 60 | 60 | Unchanged | 60 |
| Fluorspar | CaF$_2$ | 78 | 78 | CaO | 56 |
| Gypsum | CaSO$_4$·2H$_2$O | 188 | 188 | CaO | 56 |
| Lead, Red | Pb$_3$O$_4$ | 684 | 228 | PbO | 223 |
| Lead, White | 2PbCO$_3$·Pb(OH)$_2$ | 775 | 258 | PbO | 223 |
| Lead, Yellow (Litharge) | PbO | 223 | 223 | Unchanged | 223 |
| Magnesium Carbonate (Magnesite) | MgCO$_3$ | 84 | 84 | MgO | 40 |
| Manganese Carbonate | MnCO$_3$ | 115 | 115 | MnO | 71 |
| Manganese Dioxide | MnO$_2$ | 87 | 87 | MnO | 71 |
| Niter | KNO$_3$ | 101 | 202 | K$_2$O | 94 |
| Pearl Ash | K$_2$CO$_3$ | 138 | 138 | K$_2$O | 94 |
| Potassium Bichromate | K$_2$Cr$_2$O$_7$ | 294 | 294 | K$_2$O·Cr$_2$O$_3$ | 294 |
| Sal Soda | Na$_2$CO$_3$·10H$_2$O | 286 | 286 | Na$_2$O | 62 |
| Salt | NaCl | 58 | 116 | Na$_2$O | 62 |
| Silica | SiO$_2$ | 60 | 60 | Unchanged | 60 |
| Soda Ash | Na$_2$CO$_3$ | 106 | 106 | Na$_2$O | 62 |
| Sodium Antimonate | Na$_2$O·Sb$_2$O$_5$ | 386 | 386 | Na$_2$O·Sb$_2$O$_3$ | 354 |
| Sodium Bicarbonate | NaHCO$_3$ | 84 | 168 | Na$_2$O | 62 |
| Sodium Nitrate | NaNO$_3$ | 85 | 170 | Na$_2$O | 62 |
| Talc (Steatite) | 3MgO·4SiO$_2$·H$_2$O | 378 | 378 | 3MgO·4SiO$_2$ | 360 |
| Tin Oxide | SnO$_2$ | 151 | 151 | Unchanged | 151 |
| Titanium Oxide (Rutile) | TiO$_2$ | 80 | 80 | Unchanged | 80 |
| Whiting | CaCO$_3$ | 100 | 100 | CaO | 56 |
| Zinc Oxide | ZnO | 81 | 81 | Unchanged | 81 |
| Zircon (Zircopax) | ZrO$_2$·SiO$_2$ | 183 | 183 | Unchanged | 183 |
| Zirconium Oxide | ZrO$_2$ | 123 | 123 | Unchanged | 123 |

## Formula into recipe

Given a glaze formula, how do we go about weighing out the ingredients for the glaze? Before we can do this, we must turn the formula into a recipe, that is, we must find out what materials and how much of each will give us the molecular relationships called for in the formula. We shall need a table of molecular weights like the one given.

The molecular weight of a substance is the total of the weights of all of the atoms which go to make up one molecule of that substance. The hydrogen atom is the lightest one known, so its atomic weight is called one. An atom of oxygen, which is sixteen times as heavy as a hydrogen atom, has, therefore, an atomic weight of sixteen; water ($H_2O$), one molecule of which contains two hydrogen atoms and one oxygen atom, has a molecular weight of two plus sixteen, or eighteen.

If you study the table you will note that one column is labeled molecular weight and another, equivalent weight. In most cases the quantities listed in these two columns are identical but in some cases they differ. We can explain why this is if we examine white lead. The formula of white lead is $2PbCO_3 \cdot Pb(OH)_2$ but after it is fired it becomes PbO. One molecule of white lead which contains three atoms of Pb would produce three molecules of lead oxide, each of which contains only one atom of Pb. Therefore, we need only one-third as much white lead to produce the equivalent of one molecule of lead oxide and so, while the molecular weight of white lead is listed as 775, its equivalent weight is only one-third as much or 258.

Let's work out the recipe for the cone 04 glaze whose formula was given above as:

$$\left. \begin{array}{l} PbO \;\; - .55 \\ CaO \;\; - .35 \\ KNaO - .1 \end{array} \right\} Al_2O_3 - .2 \left\{ SiO_2 - 1.6 \right.$$

We must select materials which will provide all of these oxides in the proper molecular relationships. Prepare a diagram like this:

| This is the recipe | | | | This is the molecular formula |
|---|---|---|---|---|
| Material | Amount of oxide in formula | × Equiv- alent weight | = Quantity of material in recipe | PbO .55   CaO .35   $K_2O$ .1   $Al_2O_3$ .2   $SiO_2$ 1.6 |
| | | | | In these columns keep track of the oxides going into the recipe. |

When we list an ingredient in the column labeled material, we will multiply the number of molecules required by its equivalent molecular weight. The product of this multiplication will be the quantity of the material needed in the glaze recipe. At the same time we will enter the amount of each oxide supplied by the material in its proper column at the right. In that way we shall keep track of what is going into the glaze.

The first ingredient, lead, we shall obtain from white lead. Our formula calls for .55 PbO, so at the left of the diagram enter the following:

White lead .55 × 258 = 141.9

Then in the PbO column, enter .55. This indicates that 141.9 parts of white lead will be needed to supply all the PbO called for by the formula.

The next ingredient, CaO, we shall get from whiting, whose molecular weight and equivalent weight are the same, namely 100, so the second line will be:

Whiting $.35 \times 100 = 35$

We have now satisfied the entire glaze requirement for both PbO and CaO. Our diagram looks like this:

| Material | Amount of oxide in formula | $\times$ | Equiv- alent weight | $=$ | Quantity of material in recipe | PbO .55 CaO .35 $K_2O$ .1 $Al_2O_3$ .2 $SiO_2$ 1.6 |
|---|---|---|---|---|---|---|
| White lead | .55 | $\times$ | 258 | $=$ | 141.9 | $\underline{.55}$ ← This shows that we have supplied all of<br>$.00$   the PbO called for by the formula. |
| Whiting | .35 | $\times$ | 100 | $=$ | 35 | $\underline{.35}$<br>$.00$ |

The third ingredient, $K_2O$, we shall get from feldspar. If we select Buckingham feldspar, we note that its formula is: $K_2O \cdot 1.13\ Al_2O_3 \cdot 6.45\ SiO_2$. Its molecular weight is 596; so the next line will be:

Buckingham feldspar $.1 \times 596 = 59.6$

But feldspar contains other things besides potash. When we add .1 of $K_2O$, we also add .1 x 1.13, or .113 of $Al_2O_3$; and .1 x 6.45, or .645 of $SiO_2$. These must be added in the proper columns; the diagram now looks like this:

| Material | Amount of oxide in formula | $\times$ | Equiv- alent weight | $=$ | Quantity of material in recipe | PbO .55 | CaO .35 | $K_2O$ .1 | $Al_2O_3$ .2 | $SiO_2$ 1.6 |
|---|---|---|---|---|---|---|---|---|---|---|
| White lead | .55 | $\times$ | 258 | $=$ | 141.9 | $\underline{.55}$<br>$.00$ | | | | |
| Whiting | .35 | $\times$ | 100 | $=$ | 35 | | $\underline{.35}$<br>$.00$ | | | |
| Buckingham feldspar | .1 | $\times$ | 596 | $=$ | 59.6 | | | $\underline{.1}$<br>$.0$ | $\underline{.113}$<br>$.087$ | $\underline{.645}$<br>$.955$ |

This shows that we have satisfied the entire requirements for PbO, CaO, and $K_2O$ and part of the requirements for $Al_2O_3$ and $SiO_2$. We still need .087 of alumina which we shall get from china clay whose weight is 258, so the next line will be:

China clay $.087 \times 258 = 22.4$

But clay contains two parts of $SiO_2$ for every one of $Al_2O_3$; thus when we add .087 of china clay we add .087 x 2 or .174 of $SiO_2$. This reduces the $SiO_2$ requirement still further, leaving only .781 to be added. We shall obtain this from flint whose molecular weight is 60: the last line is:

$$\text{Flint } .781 \times 60 = 46.9$$

The diagram now looks like this:

| Material | Amount of oxide in formula × | Equivalent weight = | Quantity of material in recipe | PbO .55 | CaO .35 | K₂O .1 | Al₂O₃ .2 | SiO₂ 1.6 |
|---|---|---|---|---|---|---|---|---|
| White lead | .55 × | 258 = | 141.9 | .55 / .00 | | | | |
| Whiting | .35 × | 100 = | 35 | | .35 / .00 | | | |
| Buckingham feldspar | .1 × | 596 = | 59.6 | | | .1 / .0 | .113 | .645 |
| China clay | .087 × | 258 = | 22.4 | | | | .087 | .955 |
| Flint | .781 × | 60 = | 46.9 | | | | .087 / .000 | .174 / .781 / .781 / .000 |

We have satisfied all of the requirements of the molecular formula, our recipe is complete. Remember that the numbers refer to parts. The quantities could be weighed out as ounces, pounds, or even tons; but for our purposes, the gram is the best unit of weight. If you weigh these quantities in grams, the formula will produce a 300-gram batch, or about a pint of glaze.

Sometimes the potter has a choice in selecting the materials with which to work out a glaze formula. Hence the same formula might produce slightly different recipes. For example in the formula above, if we wish to use red lead instead of white, we may do so and achieve exactly the same results in the glaze. Our first line in this case will read:

$$\text{Red lead } .55 \times 228 = 125.4$$

Thus we would need to use 125.4 parts of red lead in the recipe to do the work of 141.9 parts of white lead.

### COLOR IN GLAZES

The potter's prime source of color is in the clay itself; his secondary source is in various metals which he uses as oxides, or carbonates, or soluble salts—sulphates and nitrates. The form is not important—what counts is the metal. We might say that a third source of color for the potter lies in all of the prepared pigments sold by dealers, the underglaze colors, the overglaze colors, and the various ceramic stains, but these also are merely oxides and carbonates of metals.

The color of the clay will affect the color of the finished glazed piece unless the glaze is so opaque that the body is completely hidden. Think well before you make a glaze like that. Even in majolica work, the beauty of the ware is enhanced if the warm tone of the clay shows through the glaze. It is a mistake not to use the decorative possibilities of the material out of which the piece is made. Look at some of the pottery made in other generations, and see how often, in those pieces which have stood the test of time, the color of the clay adds its part.

The colors which metals produce in glazes are affected not only by the clay underneath, but by the amount of metal introduced, the way the glaze is applied, the ingredients with which the metal is associated in the glaze, the temperature to which it is fired, the rate of firing, and the atmosphere of the kiln. In general, colors are more brilliant in alkaline glazes and at lower temperatures. Some metals change color completely when high temperatures are reached, and others change when the kiln is reduced. Here is a list of the principal metals used by potters with a description of the colors they produce. Most of these are illustrated on Color Plate 3.

### Copper

Copper is usually used as black copper oxide ($CuO$) or copper carbonate ($CuCO_3$). The former is stronger in coloring power. In a lead glaze, from I per cent to 6 per cent of copper will produce various shades of apple or grass green. In an alkaline glaze with high soda content and low alumina, with no lead or zinc present, copper produces a beautiful turquoise at cone 07. In a reducing fire, black oxide of copper reduces to a lower oxide form which is red. This gives the rich scarlet of sang-de-boeuf. Copper has a fluxing action; if more than 6 per cent is used in a glaze, it will increase the flow; hence the amount of lead should be reduced. An over-charge of copper in a glaze makes the surface dull and metallic, somewhat like gun metal.

### Cobalt

Cobalt is the strongest of all of the ceramic colorants. It is used by the potter as black cobalt oxide ($Co_3O_4$) or as cobalt carbonate ($CoCO_3$). The former is the stronger. A little bit of cobalt goes a long way, usually ½ per cent is enough to produce its characteristic blue color in a glaze. Never use more than 3 per cent. In the presence of zinc, the blue of cobalt becomes more intense. With rutile at high temperatures it becomes green.

### Iron

Iron is a good ceramic colorant, usually present in the clay anyway. It is what gives native clays their warm red tones, or, when calcium is also present, their shades of buff and yellow. It is almost always used as red iron oxide ($Fe_2O_3$)—the black oxide ($FeO$) is rarely used. In glazes, iron produces colors ranging from amber through tan to deep red brown, depending on the quantity. Between 5 per cent and 10 per cent should be used (below 5 per cent the color is pale and uninteresting). In a high lead glaze, 8 per cent iron produces a rich dark red. An overload of iron will sometimes produce a "gold stone" or "aventurine" glaze, a beautiful purple-red with gold flecks, but this effect is hard to get. In a reduction fire, iron produces the lovely pale green of celadon.

### Manganese

Manganese is used as a dioxide ($MnO_2$) or as a carbonate ($MnCO_3$). The latter is the better form to use. In quantities from 5 per cent to 10 per cent, it produces shades of purplish brown. In an alkaline glaze, it verges toward violet and will give a beautiful aubergine or eggplant color. With copper or cobalt, manganese makes black metallic surfaces, with iron it produces lustre. Its color fades above cone 4. Glazes containing manganese are apt to blister.

### Chromium

Chromium is a queer character with a strange behavior. At very low temperatures it is red, at high temperatures, green. It turns brown in the presence of zinc and makes tin pink. The potter usually uses 2 per cent to 5 per cent of green oxide of chromium ($Cr_2O_3$). Other forms occasionally used are potassium bichromate ($K_2Cr_2O_7$), lead chromate ($PbCrO_4$), and iron chromate ($FeCrO_4$). The latter gives a good gray in engobes (1 per cent to 3 per cent). Chromium is not much used in low temperature glazes but it is good up to porcelain temperature. At very low temperatures (cone 012 to cone 010) in a high lead glaze with low alumina and low silica, chromium produces a strong vermilion red. This same glaze heated higher turns brown at cone 06 and green at cone 02. Sometimes if you can stop the fire just as it is changing, the effect is pleasing. Chromium is the base of many underglaze colors and stains. Calcined with tin, it produces the red colors, pink oxide, maroon base, etc.; and with zinc, it makes many of the brown stains. Chromium won't stand reduction. Because it affects so many other substances, it can cause trouble in the kiln. Care must be taken not to place a chrome glaze near any other susceptible to its action.

### Nickel

Nickel is used by the potter as green nickel oxide (NiO), black oxide of nickel ($Ni_2O_3$), or nickel carbonate ($NiCO_3$). When used in quantities from 2 per cent to 5 per cent, it produces shades of green, brown, and purple. Nickel is not used in low temperature glazes.

### Uranium

It may seem useless to talk about uranium now, since potters will probably no longer be able to obtain it; but if only as a matter of record, it should be included among our glaze colorants. Uranium produces colors ranging from brilliant orange red to lemon yellow. At low temperatures in a high lead glaze, it is red; in an alkaline glaze, yellow. The forms usually used are black oxide of uranium (UO$_2$) and sodium uranate (Na$_2$UO$_4$). Between 5 per cent and 8 per cent is the right amount, an over-charge produces black. Uranium is good at all temperatures, but it cannot stand reduction.

### Antimony

From 3 per cent to 6 per cent of antimony oxide (Sb$_2$O$_3$) will give a yellow color, but a glaze containing raw antimony is apt to blister; most potters prefer to obtain their yellows from yellow base, which is made by calcining a mixture of red lead, antimony, and tin (see page 203 for the formula).

### Zinc

Zinc is not a colorant, but since it affects other colors, we may consider it here. As mentioned above, it heightens the blue of cobalt and makes chromium turn brown. It also affects iron, turning it a mustard color. This is something to consider whenever you use a glaze containing zinc on a red clay, for the action of the zinc on the iron of the clay will tone down its color and produce a result which may or may not be pleasing. High zinc content in a glaze will make it semi-opaque. The potter uses zinc as zinc oxide (ZnO).

### Titanium

Titanium oxide or rutile (TiO$_2$) gives a light buff color to glazes, but its main interest to the potter comes from the crystalline effects it produces. No two pieces glazed with a rutile glaze will come out of the kiln the same. Sometimes the effects are good, especially when the rutile is used with copper or cobalt. Titanium is affected by chromium in the same way as tin, becoming pink when fired near it.

### Tin

Tin is the strongest opacifier known to the potter. Instead of going into solution in a glaze, it stays in suspension, producing whiteness. The potter uses it as tin oxide (SnO$_2$), adding 10 per cent to a glaze to make it opaque. With no other colorants present, tin produces a white glaze ideal as a background for majolica decoration. With colorants added, tin makes pastel shades which can be used even over dark clay bodies.

### Zirconium

Zirconium is used as a substitute for tin. It is an opacifier but only half as strong as tin, so 20 per cent must be used to make a glaze opaque. There are several forms of zirconium. The best for the potter is zircon or zircopax (ZrSiO$_4$).

## Soluble salts

Soluble salts are the sulphates and the nitrates of various metals. They are almost never used as glaze colorants, but they are good for certain decorative treatments when used as washes on top of a glaze, and they are important in lustre work.

## Prepared ceramic colors

An important source of color for the potter is the pigments sold by ceramic supply houses as underglaze color, overglaze color, and ceramic stains. Stains are used to color glazes and sometimes clay bodies. Overglaze colors are used only for decoration on top of a glaze which has been previously fired, while underglaze colors can be used any way at all—over, under, or in a glaze. The reason for this difference is that the overglaze colors won't stand high temperatures; at cone 07 they begin to fade, and above that point they soon disappear; therefore, when they are used, the piece and the glaze must be fired first. The overglaze colors are then applied and hardened in a third firing to cone 015 or 012.

Underglaze colors, as the name implies, are intended for decoration on bisque or raw ware which is then covered with transparent glaze. Obviously these colors must be able to stand any temperature the glaze will, and it is this flexibility in their temperature range which makes them useful for majolica decoration (designs painted on top of an unfired glaze) as well as for glaze colorants. It will not be possible to list here all of the underglaze colors and stains which can be used in glazes. Consult the dealers' catalogues and do some experimenting. Some brilliant colors are available, as well as some reds which are hard to obtain any other way.

# chapter Eleven

# *Mixing Glazes*

*M*ixing a glaze is simple. You will need a scale for weighing out quantities in grams, and a 100-mesh sieve. A mortar and pestle will be handy to have, although not absolutely essential, and for experimental work you should have a glass slab about 12″ x 16″ and a spatula for mixing small amounts of glazes for tests. And that, aside from bowls and glass jars, is all you really need. A ball mill with jars and pebbles is convenient but not really necessary—don't buy one unless you plan to mix large quantities of glazes.

The ingredients of a glaze are weighed out dry and then mixed with water—about one-half cupful for a 300-gram batch.

### Using the ball mill

If you have a ball mill, put the ingredients and the water in the jar with a double handful of pebbles and let them grind for an hour—no longer. At the end of this time, dump the glaze and the pebbles into a bowl, then rinse the jar and pour the rinse water into another bowl. Remove the pebbles from the first bowl and wash them off in the second bowl, then pour the contents of both bowls into one and let the glaze settle. At the end of a few hours, the excess water may be poured off the top and the glaze put into a glass jar and labeled.

NOTE. This method does not work with alkaline glazes or any glazes containing soluble ingredients. With these you must be careful to add just enough water to make a thick creamy paste—no excess water can ever be poured off. For this reason it is best not to mix such glazes in a ball mill.

### Without a ball mill

If you haven't a ball mill, you may grind the ingredients by hand, using a mortar and pestle. But even that much grinding is not absolutely essential. In most cases, you will find it satisfactory merely to mix the ingredients and the water thoroughly, shaking them in a covered jar, and then screen-

# COLOR PLATE No. 4
Examples of decorative techniques.

*Above:* Underglaze decoration on white engobe.

*Above:* Majolica.

*Above:* Stoneware with slip trailed decoration, salt glazed.

*Above:* Majolica.

*Right:* Sgraffito decoration in copper engobe over buff body.

ing them through a 100-mesh sieve. It may be necessary to rub the material through the screen. This sieving action not only removes coarse particles but also makes the mixing more thorough. Glazes mixed this way will not be as even in color as those ground in a ball mill; pigments such as cobalt will produce a speckled effect, but this is often more pleasing than the perfectly uniform color of milled glazes.

### Settling

Fritted glazes and glazes containing especially heavy ingredients such as red lead will settle in the bottom of a container and cake into hard masses almost impossible to stir up. To prevent this, add a teaspoonful of epsom salts to the water when you mix the glaze.

### Gums

A glaze needs a binder to hold it in place on the ware until it is fired. Without this it would dust off the piece as soon as it dried. The binder must be some kind of gum which will burn out and disappear without affecting the glaze in any way. Potters have tried many substances for this purpose, among them honey, molasses, fish oil, various vegetable oils, sodium alginate, gum arabic and gum tragacanth. In my opinion, gum tragacanth is way ahead of all the rest. It is simple to prepare, easy to use, and always dependable. Buy it in powdered form. To prepare it for use, stir a teaspoonful of the powder in an ounce of alcohol, then add a half-pint of water. This will make a medium thick gum which you can add to glazes at the rate of one tablespoon to a pint of glaze.

Gum tragacanth won't keep over a long period unless a preservative such as oil of cloves is added. My preference is to mix a little at a time and use it up before it spoils.

### Experimenting with glazes

If you want to discover new glaze effects or work out a formula which is entirely your own, it will be necessary to try a lot of experiments, mixing up many different batches and then firing tests. Making large quantities is wasteful of time and material. So for experimental work, weigh out small batches and mix the ingredients on a glass slab with a spatula, adding just enough water so that the glaze can be painted on a test tile. A drop or two of gum tragacanth will help also.

### A line blend

Sometimes you will want to try mixing two different glazes to see the results when various proportions are used. To do this, make a line blend. This is a series of tests of mixtures in which proportions are systematically varied until all possible combinations are tried out. Thus if we have two glazes, A and B, the first test will be all A and no B, the second 4/5 A and

1/5 B, the third 3/5 A and 2/5 B, and so on. The complete line blend, with the proportions expressed decimally, would then look like this:

| 1 | 2 | 3 | 4 | 5 | 6 |
|---|---|---|---|---|---|
| A — 1.0 | A — 0.8<br>B — 0.2 | A — 0.6<br>B — 0.4 | A — 0.4<br>B — 0.6 | A — 0.2<br>B — 0.8 | B — 1.0 |

More steps can be made in the line blend but it is not really necessary. The series shown above will give a fairly complete picture of all the ways in which glazes A and B may be combined.

*A triaxial blend*

To test the various combinations of three different glazes, A, B, and C, make a triaxial blend like this.

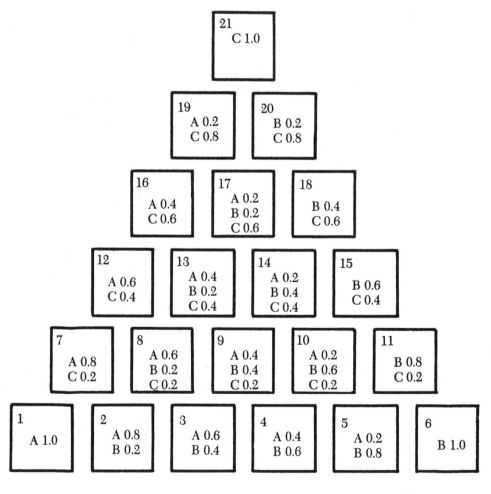

Again, you may make more steps if you wish, but the 21 tests in this triaxial should give a pretty good idea of all of the possible combinations of glazes A, B, and C. If you make such a series, number the tiles from 1 to 21 as shown, and after the firing they may be easily arranged in triangle form and studied.

*Test tiles*

If you test all of your glazes on tiles which lie flat in the kiln, you won't get an accurate picture of how they work, for a glaze which fires perfectly on a horizontal surface may run on a vertical one. Test tiles, therefore, should be fired standing on edge. Some potters prefer to make their test tiles in angle shape so that each tile provides a vertical surface on which to test the glaze. Such tiles can be made easily by throwing a ring shape on the wheel as shown in Fig. 95 and cutting it into segments when it is leather-hard.

ANGULAR TILE SHOWS HOW MUCH GLAZE RUNS

CLAY RING THROWN ON WHEEL CUT INTO TILES

FIG. 95 - TEST TILES

When you test your glazes you will find it helpful to paint a simple design over the glaze to see how much distortion is produced in the firing. Use underglaze colors for this purpose and follow the method described in the section on majolica.

*Marking tests*

All test tiles should be carefully marked and records kept of what went into the sample. Don't let yourself get into the predicament of the fellow who has several beautiful glaze tests and can't for the life of him remember how he got them. Prepare marking fluid by mixing equal parts of transparent glaze and black underglaze color and adding enough water and gum tragacanth so that you can paint with it easily. Use a small brush. This marking fluid may be used to label either raw or fired tiles, or it can be used to make designs on top of glaze tests, as described in the section above.

## APPLYING GLAZES

The way you apply your glaze will have much to do with the beauty of the finished piece. It is important to get the glaze on in a smooth, even coat, thick enough so that it can flow into a satisfactory surface during the firing and not too thick so that it crawls.

Before applying a glaze, pour off the free water from the top of the jar, stir the glaze thoroughly and bring it to the right consistency by adding as much water as is needed; then screen it through a 100-mesh sieve. See that the glaze contains enough gum. Clean the piece to be glazed by wiping it with a damp sponge; dust on the surface will cause crawling, and so will any spots of oil or grease. Make sure that your hands are clean and take care in handling the piece.

### Dipping or pouring

In glazing bisque ware by dipping, you can either saturate the piece with water first or have it dry. In the former case, the glaze must be quite thick. Soak the piece in a pail of water for several minutes, then take it out and wipe it with a towel. When there is no moisture left on the surface, pour on a little glaze as a test. You will be able to tell by the way the glaze piles up whether it is thick enough or if the piece is too wet. The trick is to get the proper balance between the moisture content of the ware and the thickness of the glaze. The wetter the piece, the thicker the glaze must be, and vice versa.

FIG. 96 —
GLAZING
A BOWL

When you have the glaze and the piece adjusted to each other, glaze the inside by pouring in glaze. Roll the glaze around until the entire inside surface is covered, and then pour out all which does not stick to the sides. Next turn the piece upside down and rest it on two sticks laid across the top of a bowl, as shown in Fig. 96. The outside surface can now be glazed by pouring glaze over it.

If you have enough glaze to fill a large container, you may find it easier to hold the piece by the foot, dip it completely into the glaze, then lift it out and allow the excess glaze to drain off, after which the piece can be rested on two sticks until the coating of glaze dries. The places where the piece rests on the supports and where your fingers grasp it will have to be touched up with a brush later. There will probably be too heavy a layer of glaze on the bottom; so when the piece is dry enough to handle, scrape the bottom clean with a spatula and brush on a thin layer of glaze. The foot should be completely free of glaze so that the piece can stand on the kiln shelf without need of stilts.

Small pieces and tiles are especially suited to dipping. Practice until you become skillful. It is not always necessary to soak the bisque piece before glazing it. You can leave it dry if you wish. In this case the glaze must be much thinner and you will have to work quickly in order not to have it pile up in thick masses. Experience will be your best teacher here.

### Brushing glaze

Applying glaze with a brush is not easy. It takes a delicate touch, and, like everything else in pottery, requires practice. Use a flat brush with soft hairs, ½" to 1" wide. Work quickly, laying the glaze on with even strokes and avoiding thick deposits of glaze where strokes overlap. As long as the glaze coating is damp you can brush over it, but once it has dried, another brush stroke is risky.

### Spraying

This method gives the best results of all, but the equipment is costly, for it requires a spray gun, a compressor, and a spray booth. An investment in these can run into several hundred dollars, but you can buy a paint spraying outfit, including compressor, for much less. This builds up a pressure of thirty pounds per square inch and does a good job spraying glazes, provided they are not too thick or heavy. You can rig up your own spray booth if you are able to buy an exhaust fan and a motor. Fig. 97 shows how one of these was built. The only difficulty you will encounter in spraying glazes is keeping the gun in good working order. Screen each glaze through a 150-mesh sieve before using it, and clean the spray gun carefully when you are through.

You can spray glaze with an ordinary flit gun if you have a lot of patience. The glaze has to be quite thin in order for the sprayer to be able

. . . 201 . . .

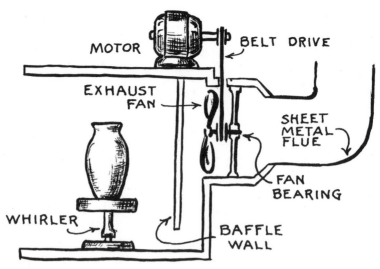

## FIG. 97- DIAGRAM OF SPRAY BOOTH

to lift it, and it takes a long time to build up a thick enough coat of glaze; still it is worth trying if no better sprayer is available.

*Glazing raw ware*

Unfired pieces can be glazed in the same manner as bisque, but of course they cannot be soaked first; care must be taken in dipping to see that the piece does not absorb too much moisture. Glazes on raw ware are best applied by brushing or spraying. If you use a brush, you will find it helpful to paint the surface first with a coat of gum tragacanth. This will allow the glaze to be brushed on without having the piece act as a sponge.

### SOME GLAZE RECIPES

Here are some glazes which you might like to make up and try. The quantities given should be weighed out in grams. Each batch will make enough glaze for several pieces. Unless otherwise noted, the coloring oxides listed for glaze No. 1 may be used for any of the glazes which follow.

When a recipe calls for feldspar, any potash or soda spar may be used. When the recipe calls for clay, use any type of kaolin. Some recipes call for ball clay. This makes the glazes easier to apply. Some call for calcined clay. You can make this by putting some dry powdered clay into your kiln when you are firing.

Most of the following glazes are illustrated on Color Plates 2, 3, and 4.

1. *Transparent lead glaze. Cone 06 to cone 02.*

| | |
|---|---|
| White lead | 142 |
| Whiting | 35 |
| Feldspar | 60 |
| Clay | 22 |
| Flint | 47 |

This is the glaze whose formula we worked out in Chapter Ten. Colors may be added to this glaze as follows:

| | | |
|---|---|---|
| For blue add | cobalt oxide | 2 |
| For dark blue add | cobalt oxide | 6 |
| For green add | copper oxide | 9 |
| For tan add | iron oxide | 8 |
| For iron red add | iron oxide | 24 |
| For crimson add | pink oxide | 40 |
| For yellow add | antimony oxide | 9 |
| | or | |
| | yellow base* | 30 |
| For gray violet add | manganese carbonate | 12 |
| For purple add | { cobalt oxide | 2 |
| | { pink oxide | 20 |
| For gray green add | chromium oxide | 3 |
| For gray add | nickel | 6 |
| | or | |
| | iron chromate | 6 |
| For black add | { manganese carbonate | 20 |
| | { copper oxide | 5 |
| | { cobalt oxide | 8 |

* Yellow base can be made as follows.

| | |
|---|---|
| red lead | 15 |
| antimony oxide | 10 |
| tin oxide | 4 |

Mix these ingredients together, and fire in a crucible in the coolest part of your kiln. After the mixture is fired and reground, it is ready for use.

Experiment by blending some of the above colorants. Often more pleasing tones are achieved that way. Remember, too, that the whole range of underglaze colors is available to you—try some of them in your glazes.

2. *Opaque white tin enamel glaze. Cone 06 to cone 02.*

This is made by adding 10 per cent of tin (30 grams) to glaze No. 1. If you have difficulty in obtaining tin, add 20 per cent of zircopax. This makes an excellent glaze for majolica work. Colors may be added as above.

The three glazes which follow use frits. The numbers refer to the frits of the Ferro Enamel Company, Cleveland, Ohio.

3. *Transparent fritted glaze. Cone 07 to cone 04.*

| Frit 3304 (high lead) | 100 |
| Ball clay | 10 |

4. *White majolica fritted glaze. Cone 07 to cone 04.*

| Frit 3304 | 100 |
| Ball clay | 10 |
| Tin oxide | 10 |
| or | |
| Zircopax | 20 |

5. *Alkaline majolica fritted glaze. Cone 07 to cone 04.*

| Frit 3124 (leadless) | 100 |
| Ball clay | 10 |
| Tin oxide | 10 |
| or | |
| Zircopax | 20 |

Any of the colorants listed for glaze No. 1 may be used in the above fritted glazes. The alkaline majolica produces a good turquoise with the addition of 1 per cent of copper oxide.

6. *Chrome red glaze. Cone 012.*

| White lead | 258 |
| Clay | 26 |
| Flint | 48 |
| Chromium oxide | 5 |

This glaze produces a bright vermilion red, but don't overfire it; it will turn brown if you do. It works best on a white body or on a piece covered with white engobe. Be sure that the piece is matured to the proper temperature before using this low fire glaze on it.

7. *Raw alkaline glaze. Cone 08.*

| Soda ash | 62 |
| Whiting | 21 |
| Feldspar | 111 |
| Flint | 24 |

Like all raw alkaline glazes, this must be ground by hand and applied immediately.

8. *Lead glaze. Cone 07.*

| | |
|---|---|
| White lead | 63 |
| Flint | 17 |
| Clay | 10 |

This glaze is particularly good on red clay. Use the same clay in the glaze that is in the body.

9. *Purple glaze. Cone 05.*

| | |
|---|---|
| Soda ash | 50 |
| Magnesium carbonate | 25 |
| Boric acid | 200 |
| Flint | 50 |
| Cobalt oxide | 5 |

This is an alkaline glaze and must be ground by hand and applied immediately. It is a tricky glaze which bubbles violently during the firing and is apt to produce some unexpected results.

10. *Turquoise blue glaze. Cone 04.*

| | |
|---|---|
| White lead | 26 |
| Barium carbonate | 10 |
| Zinc oxide | 4 |
| Colemanite | 82 |
| Feldspar | 60 |
| Clay | 10 |
| Flint | 77 |
| Copper oxide | 10 |
| Tin oxide | 20 |

11. *Mirror black. Cone 04.*

| | |
|---|---|
| White lead | 168 |
| Whiting | 17 |
| Clay | 26 |
| Flint | 67 |
| Cobalt oxide | 8 |
| Red iron oxide | 6 |
| Manganese dioxide | 6 |

12. *Brown lustre. Cone 04.*

| | |
|---|---|
| White lead | 175 |
| Feldspar | 39 |
| Clay | 13 |
| Flint | 48 |
| Manganese carbonate | 17 |
| Iron oxide | 8 |

This glaze produces an attractive lustred surface. It is quite similar to the Rockingham glaze used by early American potters.

13. *Oxidizing green glaze. Cone 04.*

| | |
|---|---|
| Soda ash | 42 |
| White lead | 77 |
| Zinc oxide | 5 |
| Feldspar | 56 |
| Flint | 42 |
| Tin oxide | 10 |
| Copper carbonate | 7 |
| Copper oxide | 3 |

This glaze has an overload of copper. Parts of the surface of the glaze will have a metallic appearance after it is fired. This is a raw alkaline glaze, so grind by hand.

14. *Raw alkaline glaze. Cone 04.*

| | |
|---|---|
| Borax | 103 |
| Feldspar | 60 |
| Whiting | 28 |
| Clay | 10 |
| Flint | 76 |
| Zinc oxide | 28 |

Since this is a raw alkaline glaze, the ingredients must be ground by hand and applied to the ware immediately. This glaze is especially good for producing various shades of turquoise blue. These colors will be effective, however, only if the glaze is used over a white body. For buff or red clay, add 10 per cent of tin oxide to the glaze batch.

| | | |
|---|---|---|
| For Egyptian blue add | copper oxide | 5 |
| For Persian blue add | { copper oxide | 10 |
| | { cobalt oxide | 0.5 |

15. *Borosilicate glaze. Cone 04.*

| | |
|---|---|
| Colemanite | 82 |
| Feldspar | 144 |
| Barium carbonate | 78 |
| Clay | 16 |
| Flint | 66 |

16. *Barium mat glaze. Cone 04 to cone 02.*

| | |
|---|---|
| White lead | 129 |
| Whiting | 20 |
| Barium carbonate | 39 |
| Feldspar | 72 |
| Clay | 34 |
| Flint | 27 |

17. *Rutile glaze. Cone 03.*

| | |
|---|---|
| White lead | 237 |
| Feldspar | 37 |
| Clay | 6 |
| Flint | 51 |
| Rutile | 23 |

This glaze produces crystalline effects. It is especially good with the following colorants:

| | | |
|---|---|---|
| Copper oxide | 8 | produces green mat surface with light and dark stripes |
| Cobalt oxide | 1 | produces light blue mat surface with yellow and brown stripes |
| Iron oxide | 16 | produces brown mat surface with yellow crystals |

This is an interesting glaze to experiment with. Try it with other colorants.

18. *Alumina mat. Cone 03.*

| | |
|---|---|
| White lead | 149 |
| Whiting | 35 |
| Feldspar | 75 |
| Clay | 13 |
| Calcined clay | 37 |

19. *Cornwall stone glaze. Cone 2 to cone 4.*

| | |
|---|---|
| Cornwall stone | 200 |
| White lead | 65 |
| Whiting | 30 |
| Zinc oxide | 12 |

This is an excellent glaze for Monmouth or Jordan clay.

20. *Stoneware glaze. Cone 8 to cone 10.*

| | |
|---|---|
| Feldspar | 120 |
| Dolomite | 55 |
| Whiting | 20 |
| Clay | 32 |
| Flint | 118 |

This glaze should be applied thick.

21. *Porcelain glaze. Cone 9. Copper red (sang-de-boeuf).*

| | |
|---|---|
| Feldspar | 40 |
| Flint | 40 |
| Calcined borax | 12 |
| Whiting | 18 |
| Copper carbonate | 0.5 |
| Tin oxide | 2 |
| Bentonite | 1 |

This glaze requires a reduction fire. Since it contains the soluble ingredient borax it must be ground by hand and applied immediately.

22. *Porcelain glaze. Cone 11. Celadon.*

| | |
|---|---|
| Flint | 134 |
| Whiting | 80 |
| Clay | 80 |
| Feldspar | 111 |
| Red iron oxide | 4 |

This glaze requires a reduction fire.

23. *Egyptian paste. Cone 07.*

This is not really a glaze. Small objects, ornaments, jewelry, etc., may be modeled of this paste and fired in the kiln. Be careful in mixing the ingredients together not to lose any of the soluble materials. It is best to mix them with a spatula on a glass slab, using just enough water to make a workable material.

| | |
|---|---|
| Feldspar | 34 |
| Flint | 34 |
| Clay | 11 |
| Sodium carbonate | 5 |
| Sodium bicarbonate | 5 |
| Copper carbonate | 3 |
| Dextrine | 8 |

# SPECIAL GLAZE EFFECTS

Ever since some Chinese craftsman of the Han period added dabs of copper to the brown glaze on the figure of a horseman and produced irregular stripes of green mingled with the brown, potters have looked for unusual effects in glazes. Variety is interesting now as it was then. That is why studio potters experiment constantly with such things as mottling, specks, oversprays, anything in fact to give their ware individuality, to make it different from the flat uniformity of most commercial products. Here are some things to try.

## Specks

Whenever the coloring oxides in a glaze are not thoroughly ground, the glaze will have a speckled appearance. This is especially true of cobalt.

Common sand does interesting things in a glaze. Try adding 10 per cent to some of your tin enamels, screening it first through an 80-mesh sieve. The results in a lead glaze will be different from those in an alkaline glaze and, in either case, will be affected by the impurities which happen to be present in the sand. It is only by experimenting that you can find out what effects you can achieve.

Other things which can be added to produce specks in glazes are granular ilmenite (a titanium iron oxide, $FeTiO_3$), 100-mesh carborundum, and 80-mesh grog.

## Mottling

The effect produced when colors put over one another at random run together in a fluid glaze is sometimes pleasing, but beware of overworking this trick and turning out ware which is "arty."

Some of the early American potters were so fond of mottled surfaces that they covered their pieces with a bright lead glaze and then used a pepper shaker to sprinkle coloring oxides over them before they were fired. Ware treated this way would come out of the kiln covered with mingled flecks of green, blue, yellow, brown, and orange. This type of glaze, called "Flint Enamel," was actually patented by the Bennington potters.

## Crackle

A crackle glaze is one that has crazed, something much easier to do than to avoid. You can make a crackle out of any glaze at all just by forgetting to put in the flint or leaving out part of the alumina; but remember, earthenware covered with such a glaze won't hold water. When the Chinese potters put crackle glazes on their porcelain vases, that was all right because the body was vitreous anyway and would have held water without any glaze at all.

It is possible to create crackle effects and at the same time produce sound ware by means of an extra firing. Fire the glazed piece first to a point two or three cones below the temperature needed for maturity. As soon as the kiln cools, take the piece out and plunge it into a pail of water. This temperature shock will make the glaze craze over its entire surface. (It may also cause the piece to break, but that is one of the chances you must take.) Now rub some underglaze color over the surface of the piece so that it penetrates all of the tiny cracks, then wipe off the excess. The pattern of the crazing will now show in color. If you fire the piece again to its proper maturing point all of the cracks in the glaze will close and the crazing will disappear but its pattern will remain as a crackle. Since both glaze and body have now matured properly, the piece is good pottery.

### Pooling

Recently there has appeared in the stores a type of pottery with a glaze called "crystalline" or "jewel glaze." This is merely an extremely fluid glaze used in large amounts so that it forms a pool on the inside of a piece. This pool, upon cooling, turns into a thick layer of glass which crazes considerably but which has beauty because of its depth. Colors may be introduced into such a glaze at random.

You can achieve this effect with almost any glaze by reducing the alumina content so that it flows more freely, and then putting a thick coating on the inside of a piece. If you wish to try an experiment, put two or three spoonfuls of some high soda frit on the inside of the piece and fire it that way. (You don't have to mix it with water, just use it dry. Frit No. 3230* is a good one to try.) For color, sprinkle some copper carbonate on top of the frit. This will produce turquoise. As an experiment, try some other oxides or some underglaze colors.

### Lustre

If you can produce controlled reduction in your kiln, you can make lustres. (See the section on reduction in Chapter Nine.) Here is a glaze you may try:

| | |
|---|---|
| Frit 3195* | 90 |
| Ball clay | 10 |
| Silver nitrate | 1 |
| Bismuth sub-nitrate | 2 |

This glaze may be applied to green ware or to bisque. It is particularly effective over colored engobes (try it over black). Fire it to cone 04, then allow the kiln to cool to cone 016 or 795° centigrade. At this point reduce

* These numbers refer to frits made by the Ferro Enamel Company of Cleveland, Ohio.

the kiln as violently as you can, either by introducing organic matter into the chamber or by closing the dampers and shutting off the air at the burners so that the flame burns yellow. After five or ten minutes of this, turn off the kiln and allow it to cool. When you open it, you should find some lustre ware. You will also find a kiln black with soot, but don't let that worry you, it will burn out completely the next time you fire.

Make a second glaze by adding 1 per cent of copper carbonate to the first, and use the second as an overspray on the first one, or for decorative brush strokes on top of it.

To put a lustre over a finished glaze, mix the lustre glaze with cornstarch and put a thick layer on the piece to be lustred. Fire it up to cone 07, then allow the kiln to cool to cone 016 and reduce as described above.

### Prepared lustres

Commercially prepared lustres of gold, silver, copper, and other metals can be bought from ceramic dealers. These lustres contain their own reducing agents, so it is not necessary to reduce the kiln when using them. They are painted over finished glazes with some oil medium such as oil of lavender, then fired to cone 012. That's all there is to it.

### Bubbling

Much of the beauty of borosilicate and colemanite glazes is caused by the action of borax during the firing. This glaze ingredient boils violently, forming bubbles which disappear after the borax is melted. As the bubbles settle down and the glaze flows smooth, however, slight markings are left. These give a glaze an interesting texture. Other glaze ingredients which bubble violently during the firing are manganese and antimony. As an experiment, try the brown lustre glaze, Recipe No. 12. Apply this to a piece of pottery and then brush a coating of white majolica glaze on top of it. The manganese in the brown lustre glaze will bubble and break through the coating of white glaze. This will produce the mottled effect shown on the vase in the middle of the top row on Color Plate 3.

A borosilicate glaze does interesting things to any design which is on top of it; the bubbling action breaks the lines slightly—not enough to destroy the design, but sufficient to give an interesting texture to it.

### Oversprays

The action of borosilicate glazes described above can be used to advantage by spraying a glaze of a different color over a borosilicate base. Again the bubbling action will give texture to the color on top.

Quite different effects are obtained by spraying a fairly viscous glaze on top of a highly fluid one. During the firing, the fluid glaze will run and will break up the glaze on top of it into patterns which may be pleasing.

# DEFECTS IN GLAZES

There is always an element of uncertainty in firing glazes. Lots of things can go wrong, and the source of trouble is sometimes hard to trace. It may lie in the glaze or in the clay itself. There may be a mistake in the formula or in the way the ingredients were weighed out. There may be faults of application or firing. Here are a few of the most common glaze defects, and some of the things which cause them.

## Crazing

When a glaze crazes it develops tiny cracks all over its surface. Sometimes these show immediately after the piece comes out of the kiln but often they do not appear until several months later. Crazing is an indication that the glaze does not fit the body.

Crazing can have many different causes. It is often a problem of the body rather than the glaze. Fire the ware higher, or add flint, or else add a body flux as described in Chapter Eight to increase the density. Bring the percentage of absorption down as far as possible—get below 10 per cent. If you are using a native clay, it may be too coarse and sandy—try screening it through an 80-mesh sieve.

If the fault is not with the body, increase the alumina and the silica content of the glaze, running a series of tests of various additions until you have secured a better fit. Sometimes changing feldspars will help.

## Crawling

When a glaze crawls, the piece comes out of the kiln with bare spots where the glaze has moved away, exposing the body underneath. This may be due to:

    a. Not enough gum tragacanth in the glaze, so that it cracked before going into the kiln.
    b. Dust on the surface of the piece when the glaze was applied.
    c. Oil on the surface of the piece.
    d. Too much grinding of the glaze.
    e. Too heavy application.
    f. Underfiring.
    g. Firing before the glaze dried.
    h. Too porous a body.
    i. Too much plastic clay in the glaze.

The remedy for each of the above, except the last one, is obvious. If the trouble is caused by the shrinkage of clay in the glaze, try firing some of the clay in powder form and use it in the glaze calcined instead of raw.

## Blistering

Blistering may be due to sulphur in the clay. To remedy, add 2 per cent of barium carbonate to the clay when it is in slip form. Blisters or craters which are caused by sulphur will eventually burn out if the piece is refired.

If blisters appear in lead glazes and not in others, the trouble is reduction. Check the kiln and the burners.

Manganese often blisters in a glaze. Other causes are too heavy application, putting a second coat of glaze over the first, and underfiring. In most cases a piece which has blistered can be refired and cured.

### Pin holes

Pin holes are often caused by air holes in the clay, especially in cast pieces. Other causes are too rapid firing or too rapid cooling. Painting over a glaze after it has dried is apt to cause this trouble.

### Running

Too much flux in the glaze or overfiring will make a glaze run. Sometimes coloring oxides act as fluxes and cause running. To remedy, cut down on the flux or increase the alumina.

### Dryness

Dryness is due to underfiring or not enough flux. In alkaline glazes, this often occurs through the loss of soda.

### Sandpaper surface

A rough surface indicates that the glaze was not applied thick enough.

### Shivering

Shivering occurs when sections of glaze lift off the piece. This is usually a body fault. To remedy, lower the silica in the body and increase it in the glaze. Another cause of shivering may be too rapid firing or cooling.

### Dunting

When a piece comes out of the surface of a pot, leaving a hole, the defect is called a "dunt." Dunting may be due to too rapid cooling or to a fragment of stone in the clay.

### Discoloration

Discoloration may be due to reduction or to the presence of chromium in the kiln.

### Chipping

Chipping usually results from lack of fit between glaze and body. The body may be too porous. Try introducing some feldspar.

### Shiny surface on mat glaze

If a glaze which should be mat comes out shiny, the piece was fired too high.

*Devitrification*

Devitrification is a dull surface on a glaze resulting from the crystallization of silica. It occurs when the kiln cools too slowly. This is a defect which studio potters rarely encounter for their kilns almost always cool too fast.

SOME POINTS ON WORKING WITH GLAZE:

*1. To get the full satisfaction of pottery, devise your own glaze formulas and make your own glazes.*

*2. Experiment, but know what you are doing. Keep accurate records of all the glazes you prepare and fire tests on carefully marked tiles.*

*3. Test every glaze before you use it on a piece.*

*4. Control your glaze effects; don't be satisfied with accidental results.*

*5. Work for glazes which fit your clay. Don't excuse crazing by saying you wanted a crackle anyway.*

*6. Let your glazes have translucence and depth. Avoid a paintlike quality.*

*7. Some mottled effects are pleasing, but beware of haphazard mingling of glazes.*

*8. Use the natural color of your clay.*

*9. Remember that form and color are both important; when you start to shape a piece of clay, have in mind the glaze which will be on the finished piece.*

# chapter Twelve

# *Decoration*

*W*e have spoken about ways of decorating clay by carving, incising, and so on. Now a word or two about decorating in color.

The most direct method of decorating pottery is by using clay of two different colors, inlaying one in the other or putting one on top of the other as a slip. Slip used this way is called engobe.

When you put liquid engobe on a leather-hard or bone-dry piece of clay, you face the problems of unequal shrinkage. If the engobe contracts more than the clay, it will crack off. To avoid this trouble, apply engobe decorations while the clay is still quite wet so that the engobe and the piece can shrink together. Another way of meeting the problems is to prepare an engobe with a high percentage of flux. Such an engobe is actually almost a glaze but it can be used as a slip and may be applied to bone-dry ware or even to bisque.

Much can be done in slip decoration by using different colored native clays. Red and buff are harmonious when used together this way. For more brilliant colors, it is necessary to prepare a white engobe and color it with metal oxides.

Here is a white engobe which can be used on wet clay:

|  | grams |
|---|---|
| China clay | 25 |
| Ball clay | 20 |
| Flint | 30 |
| Feldspar | 17 |
| Whiting | 2 |
| Magnesium carbonate | 6 |

These ingredients should be mixed in the same manner as that described for glazes in Chapter Eleven.

The following engobe contains a high proportion of flux. It can be applied to bone-dry ware or to ware which has been fired. It will not work on wet clay. This engobe contains a soluble ingredient (borax), so mix it as you would an alkaline glaze.

|  | grams |
|---|---|
| China clay | 6 |
| Ball clay | 6 |
| Feldspar | 10 |
| Flint | 20 |
| Whiting | 3 |
| Borax | 3 |
| Nepheline syenite | 12 |
| Frit 3124 (Ferro Enamel Co.) | 20 |
| Zircopax | 20 |

Both of the above engobes may be colored by adding metal oxides in the proportions listed for glaze No. 1 on page 203.

Engobe can be painted on ware with a brush, applied with a tube, sprayed, poured, or dipped. Designs may be drawn directly with engobe or may be scratched through an engobe coating. They can also be made by using stencils.

*Slip painting*

It is not easy to use a brush with engobe. The material won't flow the way paint does, and so long brush strokes are impossible. During the firing some of the engobe goes into solution in the glaze which covers it; hence it must be applied thick—delicate strokes disappear. Pleasing brush decorations can be made with engobe, however, as long as the limitations of the method are understood. Since you cannot make long brush strokes, make short ones—compose designs with direct touches of the brush heavily loaded with engobe. Look at the teapot shown in Plate IX, and see how effective simple decoration of this type can be.

*Slip trailing*

More elaborate designs in engobe can be made by trailing the material onto the piece through a tube. The best and simplest tool for this work is a piece of glass tubing slightly narrowed at one end. The tube is filled by dipping it into the engobe and using it as a straw, drawing slip up into the tube by suction (be careful not to get a mouthful). The flow of slip can be regulated by changing the slant of the tube. When you hold the tube in a horizontal position, the slip will not run out at all. As you tip it up, the slip will start to flow, increasing in speed as the tube approaches a vertical position. A little experimenting will enable you to control the flow, producing thick or thin lines as you wish. The slab built box shown on Plate II was decorated this way. Other examples of slip trailing are shown on Plates III and XX and on Color Plate 4.

### Sgraffito

"Sgraffito" means scratched. In this type of decoration, designs are scratched in a coating of engobe so that the contrasting color of the body shows through. The coating of engobe may be put on the piece with a brush or may be poured or sprayed.

Much variation is possible in sgraffito design. Lines scratched when the engobe is still wet have a different character from lines scratched after it has dried. Different tools give different effects. Color Plate 4 shows an example of sgraffito work. In this (the plate with two fish) the design was made with the end of a wooden modeling tool cutting through a copper engobe which had been brushed on a piece made out of buff clay. In the example of sgraffito shown on Plate XX (the farmer with a load of hay) an engobe containing a high percentage of tin was sprayed over a red clay body and allowed to dry. The design was then scratched with a pen.

Another kind of sgraffito decoration is possible when pieces are poured in drain molds. Engobe of one color is poured into the mold and then poured out immediately so that a thin layer is left on the inside of the mold. Before this dries, casting slip of a different color is poured in. When the piece is removed from the mold, the engobe coating will cover the entire surface. A design cut through this outer layer will show the contrasting color of the body.

Another way of using slip as a decoration in connection with molds, is to paint or trail a design on the inside of the mold before the casting slip is poured in. As the slip hardens, it will pick up the design and the finished piece will show the decoration as a colored inlay.

### Spraying

Engobe may be applied with a spray gun. It is possible to put on even coats this way in preparation for sgraffito decoration, or designs may be sprayed through stencils. The vase shown on Plate IX is an example of this method. The vase was thrown on the wheel out of buff clay. When it was leather-hard, a piece of paper cut into a scallop pattern was held at its side while red clay slip was sprayed against it. The result—contrasting bands of color on the side of the vase.

### Wax resist

Designs may be painted on green ware with melted wax. If engobe is then poured over the piece, it will stick only on those portions which are not covered by wax, hence the design will show the color of the original clay body. This method is rather complicated and only simple designs should be tried. If you dip a brush into hot wax so that the heat reaches the ferrule which holds the hairs, the hairs are apt to loosen and fall out. Dip just the tip of the brush into the wax, and don't use a good brush.

*Terra sigillata*

The Romans had a way of treating their pottery to give it a hard semi-glossy surface almost as dense as a glaze. This surface treatment is terra sigillata (the word means sealed earth). Terra sigillata is really an engobe made of very fine colloidal particles of clay which stay in suspension when the clay has been ground for a long period and deflocculated.

If you would like to experiment with terra sigillata, use 1000 grams of native clay, add 1000 grams of water and grind the mixture in a ball mill for 24 hours or longer. Remove the slip from the ball mill and put it in a tall glass container, then add water until the specific gravity of the mixture is 1.2. (You can measure the specific gravity of the slip with a hydrometer.) Add 20 grams of sodium hydroxide, stir the slip thoroughly, and let it stand undisturbed for 24 hours more. At the end of this time clay will have settled to the bottom of the container with an almost clear colorless liquid above it. This liquid contains the colloidal particles of clay you are seeking. Carefully siphon off some of this liquid into another container. When this is sprayed on raw ware, the piece will come out of the kiln with an extremely hard coating having a slight shine.

The color of terra sigillata varies; sometimes it is quite different from the clay out of which it is made. It provides a good surface treatment for sculpture, and may be used for various decorative treatments such as sgraffito or spraying over patterns. It is not possible to make terra sigillata out of all clays, so do not be discouraged if your experiment does not work.

*Ceramic colors*

There are many different ways of using ceramic pigments in decorating pottery. The colors may be painted on unglazed ware and then covered with a transparent glaze and fired (underglaze decoration), or they may be put on top of a coating of opaque glaze before it is fired (majolica). Colors may be painted on top of a glaze which has been fired (overglaze decoration) or they may be mixed in with the glaze itself and painted on the ware in decorative patterns (polychrome).

In my opinion the best type of decoration for the studio potter is majolica. The method is simple (one firing of the piece is usually enough) and the results are highly satisfying, for the colors melt into the glaze and the design becomes part of the piece itself. Ware decorated this way has a true ceramic quality often absent from underglaze or overglaze work. Let's consider majolica first.

## PLATE XX
### Examples of decorated ware.

Majolica, dry brush technique.

Sgraffito, design scratched with a pen in white engobe over red body.

Majolica, background painted over white glaze.

Majolica, decoration painted with opaque colors over a transparent glaze on a red body. The plate was made on a flop-over mold.

Underglaze painting, free brush strokes. Plate made by **Pat Lopez**.

*Majolica*

Whenever ceramic colors are used in decoration they must be mixed with a flux so that they fire properly, and with some liquid to serve as a vehicle and make them flow from a brush. Number 8 flux is generally used. (This is a frit prepared especially for ceramic color work; all dealers sell it.) A bit of glaze mixed with the color will often serve just as well. As a vehicle, water alone may suffice but a little gum tragacanth or glycerine will make the painting easier.

Provide yourself with a glass slab, a small steel spatula, an assortment of underglaze colors, and one or two fine brushes of good quality. Place a small amount of each color on the glass slab (a little underglaze color goes a long way, so use it sparingly—a mound as big as a pea should suffice), add an equal amount of Number 8 flux or glaze and mix the two thoroughly with the spatula. Now add a drop of water and a drop or two of gum tragacanth and mix again. Grind the mixture with the spatula until you have a smooth creamy liquid without any lumps. If the color is too thick for painting, add more water and gum, but beware of thinning your pigments too drastically. A little experimentation will enable you to get the mix just right.

When the colors are ready, glaze the piece, using a glaze with 10 per cent of tin oxide added to make it white and opaque (glaze Number 2 is a good one for majolica work). The glaze may be put on either raw ware or bisque and it can be applied by dipping, brushing, or spraying. Try to get a smooth coat of even thickness.

Painting over a coating of glaze is tricky. When it dries, the glaze will absorb color rapidly, and working on it will be just like painting on blotting paper. You will find it easier to apply your decoration while the glaze is still damp. If you have difficulty in painting on the surface of the glaze, spray or brush a thin layer of gum tragacanth over the glaze before you paint.

You have planned your design well in advance, of course. The next step is to sketch the design on the piece. You can't use a pencil because this would mar the coating of glaze; so use a brush dipped in india ink. India ink will burn out completely during the firing and not leave any trace; you can be as free as you wish in using it. Sketching on the piece with a brush has the added advantage of giving you a chance to practice the strokes needed in the final design.

Now go ahead and paint. The quality of your brush work is most important here. Work quickly, painting with free direct strokes. Avoid going over any portion of the design twice. Keep your colors smooth and free flowing. Try to achieve character in your line so that each brush stroke has beauty of its own.

For bands of color around the edges of plates use the banding wheel or whirler. Center the piece carefully and spin the wheel. Load your brush with color and touch it to the rim of the piece as it spins, holding the brush steady until a complete band is made. A brush with hairs about an inch long is best for banding, and the colors should be mixed with an extra amount of glycerine to help them flow.

Great variety is possible in majolica decoration through the use of different glazes and different methods of painting. Designs may be made with smooth brush strokes, or a "dry brush" technique may be used. In this method the brush is dipped into the color, then squeezed almost dry and the hairs separated so that tones rather than lines are painted. The cat design shown on Plate XX was made this way. When designs are painted over a borosilicate glaze which bubbles during the firing, the effect will be quite different from that obtained when they are painted over smooth lead glazes. If a glaze is sprayed through a coarse nozzle so that it makes a pebbly surface on the piece, brush strokes made over it will show a grain. Color Plates 2 and 4 show examples of various majolica techniques. To perfect your skill in majolica decorating, paint a number of designs on tiles. Try different methods, and practice until you have full command of the brush.

Majolica decoration is usually painted on top of an opaque glaze but this is not the only way of doing it. Interesting results are obtained by using a transparent glaze over a red clay body. When you paint on top of such a glaze, mix liberal amounts of tin oxide with some of the colors so that they will show up light against the dark background of the piece. Other colors may be used without tin. The Neptune dish on Plate XX illustrates this method.

If the colors have been mixed with enough flux, the piece will come out of the kiln with a smooth glossy surface. If some portions of the decoration are dull, the flux was not sufficient. This defect can be corrected by spraying the piece with a thin coat of transparent glaze and firing it again. Some potters who wish to make sure of a highly glossy surface on their majolica work spray a little transparent glaze over the decoration before they fire it.

Majolica decoration gives the potter a chance to make "personalized" pottery—special pieces for individuals or to commemorate special occasions, like the wedding plates of the old Pennsylvania Dutch potters. Note the dish made for a little girl who lives on a farm and loves animals, shown on Color Plate 4.

*Underglaze decoration*

Designs may be painted with underglaze colors either on raw ware or on bisque. The colors must be mixed with flux in the manner described in the section on majolica but instead of using water as a vehicle, it is necessary to use glycerine or gum for raw ware and some oil medium for bisque.

The simplest method of underglaze decoration is painting directly on the raw ware. It is best to paint on ware which is still leather-hard, for bone-dry clay is too absorbent and is apt to draw color from the brush, making it pile up in lumps instead of flowing as it should. If you have this trouble, try sponging the piece, or else brush a thin coat of gum tragacanth over the surface to be decorated.

Sketch your design on the piece with a soft pencil or with brush and india ink. Sketches which don't turn out right can be removed with a damp sponge. Use a glass slab as described in the section on majolica and mix the underglaze colors thoroughly with Number 8 flux or with glaze, adding glycerine or gum tragacanth as a vehicle.

The quality of brush work is important in underglaze painting as well as in majolica. Work freely and quickly. Keep the color from piling up in lumps, for these will stick out through the glaze and make ugly blemishes. If you make a mistake, don't try to correct it but sponge off the piece and start again.

Underglaze decorations can be made on bisque ware also—in fact this is the usual method of commercial production. Painting on bisque requires an oil medium. Mix the colors with flux as described above, but instead of using glycerine add a few drops of fat oil of turpentine and an equal amount of turpentine. If the mixture is too thick, use a little more turpentine to thin it.

Pieces with underglaze decorations can be glazed and fired in one firing if you are careful to apply the glaze without spoiling the design. It is best to spray the glaze over the decoration, although dipping is possible if you are skillful. Some potters prefer to fire the decorated piece to red heat before they glaze it. This hardens the design on the piece so that it cannot be washed off when the glaze is applied. If you have painted on bisque ware using fat oil as a medium, it will be advisable to fire the piece to red heat before you glaze it in order to burn out the oil, which otherwise might cause trouble under the glaze.

Remember in underglaze decoration that the color of your clay will affect the colors of your design. If you want bright colors, it will be necessary either to use a white clay body for making your ware or else cover the ware with white engobe. If brilliance of color is not important, however, decorations may be painted directly on buff or red clay. Examples of underglaze decoration are shown on Plate XX and on Color Plate 4.

*Overglaze painting*

Designs can be painted with overglaze colors on ware which has been glazed and fired. The method involves an additional firing but it has the important advantage of making available to the potter a range of colors not obtainable in any other way.

Overglaze colors will not stand high temperatures—most of them begin to disappear above cone 012. The piece to be decorated must, therefore, be glazed and fired to full maturing temperature before the overglaze colors are applied. The colors are then painted on and the piece is fired again, this time to a temperature just high enough to soften the glaze slightly. The colors are thus bound into the glaze.

Using overglaze colors is simple. The colors are prepared in the manner described in the section on underglaze painting, mixed with flux and with fat oil of turpentine, then thinned to the proper consistency with turpentine. Designs are then painted on the surface of a glazed piece. This method has one advantage over majolica—mistakes can be wiped off and decorations repainted as often as you wish.

Ceramic supply manufacturers have prepared a number of oils especially for use in overglaze painting. If you wish to experiment with the method you might try some of these. Try also using the prepared lustres described in the section on special glaze effects in Chapter Eleven.

### Polychrome

Designs may be made on pottery by mixing colors with glaze and painting directly on the piece. Here the problem is to keep the colors of one area from flowing into another. Various devices are used to prevent this. Flat pieces, tiles, etc., are sometimes made with raised lines which separate areas where different colors will be placed. Sometimes color areas are outlined with a glaze made with insufficient flux so that it does not run. If care is used in preparing the glazes and in firing, however, it is possible to make decorations by painting directly with different colored glazes.

Polychrome decoration is better suited to sculpture and tiles than to plates and vases. The figure on the fountain shown in the Frontispiece was decorated this way.

### Some points on ceramic decoration

Think carefully before you decorate. Remember that what counts is the shape of the piece and the clay which forms it. Too often beautiful pottery is spoiled by over-elaborate ornamentation.

Tastes vary. Some people like gaily decorated pottery while others prefer plainer wares. We cannot say that one is right and the other wrong. We can say, however, that if decoration is used it must have a relation to the way a piece is made and the purpose it will serve.

Everything that is popular is not necessarily good. The fact that a piece of pottery is pictured in an expensive magazine or sold in an exclusive store does not mean that it is good.

Don't debase a piece of pottery by letting it serve merely as a background for painting. Decorate only pieces which you have made yourself.

Don't buy plates produced in a factory and paint pictures on them. This is bad even when it is done by some celebrated artist who ought to know better.

As you work with clay your sense of design will improve. After a while you will realize that the most satisfactory decorations are usually the simplest—those which show what they are made of and how they are put on.

When you make a piece of pottery a bond is established between you and everyone else who has shaped clay ever since the world began. You are fellows in the same craft. Take a little time to study what others have done; let their work inspire you.

Drawing inspiration from potters of other times and other lands does not mean copying their work. The pottery you make must be your own yet what you see in books on ceramic history or in museum collections can suggest ways of making your pottery more beautiful and more satisfying. After all it is not possible to be entirely original in ceramic work. A cup is a cup and a bowl is a bowl—you cannot make them completely different unless you enter the realm of the fantastic. Since that is so, be familiar with the best of what has been done so that your work may be a product of knowledge and understanding.

# chapter Thirteen

# *D*o *P*otters *E*at?

*N*ow you know some of the secrets of the potter; you have mastered the wheel and have learned how to control the fire. Have you thought about pottery as a career? It must be very pleasant to earn one's living creating beautiful things out of clay. Can it be done?

The answer is yes, it can be done and it is being done but probably not exactly in the way you have in mind. Almost everyone who has worked with clay has dreamed of opening a small pottery shop by the side of a road, somewhere near a clay bank, where he could build his kiln, set up his wheel, and then throw pieces of ware all day long. This would be good pottery, of course, much better than that sold in department stores, and so, like the man with the mousetrap, the world would beat a pathway to his door. It is a romantic picture.

Places like that really do exist, but before you embark on such a venture, consider these two facts: first, throwing pottery all day long is hard work. After the first thrill has worn off it can become just as monotonous as digging ditches; and second, you will have to sell a lot of pottery to support yourself. If you employ an assistant, you will have to sell a great deal more.

We live in an industrial age which promises to become even more industrial. This gives us more efficient living, it is true, but at the same time it robs us of much satisfaction. The man who built his own home one hundred fifty years ago was not as well housed as our modern apartment dwellers but his life had something which we miss. So much is done for us by machines today. Our clothes are made in factories, our food is cooked and canned, we even have machines to sing our songs for us. Perhaps that is why many of us turn to pottery in hope that digging clay from the earth and shaping it to serve a purpose, decorating it in a way which seems good, may somehow supply a little bit of what is lacking in our lives.

But earning a living from pottery is something else again. We cannot ignore the industrial era—just turn our backs upon it and, by wishing, return to the age of crafts. If you plan to make pottery your life work, you must consider how you will do so in the midst of an industrial society, remembering that you will either have to use mass production methods or face the terrific competition of low prices which mass production makes possible, remembering also that rent must be paid and families fed even when people don't buy, and not forgetting that your plans must include provision for security later on. You must face facts realistically.

The ceramic industry in America is a large one, but that does not mean unlimited opportunities for the kind of work you want to do. The worker in a pottery plant is not much different from the worker in an automobile factory. He does not make things—he performs operations. He is a dipper or a fettler or a jiggerman, and what he does is monotonous and repetitive. That is not what you had in mind, is it?

How then does one make a living from pottery? It can be done in a number of different ways. Here is how some people have done so. Perhaps if we study what they have done it will answer some of our questions. The names which follow are all fictitious, but the people are all very real.

*The primitive potter*

Lance is a primitive potter indeed—so primitive that it is hard to imagine him existing in America today. I met him a few years ago when I thought I was driving to a house afire. It was on a back road in Alabama among scrub pine, where, as our car rounded a bend, we saw great clouds of smoke and tongues of flame shooting above the treetops. Someone in serious trouble, we thought, and raced to the spot; but there was no trouble—Lance was just firing his kiln. In fact, he wasn't even watching the kiln at the moment but was in his shop, throwing butter crocks. As we walked in, he nodded

and said "Howdy" and kept right on working. The wheel was a homemade one with a treadle and a wooden head. Lance didn't bother with plaster bats or any of that foolishness, but just threw the clay on the wheel head, shaped the pot, then cut it off with a wire and lifted it aside to dry. The place was full of un-fired ware, mostly crocks of gallon and two-gallon size with lids, and as we stood watching for a few moments, two more joined the stack. Then he changed his product in order to demonstrate his skill. "I'm fixin' to make a pitcher now," he said, as he threw a lump of clay on the wheel. In less time than it takes to tell it, he had shaped a cylinder, rolled an edge, pulled out a spout, and attached a handle; then it was off the wheel and a smaller lump of clay was in its place. In a moment this became a mug.

Lance learned how to make pottery from his father. His brother helps him now, and between them they dig their clay, make their ware, and fire it in a big down draft kiln with a wood fire. It takes about two cords of wood for a firing. They don't have time to cut their own wood, however—they buy that from a neighbor.

Lance and his brother make a living, but it is a meagre one. Some of their pottery is sold locally, but most of it they take to Birmingham, about forty miles away, where it is sold in a department store. They make good honest ware which is sold for much less than it is worth. They are able to exist through hard labor and because they dig their clay from their own land. They don't use glazes, but cover their ware with a brown clay (also dug from their land) which fuses almost as well as Albany slip. When their clay runs out they will have to go into some other kind of work.

I came back later to get the pitcher and the mug after they had been fired. They are shown on Plate IX.

### Ceramic jewelry

Irma has a tiny electric kiln, about the smallest you can buy, but it is big enough for her purposes; for everything she makes is tiny, also. She manufactures ceramic jewelry —small flower shapes, butterflies, etc., as well as abstract forms which she sets in bracelets and earrings. She does not need to know a great deal about clay, for she buys a prepared white body and uses commercial glazes. She has had some training in jewelry making—enough to enable her to make finished pieces.

Irma is a good craftsman, her work is neat and well finished. She has built up a clientele of stores who like her product and are willing to buy all she can turn out. As long as the vogue for ceramic jewelry continues, Irma should make out very well.

### A homemade factory

Harry and Joe are veterans of World War II. They were on different fronts, were both wounded and, while recuperating in hospitals, made their first acquaintance with clay through occupational therapy work. After their recovery and discharge, their interest in clay continued and they both went to a ceramic college to learn more about it. That's where they met. They are ambitious young fellows, talented, temperamental, and impatient of delay. They worked hard to learn all they could in the shortest possible time. As soon as they thought they knew enough, they left school and established their own plant.

For their shop, they got the use of an old barn on a farm near a creek with a clay bed. The clay they use comes from this bed. They built their kiln out of second-hand fire brick from an abandoned factory. The region they are in has a supply of natural gas and they were able to get a line into their kiln. Their work tables, storage bins, and racks are made of discarded pieces of furniture which they were able to pick up.

All of their ware is made in molds. They have been able to develop a good casting slip out of their clay (it fires red) and have worked out some engobes which fit it well. To speed up production they use gang molds—molds in which the bottom half of one mold is the top of the next, so that six or more pieces are poured at once. They have developed a line of tableware based on rectangular shapes—square plates and square cups —with sgraffito decoration under a clear glaze. They don't use a wheel at all. In fact their only piece of equipment other than the kiln is a spray gun for glazes. This is a paint sprayer they bought from a mail order concern. Their entire investment in their plant so far is less than $600.

The boys are artists and their product sells. Orders are piling up and they work like beavers to fill them. They are able to show a good margin of profit and they expect soon to be able to get some better equipment and a larger kiln. They are having a wonderful time.

At the moment they are able to do all the work of their factory themselves. If they decide to expand, however, and hire additional workers, they will move into a different category with an entirely new set of problems to worry about. This was the case with Harris, whom we shall talk about next.

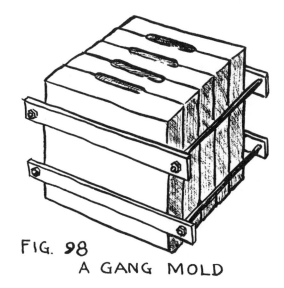

FIG. 98

A GANG MOLD

*Big business*

Harris started out as a painter. He studied at various art schools here and abroad and did a little sculpture as well. When he saw some pottery made by a friend, his interest was aroused and he started a year of intensive study of ceramics, during which he experimented with clay bodies and glazes, finally working out a cream-colored casting body and three or four very beautiful glazes to go along with it. At the end of the year he started producing tableware. His artistic skill and his talent as a sculptor helped him to design good shapes and to make satisfactory molds. All of this ware was cast. It was immediately popular.

Harris started his production in a wooden garage in a small town, with two hired helpers and a gas-fired muffle kiln. The demand for his product forced him to expand almost at once. The kiln was replaced by a larger one and then another was installed. Additions were made to the garage. Finally, the growth of the business was such that the first buildings were

abandoned entirely and a new factory erected. In this, a continuously operating tunnel kiln was installed.

Harris now employs a staff of sixty workers and has a plant which represents an investment of more than $100,000. The casting slip is mixed by mechanical blungers and piped to the pouring racks where the operators fill the molds merely by turning a spiggot. When the molds are emptied, the excess slip is carried in troughs back to the blungers for reclaiming and re-use. His plant is divided into departments—mold shop, decorating room, clay shop, shipping room, etc. His workers all perform specialized operations.

Harris has had a phenomenal success. His ware is offered for sale in stores in every city in this country and in many foreign countries as well. His rise has been due in part, of course, to the fact that he is a good designer and a talented artist, but in much greater measure it has been due to his ability as an organizer and administrator. He is a rare combination of artist and businessman. It is doubtful if one could call him a potter now. He no longer handles clay. His problems today are those of any big business executive—labor relations, operating overhead, sales, invoices, costs, and the like.

### Buy it, decorate it, and sell it again

The Johnson brothers are good businessmen too and their business is pottery, yet they don't know anything about ceramics. In fact, it is probable that they would not recognize a lump of potter's clay if someone handed it to them—certainly they would not know what to do with it. Yet they

operate a thriving business selling decorated chinaware to the trade. How do they do it? They buy blanks—porcelain dishes, which have been fired but not glazed—hire some girls to paint on floral decorations, spray the ware with transparent glaze, refire it, and sell it. On some of their ware they don't even paint the decoration, but apply ceramic decalcomanias which they buy from another firm.

Doesn't sound too attractive, does it? Still, the Johnson brothers are making out very well, and they are just one of many small firms doing the same thing.

### Thrown ware only

Betty is an artist and a fine ceramist. She is an expert at the wheel, doesn't like any other kind of pottery as a matter of fact. It is a pleasure to watch her work, to see the ease and the speed with which she can throw a dozen cups, all alike but all having the true plastic quality which handmade pottery should have. She has developed some good styles of decoration also, decoration which complements the form, which is right. She makes nothing but tableware.

Betty has fitted up a studio in lower New York City. She has a gas-fired kiln, a wheel, and enough space to work in—that's all she needs. The stores will buy all she makes and more, but she has no intention of expanding. Her reputation is growing. She is going to succeed, and she deserves to.

*Industrial design*

Jeffry started as an architect but when he got tired designing houses he started designing automobiles, nursing bottles and plumbing fixtures. In other words, he became an industrial designer. In an era in which manufacturers were willing to pay a $1500 fee to someone who would show them how to streamline an icebox by rounding the corners and fastening a strip of chromium down the front, Jeffry did all right. Then he turned his hand to pottery.

Some of his shapes are pretty startling.

### A ceramic designer

Van is an industrial designer, also, but a different kind. He studied ceramic engineering at college and after he graduated, went to work for a porcelain firm in their designing department. His job was not appear-

ance design. His problems were concerned with production. He had to design things which could be manufactured easily and which would stand up under use. Since he is a man of good taste, his designs turned out to be pretty good in appearance.

Van left the porcelain firm after a while and went out on his own as a freelance designer. During this time he designed some good tableware, original and highly functional. He designed a few ceramic novelties also and some porcelain containers for cosmetics. He ventured out of the ceramic field once or twice but here he was beyond his depth (among the things he designed was a juke box, but we hope someday he may be pardoned for that).

Now he has a regular job again as head designer for one of the largest pottery firms in America. He gets an excellent salary. His technical training, his sound artistic judgment, and his experience make him worth it.

### Molds to order

Rosario has a lot of ability as a sculptor and he is a good mold maker. His skill at carving delicate detail is amazing. I once saw him make a pair of statuettes, 10″ high, depicting a cavalier and his lady. The cavalier had lace on his cuffs and the lady held a pair of gloves in her hand. Both had plumes in their hats. The detail was all there and all perfect.

After he had finished the figurines he made molds of them—complicated molds requiring many separate parts—and then delivered them to the manufacturer who had ordered them. I have since seen editions of this cavalier and his lady on sale in several stores.

That's the kind of work Rosario does. He has no regular job, but manufacturers of ceramic novelties call on him constantly for molds of lamp bases, cigarette boxes, animals, ash trays—in fact, anything imaginable. He has all the work he can handle. The pair of figurines of the cavalier and his lady took him about four days. His price for such a job is $150.

### Part-time potters

Mr. and Mrs. Robbins both work. Mrs. Robbins teaches school—not pottery, just grammar, arithmetic, and so on; Mr. Robbins is a structural draftsman. But they both love working with clay and devote all of their spare time to it. Their home is in the suburbs and they have a back yard in which Mr. R. has built a kiln, which he fires with kerosene, and has set up a motor-driven wheel with a jigger attachment. He is an excellent craftsman and, working with the jigger, is able to make several plates in an evening.

Mrs. R. is the artist of the family, so while Mr. R. makes plates, she decorates them. Between them they turn out some beautiful dishes which they sell through local gift shops. Since both members of the family have regular salaries, they need not worry about what they earn from their pottery, and this is good, for it means they don't have to cut corners nor work against time. Every piece they sell is an individual work of art. They could never make a living working as they do, but their pottery gives them a little profit and a lot of pleasure.

### Ceramic sculpture

Leni was born in Austria and had her training in pottery there. When she came to America she brought with her a fund of knowledge about making things out of clay and a lot of talent as a sculptor, plus an irrepressible good humor.

Everything was fun to Leni, and the figures she modeled looked as though they were having fun too. Her work ranged from tiny figurines to pieces of garden sculpture eight feet high. She used to have these fired for her at brick yards. Leni opened the door for a new kind of sculpture in this

country—playful, gay, amusing. I once watched her model the head of a bacchante. She had built the figure by the coil method, and as it neared completion, she bent a strip of clay into a hair ribbon and stuck it at a rakish angle on a vagrant curl, squeezed the lips into a smile and immediately the figure came to life—a roguish, happy bacchante indeed.

Leni's work was mainly sculpture, although she made such things as dishes and teapots also. Some of her pieces were made to order to fill commissions, but most of her ware was sold by stores. She was a master of the potter's wheel, too, and even there her work was highly individual. Some gay touch would proclaim it as Leni's.

Leni had a host of friends. She never became wealthy but she earned her way. She had lots of good times. She had a good life.

### The teacher

Eric went to college to study ceramic engineering, but when he was graduating, a call came from a midwestern university for someone to organize a department in ceramics and instruct in the subject. Eric went.

Eric knows a lot about pottery. He's pretty good as an artist also and turns out some excellent pieces of thrown ware. When he took over his new post he found little equipment to work with and a small budget for supplies; but he met the challenge and has been able, with the help of students, to build a gas kiln and set up a number of wheels. His classes are exploring the state right now and experimenting with clay from a number of local beds.

Eric is quite popular with his students, being in their eyes not so much a teacher as a fellow craftsman whose greater experience enables him to lead the way. He has time to do a lot of his own work in addition to teaching. He is very happy.

Teaching pottery is a field which offers much. As its values become recognized, the subject is being included in the curriculums of more and more schools on all levels, from primary grade through college. Many potters have found positions which make possible a satisfactory combination of teaching and individual creative work.

### The research worker

Everett is a born scientist. He likes to know the "why" of things as well as the "how." When he became interested in ceramics, it was the technical side which appealed to him, so he went to college and studied ceramic engineering.

When he graduated several years ago, he got a job with a manufacturer of hotel china. He is still there. His work consists of testing raw materials, developing clay bodies, devising better glazes. Right now he is seeking a ware more resistant to thermal shock, one which can go in and out of the oven with no danger of breaking.

Everett's work is important and well paid. He enjoys doing it.

*A late start*

Walt lives in New England. He was in his fifties when he became interested in ceramics. He was a widower then, and his only daughter had married and moved to the Pacific Coast. He had retired from his work as a research chemist for a large photographic organization (he had been responsible for some of the developments in color photography) and time was heavy on his hands.

Walt hated inactivity, so he looked around for something he could do. As he says, "I wanted work which presented a challenge, which had to be puzzled out, and I wanted to meet some interesting people." He chose pottery. His training as an engineer and his experience as a chemist made it possible for him to learn a lot about ceramics during a short period of intensive study. Then he went home and built himself an electric kiln.

The electrical inspector of his city had never seen such a contraption before and refused to approve it. Walt did his best to convince him that the kiln was perfectly safe (as it is) but had no luck. He realized he could not hope to make any headway in this direction, so he packed up and moved out into the country, taking his kiln with him, and set up shop in a small farm house he was able to rent. No inspectors bother him here and he has lots of room to work. He likes it much better than his place in town.

Walt has started to produce a line of tableware decorated with fish and marine motifs which he sells to small stores (mostly gift shops) along the New England coast. He casts his pieces in molds. The kiln he built is a beauty—it uses Kanthal wire and can fire easily to cone 6 or 8, but for his work it is not necessary to go above cone 2. He has not made much money yet but his ware is becoming popular. He has hopes.

Walt has found a challenge in his work, it keeps him busy, and he has certainly met lots of people. It looks as if he has made a good choice.

Well there they are, a dozen and a half different people, each making a living or a partial living from some type of ceramic work. Among these case histories you may find a suggestion helpful to you. Note that those who have achieved outstanding success have done so either because they possessed unusual talent like Leni or were good businessmen like Harris, or had a thorough technical education in ceramic science like Van and some of the others.

There are many other ceramists who might have been described in these pages—George, for example, who is curator of a ceramic collection in a large museum, and conducts a special class in the subject, Edgar who set up his pottery shop and found he could supplement his income very nicely by firing ware for other potters, Jean who is in charge of ceramics at a settlement house, Elaine who makes special lamps to order for interior decorators. While ceramics is not an Eldorado by any means, it does hold out many possibilities. And—oh yes, we almost forgot—some people write books about it.

So long, good luck.

# Index

*Produced under the editorial supervision of*
ELLIOTT W. McDOWELL
*Designed by* FAY TRAVERS